Teaching English Language Variation in the Global Classroom

Teaching English Language Variation in the Global Classroom offers researchers and teachers methods for instructing students on the diversity of the English language on a global scale. A complement to Devereaux and Palmer's *Teaching Language Variation in the Classroom*, this collection provides real-world, classroom-tested strategies for teaching English language variation in a variety of contexts and countries, and with a variety of language learners.

Each chapter balances theory with discussions of curriculum and lesson planning to address how to effectively teach in global classrooms with approaches based on English language variation. With lessons and examples from five continents, the volume covers recent debates on many pedagogical topics, including standardization, stereotyping, code-switching, translanguaging, translation, identity, ideology, empathy, and post-colonial and critical theoretical approaches. The array of pedagogical strategies, accessible linguistic research, clear methods, and resources provided makes it an essential volume for pre-service and in-service teachers, graduate students, and scholars in courses on TESOL, EFL, World/Global Englishes, English as a Medium of Instruction, and Applied Linguistics.

Michelle D. Devereaux is Associate Professor of English Education at Kennesaw State University, USA.

Chris C. Palmer is Professor of English at Kennesaw State University, USA.

Teaching English Language Variation in the Global Classroom

Models and Lessons from Around the World

Edited by Michelle D. Devereaux and Chris C. Palmer

NEW YORK AND LONDON

Cover image: © Getty Images

First published 2022
by Routledge
605 Third Avenue, New York, NY 10158

and by Routledge
2 Park Square, Milton Park, Abingdon, Oxon, OX14 4RN

Routledge is an imprint of the Taylor & Francis Group, an informa business

© 2022 selection and editorial matter, Michelle D. Devereaux and Chris C. Palmer; individual chapters, the contributors

The right of Michelle D. Devereaux and Chris C. Palmer to be identified as the authors of the editorial material, and of the authors for their individual chapters, has been asserted in accordance with sections 77 and 78 of the Copyright, Designs and Patents Act 1988. All rights reserved. No part of this book may be reprinted or reproduced or utilised in any form or by any electronic, mechanical, or other means, now known or hereafter invented, including photocopying and recording, or in any information storage or retrieval system, without permission in writing from the publishers.

Trademark notice: Product or corporate names may be trademarks or registered trademarks, and are used only for identification and explanation without intent to infringe.

Library of Congress Cataloging-in-Publication Data
A catalog record for this book has been requested

ISBN: 978-0-367-64470-3 (hbk)
ISBN: 978-0-367-63025-6 (pbk)
ISBN: 978-1-003-12466-5 (ebk)

DOI: 10.4324/9781003124665

Typeset in Bembo
by Apex CoVantage, LLC

Access the Support Material: www.routledge.com/9780367644703

Contents

List of Contributors	viii
Acknowledgements	x
Introduction	xi
How to Use This Book	xxv

Part 1: Methods and Strategies   1

1 English Words in the English World: Integrating World Englishes in the Linguistics Classroom   3
LUCA RAIMONDI

2 Using Learning Stations at College: An Introduction to Linguistic Shift and Change for English Proficiency Development   13
YOLANDA MORATÓ

3 Balancing the Focus on Local and Global Varieties of English: Can Teaching Pedagogy Take the Multilingual Turn?   25
AICHA RAHAL

4 Translation as an Asset to Raise Global Englishes Awareness in the English Classroom   34
ELIF KEMALOGLU-ER

5 Practical Suggestions for Integrating Translanguaging in Secondary EFL: Using a Wordless Picture Book and Book Club Discussions   43
EUN YOUNG YEOM

6 L1 Use and Translanguaging in ELL Peer Interaction: A Problem or a Useful Tool?   52
DMITRII PASTUSHENKOV, CURTIS A. GREEN-ENEIX AND OLESIA PAVLENKO

Part 2: Literature and Writing   61

7 A Conversation-Analytic Approach to Translanguaging Practices in Literature Courses in Turkish Higher Education   63
VILDAN INCI-KAVAK AND YASEMIN KIRKGÖZ

8 The Subtle Case of Beirut: Translingualism in the English-Medium Undergraduate Literature Classroom   74
SALMA YASSINE AND VICKY PANOSSIAN

9 Integrating Global Englishes Into Literature and Writing Units: Advice for Secondary Teachers   82
VICTORIA E. THOMPSON

10 Language Diversity, Cross-Cultural Awareness, and Digital Media in the Writing Classroom   92
FLORENCE ELIZABETH BACABAC

11 Trans-/Multilingual Language in Different Contexts: Using Scaffolding to Assist Multilingual Learners   102
VERBRA PFEIFFER

Part 3: Perceptions and Ideologies   111

12 Speak Locally, Listen Globally: Training Listeners to Understand the Diverse Accents of Englishes Around the World   113
VANCE SCHAEFER AND ISABELLE DARCY

13 Implementing Global Englishes Real-World Activities in a Thai Tertiary Setting   123
YUSOP BOONSUK AND ERIC A. AMBELE

14 Code-Switching in Hong Kong: Key to Implementing a
   Hong Kong English Curriculum?   132
   KA LONG ROY CHAN

15 Translanguaging in University Direct-Entry Pathway English
   Courses: An Australian Case   142
   MICHELLE OCRICIANO

16 Global Englishes and Oral Communication: Perceptions of
   Multilingual Speakers   152
   NASIBA NOROVA

17 Using (Critical) Applied Linguistics to Negotiate the Teaching
   of Dominant Englishes   163
   RIBUT WAHYUDI

   Index   *174*

Contributors

Eric A. Ambele is a lecturer and researcher at Mahasarakham University, Thailand, with research interest in Global Englishes, Sociolinguistics, Teacher Education and English language teaching, and Discourse Analysis.

Florence Elizabeth Bacabac is a professor of technical writing and digital rhetoric at Dixie State University in St. George, Utah (USA), and author of several refereed articles on rhetoric and composition.

Yusop Boonsuk is an English lecturer at Prince of Songkla University, Thailand, and his research interest focuses on Global Englishes, intercultural and transcultural communication, and English language teaching.

Ka Long Roy Chan is a postdoctoral fellow at the Hong Kong Polytechnic University; his research interests include language attitudes, language education, and World Englishes.

Isabelle Darcy is a professor in the Department of Second Language Studies at Indiana University (USA) and publishes on pronunciation pedagogy, second language phonology, and the bilingual mental lexicon.

Michelle D. Devereaux is an associate professor of English and English Education at Kennesaw State University (USA), and her research focuses on integrating linguistic and sociolinguistic concepts in secondary and post-secondary classrooms.

Curtis A. Green-Eneix is a PhD student in the Second Language Studies Program at Michigan State University (USA), where he is examining issues around equitable language education and language policy.

Vildan Inci-Kavak is a lecturer at Gaziantep University, Turkey, and her research interests are conversation analysis, teacher professional development, first and second language acquisition, and teaching English to young learners.

Elif Kemaloglu-Er is an assistant professor at Adana Alparslan Türkeş Science and Technology University in Adana, Turkey; her research focuses on applied linguistics and Global Englishes.

Yasemin Kırkgöz is a professor at Çukurova University in Adana, Turkey, and her research interests are language policy and practices, curriculum design, EMI in higher education, and pre-service and in-service teacher education.

Yolanda Morató is a senior lecturer at the University of Seville, Spain, where she teaches Applied Linguistics courses (Translation and Methodology of English as a Foreign Language).

Nasiba Norova is a PhD student and research assistant at the University of Massachusetts Boston (USA), where she also teaches pre-collegiate ESL classes.

Michelle Ocriciano was an ESL teacher for 20 years and currently is a PhD candidate and lecturer in the school of education at the University of Queensland in Australia. Her main interests are epistemic justice, teacher education, and educational policy in Higher Education.

Chris C. Palmer is a professor of English at Kennesaw State University (USA); he publishes on topics such as historical word-formation, linguistics pedagogy, and teaching variation in American and Global Englishes.

Vicky Panossian is an emerging scholar of Sociology and Social Anthropology from the Central European University in Vienna, Austria; she is currently serving as Editor in Chief of *Afkar: The Undergraduate Journal of Middle East Studies*, and her research interests range from cultural identity studies to contemporary Middle East studies.

Dmitrii Pastushenkov is a PhD candidate in the Second Language Studies Program at Michigan State University (USA); his primary areas of research are second language interaction and individual differences.

Olesia Pavlenko is a graduate assistant in the MA TESL program at Kent State University (USA), where she specializes in second language interaction and game-based learning.

Verbra Pfeiffer is a senior lecturer at the University of South Africa, and her research focus is on academic literacy, English language pedagogy, and multilingualism.

Aicha Rahal, the laureate of the Africa Award 2019, is a researcher in English linguistics, focusing on sociolinguistics, ELF, language policy, psycholinguistics, and language pedagogy.

Luca Raimondi is a Marie Skłodowska-Curie Global Fellow at King's College London, UK, and at the University of the Witwatersrand, Johannesburg; he was previously a postdoctoral research fellow at CISA, University of the Witwatersrand, and lecturer in English linguistics at Fondazione Milano, Italy.

Vance Schaefer is an associate professor of Applied Linguistics and TESOL in the Department of Modern Languages at the University of Mississippi (USA) and publishes on pronunciation pedagogy and teaching language variation.

Victoria E. Thompson is a secondary English teacher at Riverwood International Charter School in Georgia (USA) who received her Master of Arts in Teaching Secondary English Education at Kennesaw State University.

Ribut Wahyudi is a lecturer at Universitas Islam Negeri Maulana Malik Ibrahim Malang, Indonesia; he has published chapters with Palgrave Macmillan (2016, 2017), Routledge (2018, with Chusna), and Multilingual Matters (2021).

Salma Yassine is an emerging scholar of gender studies from the Central European University in Vienna, Austria; her academic interests mainly tackle gender and sexuality in Middle Eastern contexts of culture, literature, and media.

Eun Young Yeom was an in-service middle school English teacher in South Korea and is currently a doctoral student in the Language and Literacy Education Department at the University of Georgia, USA.

Acknowledgements

This volume is indebted to the scholars, students, teachers, and colleagues who have supported, engaged, and inspired our work and thinking about global language variation. We would first like to thank Fulbright for the opportunity to teach abroad and learn about Global Englishes on the ground. We were humbled to work with our gracious hosts, Dr. Natalia Orlova at Jan Evangelista Purkyně University in Ústí nad Labem and the Czech Republic Fulbright Commission, as well as the University of Debrecen English Department and the Hungarian Fulbright Commission. We would be remiss without thanking our amazing students in both the Czech Republic and Hungary. Their grace and patience helped lay the foundations for this volume, and we are grateful for everything they taught us.

There were many people in the United States who also supported and encouraged this work. We are grateful to our graduate research assistants: Ashley Banks, who was instrumental in the beginning stages of this volume, and Marielena Zajac, who helped finalize the manuscript with copyediting and index preparation. We thank our students in our courses at Kennesaw State University, who thoughtfully engaged with the ideas found in the volume, helping grow our own understanding of Global Englishes. We are indebted to Victoria E. Thompson, a former student and current high school English teacher, who collaborated with us on an early project in which she taught a Global Englishes curriculum in her secondary English classroom. Her collaboration helped us understand what such curricula looked like in real-world contexts, and we are so happy to have worked with her.

We are grateful to Nicola Galloway, Suresh Canagarajah, and Jennifer Jenkins for their scholarship, correspondence, and guidance during the early stages of this volume, particularly in terms of advising us on ways to define and amplify the call for submissions. We are thankful to several anonymous reviewers for their helpful comments and to Routledge and Kennesaw State University for their support of scholarship about teaching. We would like to thank the wonderful editorial team at Routledge for their thoughtful support, particularly Karen Adler, Bethany White, and Aruna Rajendran. And, of course, we must bow to our wonderful families for their continued support of our academic work—in particular our spouses, George Koulouris and Paul Padur.

Introduction

Language Variation in Global Classrooms—Critical Questions for Teachers and Students

Michelle D. Devereaux and Chris C. Palmer

We (Chris and Michelle) have been English teachers for a while now. And we have found that one of the hardest ideas to teach students is that *language lives*. Because language reflects the people who speak it, and because that language exists in unique ecosystems of culture, society, identity, history, and power (Matsuda & Friedrich, 2011), it is dependent upon the spaces in which it is used, even as it changes and grows.

This can be a difficult concept for students to grapple with because, so often, students are taught that language is static—that it is codified in grammar and style books, that it lives a life of rules created by people long dead. And often, language instruction supports this narrative with worksheets and answer keys and words like *right, correct*, and *good*.

In this introduction, we consider how English, as a living language, exists in both academia and the larger world. In our first edited collection, *Teaching Language Variation in the Classroom: Strategies and Models from Teachers and Linguists* (2019a), authors were invited to discuss how they taught English language varieties in predominantly secondary spaces in the United States. Both of us have taught English internationally and felt that a new edited collection focused on teaching Global Englishes (defined later) could benefit students in a variety of classroom contexts around the world.

We began our journey with Global Englishes by implementing a study in a tenth-grade English classroom with a former university student who now teaches at an international school in the southeastern United States (Devereaux et al., 2021). The study focused on a pandialectal curriculum, defined as one "that does not center on a single dialect of English but rather encourages explorations of language variation and English communication in multiple global cultural contexts" (Devereaux et al., 2021, p. 236).

Through this study, we, along with our teacher-researcher Victoria (see Chapter 9), found that students appreciated what Global Englishes could teach them about the world:

> Reading different things that sound or look different . . . [gives] me a new way to view the language being used around the world.
>
> (Mateo[1])

Students also began to understand how English as a global language might impact larger socio-cultural issues:

> We also have to understand that some countries won't like the Western influence in their community because maybe they think that they are being manipulated by them.
>
> (Mariana)

In this introduction and the larger volume, our goal is to explore how Global Englishes material manifests both in the classrooms where it is taught and with the students who learn it. Because language cannot be separated from the people who speak it or the spaces in which it is spoken, English, as a language used by more than two billion people across the globe (Crystal, 2008),[2] is a ripe space to explore language instruction. It is also an ideal platform to discuss English language variations and how they act with and act upon societies, cultures, identities, histories, and power structures.

What Is a Global Classroom?

Like many terms in academia, *global classroom* has various definitions across multiple disciplinary contexts. The term can be conceptualized in the framework of global markets (Flores, 2013) and can include a variety of components, including pedagogy, curriculum, and evaluation (Bates, 2005). A global classroom has also been defined in terms of technological advances, such as digital, remote, and online asynchronous platforms that enable students to collaborate with one another in a virtual space while physically living in different parts of the world (Lock, 2015). For the purposes of this introduction, we will consider an *English language instruction* global classroom, including a brief exploration of how we discuss language, how we name language, and how we teach language in this space.

Discussing English in Global Classrooms

It might seem odd to begin with an exploration of how we *discuss* language before how we *name* language. We begin with the idea of *discussion* because words alone have little meaning without the context surrounding them.[3]

---

1 We have used pseudonyms to protect students' identities.
2 Global counts of language speakers are always difficult to estimate. *Ethnologue* (Eberhard et al., 2021) suggests a lower (and yet still immense) number of English-speakers globally, around 1.35 billion.
3 Just think of poor Hamlet when, still attempting to feign mental incapacitation, he tells Polonius that he is only reading "words, words, words" (Shakespeare, 1599/2020, 2.2.210). Hamlet knows that words without context don't scream sanity.

Although language is codified by grammar and style books, it is not *bound* by these books. However, in classrooms across the globe, instructors and students alike tend to conceptualize language as bound systems, typically defined by national and state boundaries (Otheguy et al., 2015). This idea of bound languages reflects a *monoglossic ideology*, languages as separate and distinct. Yet languages are living, diverse things; therefore, a global classroom embraces a *heteroglossic ideology*, where languages aren't seen as bound systems belonging to nation-states. A heteroglossic ideology invites "multilingual speakers' fluid language practices in their full complexity" (Flores & García, 2013, p. 245). A global classroom pushes against monoglossic ideologies that inform traditional curricula. Indeed, it does more than push against—a global classroom invites students to critique and criticize what makes a monoglossic ideology "standard." We will explore these ideas further in the following sections.

Naming English in Global Classrooms

The fact that many hundreds of millions of people across the globe speak English means that the plurality of English is undeniable, and a global classroom embraces this plurality. We can't consider English as an international language if it doesn't use an international lens for definition (Anchimbe, 2009), which must include both the colonial history that has been a part of English language learning (Subedi, 2013) and English plurality based on "culture, linguistic, and other values" (Matsuda & Friedrich, 2011, p. 338).

Throughout the chapters in this collection, the authors have chosen a variety of terms to name the English language variations found in their particular contexts. As the editors of this volume, we did not require any specific terminology in order to allow author-autonomy in naming their worlds. Indeed, this stance is, we believe, a realistic solution to what Anchimbe (2009) calls the "naming disease" of academia.[4] He lists the names given to Global Englishes over the past decades, including *New Englishes, Indigenized Englishes, Nativized Englishes, second language Englishes,* and *English as an International Language,* to name a few (pp. 275–277; for a further discussion of naming Global Englishes, see Rose & Galloway, 2019; Jenkins, 2006). Anchimbe argues, and we agree, that regional and national conventions of English must be embraced for English as an international language to thrive, and the naming of those English conventions belongs to those who speak them.

Discussions such as these—what we name the varieties of English spoken across the globe and who has the authority to do so—are foundational elements of a global classroom's teaching.

Teaching English in Global Classrooms

A global classroom not only embraces the plurality of English but creates a space to discuss the cultures and histories that act as frames for that plurality. It invites

---

4 We honor the fact that names and naming are critical considerations in a global classroom. However, we also understand that names can be placed in multiple contexts. We encourage explorations not just of names but of names within the contexts that they occur.

explorations of how colonization, power, and politics have affected the spread of the English language. It also invites students to explore similarities and differences among varieties of English and various speakers' experiences with language learning around the world, without oversimplifying those comparisons. Next, we discuss some of the specific considerations for embracing Global Englishes in the classroom.

Multiple Englishes

First, a global classroom focuses on the truth that language is multifaceted and fluid, and that the English language does not "belong" to any single nation-state or people. Beyond this, a global classroom invites students to explore the many ways English manifests in their own worlds and others' worlds. Through exploring multiple Englishes, there must be an emphasis on communication across peoples and communities. Effective communication highlights that "trying to understand others is not the sole responsibility of the nonnative speakers or speakers of 'less standard' English varieties (however that is defined). Everyone is responsible for overall successful communication, whether it is international or not" (Matsuda & Friedrich, 2011, p. 340). Thus, a global classroom emphasizes that "[m]eaning is achieved through communication and negotiation, not through adherence to a native English-speaking norm" (Galloway & Rose, 2015, p. xi). To promote effective communication without centering or privileging only native-speaker or standard varieties of English, a global classroom offers a space where teachers may take up translanguaging as a legitimate pedagogical practice (Flores & García, 2013; see the following sections for a discussion of *translanguaging*).

Multiple Narratives

In addition to embracing multiple Englishes, a global classroom considers whose knowledge is being taught and for what purposes (Vodopija-Krstanovic & Marinac, 2019). In traditional global classrooms, inner-circle (Kachru, 1982) narratives, knowledge, and Englishes are centered. Yet this focus dismisses "critical, controversial, and complex aspects of global knowledge . . . This absence is a reflection of factors such as institutionalization of a narrow nationalistic curriculum . . . that deemphasizes the global dimensions of citizenship" (Subedi, 2013, p. 621). In other words, honoring knowledge from multiple spaces, particularly those from marginalized communities and cultures, helps us all become better global citizens.

In a global classroom, narratives of difference (and similarity) are taught so that students embrace empathy in critical and conscious ways (see discussion of *empathy* next). A global curriculum focuses on both the local and the global, emphasizing questions of sustainability, including traditionally excluded voices, and empowering students to become agents of transformation (Caniglia et al., 2018).

What Is Valued in a Global Classroom?

In the previous section, we offer a framework for considering a global curriculum, which includes multiple Englishes and multiple narratives. In this section, we offer descriptions of concepts that should be a central part of a global curriculum.

Problematizing "Standard"

There is a lot of debate about what to name Standardized English and whether a Standardized English even exists (i.e., how we decide to bind or standardize a language is done through arbitrary choices fueled more by power structures than how language is actually used). Sociolinguists, people who study language in the real world, agree that there isn't a single "standard" English because they know that the follow-up question is always "whose standard?"

All variations of English around the globe follow conventions and patterns, which linguists sometimes document as *descriptive rules* (i.e., statements that merely describe patterns of language without judging the social worth of those patterns). Some conventions (using "I" only as a subject pronoun, as in *I like cheese*, and never as an object, as in the prepositional phrase *between Michelle and I*) become codified in grammar books and style guides as models of "proper" or "professional" language. Linguists refer to these codified conventions as *standards* or *prescriptive rules* (i.e., statements that tell speakers and writers how to communicate the "correct" or "best" forms of language; see online Support Material for more examples). At the same time, some dialectal conventions (e.g., use of *ain't*) are stigmatized as "incorrect" or "bad" and thus "non-standard"; varieties that exhibit non-standard conventions are then deemed by language authorities as themselves "non-standard."

Approaching this idea of standard language from a global perspective raises several critical questions:

- Who gets to decide which language conventions and which varieties are standard or stigmatized?
- Since different cultures and nations codify different standard varieties (e.g., Standard British versus Standard American Englishes), how do schools around the world decide which standard to promote in a curriculum?
- Should English classes even be teaching or promoting a single standard variety of language?
- If teachers integrate multiple Englishes into their curriculum, how do they avoid privileging certain varieties over others?
- When teaching "English" in a global classroom, which English(es) are being taught?

These are important questions for teachers, their students, and their school administrators; the answers will necessarily reflect global differences in culture, society, identity, and history. Questions about standard English in a global classroom must consider how colonization, slavery, and power both influenced and continue to influence the idea of one "right" way of using English.[5]

Hence, a global classroom critiques standard English. It invites questions around how idealizing a standard devalues local varieties of English and, furthermore, how that devaluation affects users' identities (see "identity" discussion later). Such questions open spaces for inclusive teaching: honoring variations, their histories, and the power constructs under which they develop. These questions also allow an

---

5 For further reading on colonization and English instruction, see Anchimbe, 2009 and Subedi, 2013.

exploration of naming. In the introductory chapter of our previous edited collection (Devereaux & Palmer, 2019b, pp. xvii–xviii), we encouraged classroom discussion around naming English varieties: who gets to name varieties and why? But we also advocate encouraging students to take ownership in naming their own varieties—those spoken by their own communities and families—without measuring the value of those varieties or their own identities against the social status of a standard.

Identity

Language is intricately tied to identity (Devereaux, 2015; Wolfram & Schilling, 2015). Through our language use, we both produce (Bucholtz & Hall, 2004) and perform (Curzan & Adams, 2012, p. 267) our identity. Indeed, Norton (1997) says that every time second language speakers speak, they are engaged in "identity construction and negotiation" (p. 410).

Exploring the connections between language and identity is crucial in a global classroom because, often, students might feel that they are limited by fixed-language identities, defined by nation-states (García & Li, 2014). However, a global classroom invites students to critique and resist the identities and ideologies assigned to them in their education (Seltzer, 2019). Teachers and students embrace the plurality of both their language stories and their language uses. Beyond exploring their own language stories, students are introduced to global language stories and how speakers of English across the globe identify with English. Language stories provide an entry to consider how power structures both introduce and perpetuate English instruction throughout the world (Devereaux et al., 2021). However, when learning about others' experiences with language, teachers must expand their curriculum to include critical empathy.

Empathy

Much in the same way the English language has been standardized for supposedly easy consumption, empathy has been simplified as a goal to make the world nicer (Mirra, 2018). The Atticus Adage[6] is a potentially problematic version of empathy because it often simplifies another person's experience. It isn't enough to walk around in someone else's shoes. Such advice might allow students to examine others' stories only through their own personal histories and identities. It could allow students to believe that people across the globe (and across their town) have similar access to power and resources. This type of empathy, an empathy that is uncritical and unconscious, consumes the histories, cultures, and identities of others' stories (because others' histories, cultures, and identities are not entirely like our own).

---

6 In *To Kill a Mockingbird*, Attitcus tries to teach his children about empathy by telling them "You never really understand a person until you consider things from his point of view . . . until you climb in his skin and walk around in it" (Lee, 1982, p. 30).

A concrete example of this type of empathy emerged in our work with tenth-graders in the United States. After two weeks of learning about English as a Lingua Franca and differences among World Englishes, we noticed that a majority of students demonstrated increased empathy for speakers of non-US English language varieties (Devereaux et al., 2021). Yet at the same time, they also showed an increased desire for speakers to learn a lingua franca and to embrace a single, standard variety of English. We speculated that such empathy might have been more passive and uncritical rather than active and critical. In other words, even as students felt bad about the negative experiences of other speakers learning English around the globe (who are often pressured to shift away from heritage languages or judged harshly for speaking non-dominant varieties), they may have defaulted to a problematic point of view: "Wouldn't the world be more harmonious and humane if we were all taught the same language?" Such a position might seem rooted in empathy, but it neglects significant power differentials in the world: it doesn't take much effort for a speaker of American English to expect the rest of the globe to speak (American) English. In contrast to embracing a globally dominant or standard variety of language, a more actively empathetic position might have been the following: "What can *I* do to help change global systems that perpetuate linguistic stigma, prejudice, and marginalization?" A key task for teachers, then, is to help students move from such passive forms of empathy to active ones.

Pedwell (2016) offers an accessible framework to discuss empathy with students: empathy as translation. For example, when someone translates a work from one language to another, translating the words isn't enough. The translator must understand the social, political, and historical context of the work that is being translated in order to create a fair translation. Such engagement creates a critical examination of the text. In the same way, a global classroom should consider *story as translation*, examining the social, political, and historical contexts in which English moves through the world.

The concept of empathy as translation offers a framework for discussion, but empathy doesn't become *critical* empathy without the goal of creating a more just and equitable world. Mirra (2018) outlines how to move beyond a traditional empathy (i.e., Atticus Adage), one that incites pity instead of empowerment. Instead, Mirra advocates for a "critical civic empathy" that dismantles "dominant ideas that perpetuate inequality" (p. 8) with three accessible steps:

1. It [critical civic empathy] begins from an analysis of the social position, power, and privilege of all of the parties involved.
2. It focuses on the ways that personal experiences matter in the context of public life.
3. It fosters democratic dialogue and vivid action committed to equity and justice (p. 7).

Thus, narratives that do not take into account the politics and power surrounding the global spread and use of English can never move us toward justice and equity. As we must complicate and question the idea of a standard English, so too must we complicate and question how stories are told, whose stories are told, and how those stories are positioned.

Confronting Stereotyping

Another important complication for teachers in a global classroom is that English language teaching concerns not only variation among groups of speakers around the world but also variation within groups: not all speakers within a community speak entirely the same way. And linguistic features (e.g., deletion of /r/ after vowels; use of multiple modals such as *might could*) can exist in multiple varieties of English, with different speakers using those features at varying rates in different contexts (from *quite often* to *not at all*). Despite this intradialectal variation, many people stereotype dialects and speakers of those dialects as if they spoke uniformly—singling out, exaggerating, or even mocking certain linguistic qualities, most typically the voices of marginalized communities. And speakers themselves sometimes construct identities based in part on linguistic stereotypes. They may embrace and/or reject various stereotyped features in their individual repertoire (i.e., the set of linguistic features and varieties that a speaker draws upon to communicate), often feeling social pressure to speak or avoid speaking certain ways that are seen as stereotypical of group identities (Bucholtz, 2004).

When talking with our own students about the use of dialects in literature or creative writing, stereotyping is often mentioned as a top concern. Many of them worry about the harm caused by writers intentionally or unintentionally stereotyping varieties when writing with them. For example, while revising a screenwriting prompt that Chris had assigned in class, even students writing in a dialect that was part of their own repertoire reported concerns that they may have relied on stereotyping. Students often fell back on stereotyped features to create comic effects or to provide a quick signal to readers that a character was from a certain region or community. Teachers, too, have told us that they worry about how to integrate practice with listening to, writing, or speaking different Global Englishes in their classrooms without students resorting to stereotyping or mimicry of particular varieties.

It can be beneficial for teachers to directly address these concerns about stereotyping to students as critical thinking questions: How do we recognize and avoid negative stereotypes when encountering dialects and other language varieties in our speaking, listening, reading, and writing, both inside and outside the classroom? Why do some speakers feel the need to ridicule how people talk? Is there ever a place to include linguistic stereotypes in writing (e.g., a satire about stereotyping)? What are strategies that students can use to incorporate ethical, sensitive practices in the use of global dialects and other variations in their writing?

Code-Switching, Code-Meshing, Translanguaging

To reflect the dynamic and varied linguistic practices of the worlds students live in, increasing numbers of scholars and teachers in recent years have been integrating strategies such as *code-switching*, *code-meshing*, and *translanguaging* in their work with global classrooms. Our own students, many of whom are pre-service teachers, occasionally come into our classes with some passing knowledge of these linguistic phenomena. But they often feel confused about the differences in terminology and unsure about what role these processes play in language learning.

Code-switching is one way to describe moments in which speakers shift between languages (e.g., Japanese and English); between dialects or accents (e.g., Scottish English and Standardized British English/Received Pronunciation); between sociolects (e.g., gay male Englishes and standardized Englishes); or between other varieties (e.g., Cameroon English and Kamtok/Cameroon Pidgin English). From the perspective of code-switching, all such languages and varieties are assumed to be named, discrete, and separate entities making up part of a speaker's repertoire. Code-switching also tends to assume that speakers switch between varieties for contextual or other rhetorical purposes—for example, one dialect is deemed by the speaker, often unconsciously, to be a better fit for one audience or situation than another.

Some pedagogical approaches, such as Wheeler and Swords (2006), encourage instructors to teach students code-switching as a more conscious linguistic strategy. This is recommended as a way to help students learn how conventions in their home languages or dialects compare and contrast with patterns in standardized varieties, which are commonly taught as the preferred forms of language for school and other professional contexts. Wheeler (2019) argues that such an approach keeps teachers from presenting non-standard variants in the classroom as errors and allows students to "build on the patterns of the home to add the patterns of the school" (p. 117). But some scholars, such as Baker-Bell (2020), have criticized code-switching pedagogical approaches that teach students to switch between "home" and "school." Even if the intent is to bring varieties of English into classroom practice and honor students' fluency with these varieties, the home/school dichotomy upholds a linguistic hierarchy that places standardized Englishes on a pedestal and unfairly and unjustly relegates other varieties, such as Black English, as supposedly inappropriate for formal and professional contexts. Even so, some proponents of code-switching argue that it can disrupt linguistic prejudice (Wheeler, 2019). Others maintain that the technique can destabilize linguistic hierarchies (e.g., Brown, 2009; Hudgens Henderson, 2019), as long as students are asked *to critically engage with the effects of switching* (e.g., thinking about the impacts of using different varieties for different audiences) and aren't solely or constantly being asked to switch from their own varieties into a standard variety.

Like code-switching, both *code-meshing* and *translanguaging*[7] are phenomena that describe speakers' mixing and combining of different variants within the same communicative act. But proponents of *code-meshing* (e.g., Young et al., 2011; Canagarajah, 2011) and *translanguaging* (García & Li, 2014) generally assume that different varieties within a speaker's repertoire are not fundamentally distinct and completely separate from one another: they are part of the same system rather than disparate systems that speakers switch into and out of. Code-meshing and translanguaging describe how speakers dynamically draw from different parts of their repertoire, mutually negotiating forms and meanings in real time when they

---

7 Canagarajah (2011, p. 273) sees these terms as closely related, though used in different disciplinary contexts: *code-meshing* (along with other terms such as *transcultural literacy* and *translingual writing*) in composition and communication, and *translanguaging* (along with *plurilingualism, third spaces,* and *ludic Englishes*) in applied linguistics. García and Li (2014) describe other related terms such as *bilanguaging, multivocality, metrolingualism, polylingualism, transidiomatic practice,* and *crossing* (pp. 36–41); they emphasize that "whereas codemeshing is seen as a form of resistance" to norms in academic discourse, "translanguaging is positioned as the discursive norm that names a reality other than a monolingual one" (p. 40).

communicate with one another. The names that are ascribed to certain sets of linguistic variants (typically the names of national, regional, or social languages and lects) are driven more by ideological than inherent or static properties of those varieties: in other words, we name certain varieties "English" or "Standard English" or "a dialect of English" or "not English" mostly for historical, political, and social reasons. Canagarajah (2011) explains how this perspective on labels relates to assumptions about speaker competence: "Multilinguals do not have separate competences for separately labeled languages (as traditional linguistics assumes) but an integrated competence that is different in kind (not just degree) from monolingual competence" (p. 274).

Thus, when applying code-meshing and translanguaging approaches to classrooms, teachers are encouraged to draw on multilingual students' integrated competence as a direct teaching strategy. Canagarajah (2011) makes the point that students often mesh codes or translanguage in their daily lives and in classrooms, even in secret (e.g., chatting with other students in different languages when the teacher is out of earshot), especially in those monolingual classrooms that formally disallow language use other than a single, standardized variety of the dominant language. So why not develop teaching strategies for language learning that overtly draw on multilingual students' existing competence in navigating multiple varieties to understand and make meaning? Even "monolingual" students typically navigate multiple dialects, sociolects, and other varieties in their daily communicative practices, so couldn't they too benefit from code-meshing or translanguaging in classrooms to reflect their individual identities and better understand the course material?

As pre-service teachers learn about these different language variation approaches, the most frequent pedagogical concerns we hear from them regard:

1. confusion about overlap in the concepts;
2. lack of confidence in knowing which technique would be best for their classroom;
3. uncertainty about how they should implement a technique; and
4. nervousness about their own repertoire, especially if they don't speak the languages or dialects of their students.

While there are interesting and valuable debates in the scholarship about the ideologies and efficacies of code-switching, code-meshing, translanguaging, and other related concepts, we argue that it's important for teachers not to get too bogged down by the names or technical differences among approaches and to be willing to incorporate at least one of them in their classrooms. Even if teachers don't know all of the languages or dialects used by their students, they can learn about those varieties by encouraging their students to use and analyze them in discussions and activities—to work alongside students to draw upon the classroom repertoire, so to speak. It's important to remember that students are brilliant users of language(s)—experts in their ways of speaking and communicating. Inviting them to share their expertise is an easy way to incorporate these ideas into the classroom.

In teaching there is rarely (if ever) a "one-size-fits-all" method that works for all students at all grade levels in all situations. As the different chapters of this book demonstrate, different classroom contexts may benefit from different techniques.

So it's imperative that teachers be aware of the tools, be willing to try them, and be willing to revise their use of them and/or try different tools in future classes.

When advising teachers on the implementation of English-language-variation-based techniques in a global classroom, we emphasize the value of any pedagogical approach that:

- centers a student's home varieties in the classroom and not just standard varieties or language(s);
- asks students to learn about and reflect on other students' varieties (and not just their own) within critical frameworks of history, power, and culture;
- considers intralinguistic diversity (e.g., variation within a particular language, creole, pidgin, dialect, or other variety) as much as interlinguistic diversity (i.e., diversity among languages, creoles, pidgins, dialects, and other varieties); and
- encourages critical thinking about and problematizing of linguistic labels such as *standard, non-standard, formal, informal, native, non-native, home, school, mainstream, everyday, (in)appropriate, dialect, language,* and, of course, *English.*

Conclusion: Critical Questions for English Teachers in a Global Classroom

Considering the various issues relevant to global classrooms outlined earlier, the authors in this volume have provided valuable, classroom-tested ideas and strategies for teaching English language variation in a variety of contexts. Each chapter balances theory with discussions of curriculum and lesson planning—all of which should interest English teachers around the world who work with students of varied linguistic backgrounds, as well as researchers in the field of Global Englishes. Contributors to this volume present ideas that intersect with a number of fields, such as World Englishes, English as a Lingua Franca, English as an International Language, English as a Medium of Instruction, Sociolinguistics, Applied Linguistics, Educational Linguistics, Literature, and Writing Studies. The book presents important questions and helpful models for those working in the area of Teaching English to Speakers of Other Languages, which can benefit from global and variationist perspectives on language instruction. Moreover, this material is also important for those teaching students whose first language is English. In fact, any curricula for English classes built on culturally sustaining pedagogies (Paris, 2012) must also reckon with global variation in English: an inclusive, pluralistic classroom is neither inclusive nor pluralistic if it engages exclusively with a standard, native-speaker variety of a single nation (Devereaux et al., 2021).

As reflected in the book's structure, the chapters present and offer answers for several critical questions that teachers face when they integrate and involve students in linguistically diverse material:

I: Methods and Strategies

- What methods can teachers develop to incorporate different languages, dialects, and other varieties in the teaching of English?

- Which classroom techniques can be employed for specific teaching contexts, such as small-group work and research on/within local communities?
- What methods have teacher-researchers developed to experiment with and refine different teaching strategies for Global Englishes material?

II: Literature and Writing

- What models can teachers follow to smoothly blend global language variation approaches with the teaching of literature and writing?
- How can teachers integrate linguistic material into an existing curriculum, already full of objectives for teaching literature and writing, without adding an impossible burden to their workload?

III: Perceptions and Ideologies

- Why is it important for teachers and students to discuss ideologies about language and perceptions of dialects and of other varieties from around the world?
- What sorts of activities best engage students in questions of attitudes about different Englishes as well as perceptions of English speakers from different backgrounds?
- How can classroom strategies invite students to listen, speak, read, write, and think critically about the ideologies underlying English language use in different institutional contexts, and in daily life more generally?

These questions don't have single or simple answers, of course. And while this introduction, and the various chapters of this book, don't pretend to offer simple solutions, the collection as a whole aims to provide practical, implementable strategies for addressing these critical questions about teaching English in global contexts. It is our hope that—by focusing on language variation approaches—students, teachers, and researchers will discover new, effective, and exciting avenues for learning about language and equitable education in all kinds of classrooms around the world.

References

Anchimbe, E. A. (2009). Local or international standards: Indigenized varieties of English at the crossroads. In F. Sharifian (Ed.), *English as an international language: Perspectives and pedagogical issues* (pp. 271–286). Multilingual Matters.

Baker-Bell, A. (2020). *Linguistic justice: Black language, literacy, identity, and pedagogy*. Routledge. https://doi.org/10.4324/9781315147383

Bates, R. (2005). Can we live together?: Towards a global curriculum. *Arts and Humanities in Higher Education, 4*(1), 95–109. https://doi.org/10.1177/1474022205048760

Brown, D. W. (2009). *In other words: Lessons on grammar, code-switching, and academic writing*. Heinemann.

Bucholtz, M. (2004). Styles and stereotypes: The linguistic negotiation of identity among Laotian American youth. *International Pragmatics Association, 14*(2–3), 127–147. https://doi.org/10.1075/prag.14.2-3.02buc

Bucholtz, M., & Hall, K. (2004). Language and identity. In A. Duranti (Ed.), *A companion to linguistic anthropology* (pp. 369–394). Blackwell. https://doi.org/10.1002/9780470996522

Canagarajah, A. S. (2011). World Englishes as code-meshing. In V. A. Young & A. Y. Martinez (Eds.), *Code-meshing as world English: Pedagogy, policy, performance* (pp. 273–281). National Council of Teachers of English. https://doi.org/10.1080/15235882.2012.731590

Caniglia, G., Beatrice, J., Bellina, L., Lang, D. J., Wiek, A., Cohmer, S., & Laubichler, M. D. (2018). The *glocal* curriculum: A model for transnational collaboration in higher education for sustainable development. *Journal of Cleaner Production, 171,* 367–376. https://doi.org/10.1016/j.jclepro.2017.09.207

Crystal, D. (2008). Two thousand million? *English Today, 24*(1), 3–6. https://doi.org/10.1017/S0266078408000023

Curzan, A., & Adams, M. (2012). *How English works: A linguistic introduction.* Pearson.

Devereaux, M. D. (2015). *Teaching about dialect variations and language in secondary English classrooms: Power, prestige, and prejudice.* Routledge. https://doi.org/10.4324/9780203581261

Devereaux, M. D., & Palmer, C. C. (Eds.). (2019a). *Teaching language variation in the classroom: Strategies and models from teachers and linguists.* Routledge. https://doi.org/10.4324/9780429486678

Devereaux, M. D., & Palmer, C. C. (2019b). Introduction: Teaching language variation and ideologies—Questions and strategies. In M. D. Devereaux & C. C. Palmer (Eds.), *Teaching language variation in the classroom: Strategies and models from teachers and linguists* (pp. xv–xxiv). Routledge. https://doi.org/10.4324/9780429486678-1

Devereaux, M. D., Palmer, C. C., & Thompson, V. E. (2021). Pandialectal learning: Teaching global Englishes in a tenth-grade English class. *American Speech, 96*(2), 235–252. https://doi.org/10.1215/00031283-9089613

Eberhard, D. M., Simons, G. F., & Fennig, C. D. (Eds.). (2021). *What are the top 200 most spoken languages? Ethnologue: Languages of the world* (24th ed.). Retrieved May 6, 2021, from www.ethnologue.com/guides/ethnologue200

Flores, N. (2013). The unexamined relationship between neoliberalism and plurilingualism: A cautionary tale. *TESOL Quarterly, 47*(3), 500–520.

Flores, N., & García, O. (2013). Linguistic third spaces in education: Teachers' translanguaging across the bilingual continuum. In D. Little, C. Leung, & P. V. Avermaet (Eds.), *Managing diversity in education: Languages, policies, pedagogies* (pp. 243–256). Multilingual Matters.

Galloway, N., & Rose, H. (2015). *Introducing global Englishes.* Routledge. https://doi.org/10.4324/9781315734347

García, O., & Li, W. (2014). *Translanguaging: Language, bilingualism, and education.* Palgrave Macmillan. https://doi.org/10.5565/rev/jtl3.764

Hudgens Henderson, M. (2019). Grammar in the Spanish/English bilingual classroom: Three methods for teaching academic language. In M. D. Devereaux & C. C. Palmer (Eds.), *Teaching language variation in the classroom: Strategies and models from teachers and linguists* (pp. 101–108). Routledge. https://doi.org/10.4324/9780429486678

Jenkins, J. (2006). Current perspectives on teaching world Englishes and English as a lingua franca. *TESOL Quarterly, 40*(1), 157–181.

Kachru, B. B. (Ed.). (1982). *The other tongue: English across cultures.* University of Illinois Press.

Lee, H. (1982). *To kill a mockingbird.* Warner Books.

Lock, J. V. (2015). Designing learning to engage students in the global classroom. *Technology, Pedagogy and Education, 24*(2), 137–153. https://doi.org/10.1080/1475939X.2014.946957

Matsuda, A., & Friedrich, P. (2011). English as an international language: A curriculum blueprint. *World Englishes, 30*(3), 332–344. https://doi.org/10.1111/j.1467-971X.2011.01717.x

Mirra, N. (2018). *Educating for empathy: Literacy, learning, and civic engagement*. Teachers College Press.
Norton, B. (1997). Language, identity, and the ownership of English. *TESOL Quarterly*, *31*(3), 409–429. https://doi.org/10.2307/3587831
Otheguy, R., García, O., & Reid, W. (2015). Clarifying translanguaging and deconstructing named languages: A perspective from linguistics. *Applied Linguistics Review*, *6*, 281–307. https://doi.org/10.1515/applirev-2015-0014
Paris, D. (2012). Culturally sustaining pedagogy: A needed change in stance, terminology, and practice. *Educational Researcher*, *41*(3), 93–97. https://doi.org/10.3102/0013189X12441244
Pedwell, C. (2016). De-colonising empathy: Thinking affect transnationally. *Samyukta: A Journal of Women's Studies*, *16*(1), 27–49. https://doi.org/10.1057/9781137275264
Rose, H., & Galloway, N. (2019). *Global Englishes for language teaching*. Cambridge University Press. https://doi.org/10.1017/9781316678343
Seltzer, K. (2019). Reconceptualizing "home" and "school" language: Taking a critical translingual approach in the English classroom. *TESOL Quarterly*, *53*(4), 986–1007. https://doi.org/10.1002/tesq.530
Shakespeare, W. (2020). *Hamlet, prince of Denmark* (B. Mowat & P. Werstine, Eds.). https://shakespeare.folger.edu/shakespeares-works/hamlet/download/ (Original work published 1599).
Subedi, B. (2013). Decolonizing the curriculum for global perspectives. *Educational Theory*, *63*(6), 621–638. https://doi.org/10.1111/edth.12045
Vodopija-Krstanovic, I., & Marinac, M. (2019). English as an international language and English language teaching: The theory vs. practice divide. *Iranian Journal of Language Teaching Research*, *7*(2), 19–38.
Wheeler, R. S. (2019). Attitude change is not enough: Changing teacher practice to disrupt dialect prejudice in the classroom. In M. D. Devereaux & C. C. Palmer (Eds.), *Teaching language variation in the classroom: Strategies and models from teachers and linguists* (pp. 109–119). Routledge. https://doi.org/10.4324/9780429486678
Wheeler, R. S., & Swords, R. (2006). *Code-switching: Teaching standard English in urban classrooms*. NCTE.
Wolfram, W., & Schilling, N. (2015). *American English: Dialects and variation*. Wiley Blackwell.
Young, V. A., Martinez, A. Y., & Naviaux, J. A. (2011). Introduction: Code-meshing as world English. In V. A. Young & A. Y. Martinez (Eds.), *Code-meshing as world English: Pedagogy, policy, performance* (pp. xix–xxxi). National Council of Teachers of English.

How to Use This Book

The chapters in this volume are organized to invite both connections and contrasts among the theories, ideas, approaches, and pedagogical strategies described by the authors. In the following sections, we offer different ways readers may want to explore this book. First, we explain some of the most commonly used terminology throughout the collection. Next, we briefly discuss variation in some of the written conventions of the global dialects of English used by different chapter authors. Following that appears an overview of the volume's structure: a description of the three parts of the volume, with short summaries of each chapter. We then group chapters according to common themes or topics that cut across the book's three parts. This chapter concludes with a list of lesson plans and other teaching materials appearing in the volume or on its related Support Material site.

Global Englishes: The Challenge of Terminology

In the introduction chapter, we discussed the challenges of naming Global Englishes and how English manifests across the globe. However, beyond this challenge of terminology, scholars who work with Global Englishes must also address how school terminology differs across global classroom contexts. The authors of this volume are from five continents; therefore, the naming practices of schooling levels differ throughout the volume. Rather than asking the authors to standardize their naming practices (because then the question becomes "whose standards?"), we have created this short explanation of how schooling levels are referred to throughout this volume.

- **Primary/First-level:** Schooling in the lower grades, approximately five-year-olds to ten-year-olds[1]
- **Secondary/Second-level:** Schooling in upper grades, approximately 11-year-olds to 18-year-olds
- **Tertiary/Post-Secondary/Third-Level:** University, college, or trade school
- **K-12:** Schooling from approximately five-year-old to 18-year-old
- **K-16:** Schooling from approximately five-year-old through university or college

---

1 All of the ages included in this section are approximate and may differ according to country or area.

Naming multilingual speakers and the classrooms and programs in which they learn English also varies greatly across the globe. For this reason, we provide a short list here with some of the terms our authors use throughout this volume.

- **EFL:** English as a foreign language
- **EIL:** English as an international language
- **ELA:** English language arts
- **ELF:** English as a lingua franca
- **ELL:** English language learner
- **ELT:** English language teaching
- **EMI:** English as a medium of instruction
- **ESL:** English as a second language
- **ESOL:** English to speakers of other languages
- **GE:** Global Englishes
- **GELT:** Global Englishes language teaching
- **L1:** first language
- **L2:** second language
- **SLA:** Second language acquisition
- **TESOL:** Teaching English to speakers of other languages

Finally, many of our authors used the Common European Framework of Reference for Languages (CEFRL)[2] throughout their chapters. This framework levels groups of language learners, beginning with A1 and A2 for basic users to C1 and C2 for proficient users.

Global Englishes: Diverse Language Conventions in Publications

One of the quandaries we faced when assembling this collection was how to balance publisher demands for consistency in language use across a single volume with the fact that written language conventions in English vary around the world. Our authors reflect regions from five different continents, as well as a variety of Englishes from these regions. So requiring use of a standardized variety of English (such as Standard American or Standard British) would contradict and undermine what we are arguing for: that English manifests differently across the globe and that such differences need to be embraced rather than standardized or erased.

To accommodate the needs of both the publisher and our authors, we aimed for a mixture of consistency and variation. Formatting of lesson plans, citations, and references, for example, are consistent across the book, as are punctuation conventions such as the Oxford comma. But authors were encouraged to use their local or regional English spellings and lexicon consistently within their individual chapters; hence, readers may notice differences in orthography or word choice when comparing different parts of the book.

---

2 www.coe.int/en/web/common-european-framework-reference-languages/level-descriptions

Chapter Summaries

Part 1: Methods and Strategies

Part 1 highlights particular pedagogical methods and strategies that the authors have researched and implemented in order to effectively teach English language variation in global classrooms.

English Words in the English World: Integrating World Englishes in the Linguistics Classroom Luca Raimondi, King's College London, UK and University of the Witwatersrand, Johannesburg, South Africa

Using a World Englishes approach within a postmethod pedagogical framework, Luca Raimondi describes how to develop a unit on word-formation using examples from multiple global varieties of English.

Using Learning Stations at College: An Introduction to Linguistic Shift and Change for English Proficiency Development Yolanda Morató, University of Seville, Spain

Yolanda Morató presents strategies for using learning stations to increase student participation and facilitate work on global variation in the English language, with a special focus on American and British Englishes.

Balancing the Focus on Local and Global Varieties of English: Can Teaching Pedagogy Take the Multilingual Turn? Aicha Rahal, Aix-Marseille University, France

Incorporating listening and role-play exercises, Aicha Rahal presents classroom models to teach students appreciation and understanding of multiple varieties of English from around the world.

Translation as an Asset to Raise Global Englishes Awareness in the English Classroom, Elif Kemaloglu-Er, Adana Alparslan Türkeş Science and Technology University, Turkey

Elif Kemaloglu-Er demonstrates how translation can be used as a pedagogical tool to improve multilingual students' linguistic, analytical, and critical thinking skills, as well as their understanding of Global Englishes.

Practical Suggestions for Integrating Translanguaging in Secondary EFL: Using a Wordless Picture Book and Book Club Discussions, Eun Young Yeom, University of Georgia, USA

Eun Young Yeom describes the benefits of both teachers and students using translanguaging strategies along with a wordless picture book to promote English language learning among Korean-speaking secondary students.

L1 Use and Translanguaging in ELL Peer Interaction: A Problem or a Useful Tool? Dmitrii Pastushenkov, Michigan State University, USA, Curtis A. Green-Eneix, Michigan State University, USA, and Olesia Pavlenko, Kent State University, USA

Dmitrii Pastushenkov, Curtis A. Green-Eneix, and Olesia Pavlenko highlight how translanguaging can support learners' acquisition of English by completing an assortment of tasks such as consensus, conversation, spot-the-difference, interview, and role-playing activities.

Part 2: Literature and Writing

Part 2 demonstrates how teachers can use a variety of literature and writing tasks to integrate Global Englishes material into their own curriculum.

A Conversation-Analytic Approach to Translanguaging Practices in Literature Courses in Turkish Higher Education*, Vildan Inci-Kavak, Gaziantep University, Turkey, and Yasemin Kırkgöz, Çukurova University, Turkey*

Analyzing data from a post-colonial literature class, Vildan Inci-Kavak and Yasemin Kırkgöz demonstrate how students can use translanguaging as a practical communicative device that serves particular pedagogical functions such as deeper understanding, checking and co-constructing meaning, building on previous knowledge, and identity formation.

The Subtle Case of Beirut: Translingualism in the English-Medium Undergraduate Literature Classroom*, Salma Yassine and Vicky Panossian, Central European University, Austria*

Discussing uses of both Arabic and English in a literature classroom, Salma Yassine and Vicky Panossian illustrate how translingualism serves as an effective pedagogical tool to combat socio-cultural prejudices, particularly regarding gender and sexuality.

Integrating Global Englishes into Literature and Writing Units: Advice for Secondary Teachers*, Victoria E. Thompson, Riverwood International Charter School, Georgia, USA*

Victoria E. Thompson, considering her own work with Global Englishes in her tenth-grade English classroom, offers reflections, resources, and recommendations for teachers who want to integrate Global Englishes in their own classrooms.

Language Diversity, Cross-Cultural Awareness, and Digital Media in the Writing Classroom*, Florence Elizabeth Bacabac, Dixie State University, USA*

Florence Elizabeth Bacabac highlights the use of digital media and technology to promote Global English variation and cross-cultural awareness in the writing classroom.

Trans-/multilingual Language in Different Contexts: Using Scaffolding to Assist Multilingual Learners*, Verbra Pfeiffer, University of South Africa, South Africa*

Verbra Pfeiffer describes how to use techniques such as scaffolding and semantic mapping to help pre-service teachers understand the benefits of translanguaging for students learning academic writing in English.

Part 3: Perceptions and Ideologies

Part 3 provides methods and frameworks to discuss how global English variations are perceived as well as the ideologies attached to them; these chapters work towards a more inclusive understanding of language variation in global contexts.

Speak Locally, Listen Globally: Training Listeners to Understand the Diverse Accents of Englishes Around the World*, Vance Schaefer, The University of Mississippi, USA, and Isabelle Darcy, Indiana University, USA*

Describing types of phonological features of World Englishes and the mechanisms of accent perception, Vance Schaefer and Isabelle Darcy illustrate how increasing awareness and understanding of diverse accents are key to spoken communication in a globalized world.

Implementing Global Englishes Real-World Activities in a Thai Tertiary Setting
Yusop Boonsuk & Eric A. Ambele, Prince of Songkla University, Thailand

Incorporating in-class and field-trip activities such as presentations and tourist interviews, Yusop Boonsuk and Eric A. Ambele demonstrate how university students in Thailand changed their ideologies and attitudes about English language use by interacting with speakers in the real world.

Code-Switching in Hong Kong: Key to Implementing a Hong Kong English Curriculum? Ka Long Roy Chan, *The Hong Kong Polytechnic University, Hong Kong*

Considering various attitudes about language and dialect use in Hong Kong, Ka Long Roy Chan provides theoretical background and practical strategies for integrating Hong Kong English into the local English curriculum, including a task-based guided role-play involving code-switching.

Translanguaging in University Direct-Entry Pathway English Courses: An Australian Case, Michelle Ocriciano, *The University of Queensland, Australia*

By incorporating translanguaging and multimodal approaches, Michelle Ocriciano discusses how to adapt a prescriptive curriculum in a direct-entry university pathway so that it challenges ideologies such as linguistic purism, allows students' voices to be heard, and encourages use of their full repertoires.

Global Englishes and Oral Communication: Perceptions of Multilingual Speakers, Nasiba Norova, *University of Massachusetts, USA*

Exploring topics such as standard varieties, linguistic discrimination, and perceptions of different dialects and their speakers, Nasiba Norova presents research on how and why to integrate Global Englishes perspectives into an English for Academic Purposes oracy course.

Using (Critical) Applied Linguistics to Negotiate the Teaching of Dominant Englishes, Ribut Wahyudi, *Universitas Islam Negeri (UIN) Maulana Malik Ibrahim Malang, Indonesia*

Ribut Wahyudi explains how to design and teach a course on Critical Applied Linguistics with an emphasis on helping students critique and negotiate language ideologies that uphold dominant Englishes in Indonesia and broader global contexts.

Topics

Selected chapters have been organized here into topical groups, demonstrating how different courses of study or areas of research might use this book. These groupings are meant to be a rough guide rather than an exhaustive listing of all topics covered and of all chapters touching on each topic. (Readers who don't see a topic they have in mind are encouraged to use the index to seek out other topical threads among chapters.)

Literature, TV, Film, and Media

　　Raimondi (pp. 3–12)
　　Kemaloglu-Er (pp. 34–42)
　　Inci-Kavak & Kırkgöz (pp. 63–73)
　　Yassine & Panossian (pp. 74–81)
　　Thompson (pp. 82–91)
　　Bacabac (pp. 92–101)
　　Schaefer & Darcy (pp. 113–122)
　　Ocriciano (pp. 142–151)
　　Norova (pp. 152–162)

Reading and Writing

Morató (pp. 13–24)
Yeom (pp. 43–51)
Inci-Kavak & Kırkgöz (pp. 63–73)
Yassine & Panossian (pp. 74–81)
Thompson (pp. 82–91)
Bacabac (pp. 92–101)
Pfeiffer (pp. 102–110)
Ocriciano (pp. 142–151)
Wahyudi (pp. 163–173)

Speaking and Listening

Morató (pp. 13–24)
Rahal (pp. 25–33)
Kemaloglu-Er (pp. 34–42)
Yeom (pp. 43–51)
Pastushenkov, Green-Eneix, & Pavlenko (pp. 52–60)
Inci-Kavak & Kırkgöz (pp. 63–73)
Yassine & Panossian (pp. 74–81)
Schaefer & Darcy (pp. 113–122)
Boonsuk & Ambele (pp. 123–131)
Ocriciano (pp. 142–151)
Norova (pp. 152–162)

Code-Switching and Translanguaging

Yeom (pp. 43–51)
Pastushenkov, Green-Eneix, & Pavlenko (pp. 52–60)
Inci-Kavak & Kırkgöz (pp. 63–73)
Yassine & Panossian (pp. 74–81)
Pfeiffer (pp. 102–110)
Chan (pp. 132–141)
Ocriciano (pp. 142–151)
Wahyudi (pp. 163–173)

Colonial and Post-Colonial Contexts

Raimondi (pp. 3–12)
Kemaloglu-Er (pp. 34–42)
Inci-Kavak & Kırkgöz (pp. 63–73)
Yassine & Panossian (pp. 74–81)
Thompson (pp. 82–91)
Chan (pp. 132–141)
Norova (pp. 152–162)
Wahyudi (pp. 163–173)

Language Ideologies

Morató (pp. 13–24)
Yassine & Panossian (pp. 74–81)
Thompson (pp. 82–91)
Schaefer & Darcy (pp. 113–122)
Boonsuk & Ambele (pp. 123–131)
Chan (pp. 132–141)
Ocriciano (pp. 142–151)
Norova (pp. 152–162)
Wahyudi (pp. 163–173)

Dialects of English

Raimondi (pp. 3–12)
Morató (pp. 13–24)
Rahal (pp. 25–33)
Kemaloglu-Er (pp. 34–42)
Thompson (pp. 82–91)
Bacabac (pp. 92–101)
Schaefer & Darcy (pp. 113–122)
Chan (pp. 132–141)
Norova (pp. 152–162)

Linguistic areas[3]

Raimondi (pp. 3–12)

- Morphology
- Lexicon

Morató (pp. 13–24)

- Orthography
- Morphology
- Syntax
- Pragmatics
- Lexicon

Rahal (pp. 25–33)

- Phonology

Pastushenkov, Green-Eneix, & Pavlenko (pp. 52–60)

- Lexicon

Inci-Kavak & Kırkgöz (pp. 63–73)

- Discourse Analysis
- Lexicon

---

3 The listing here mentions areas other than sociolinguistics, applied linguistics, educational linguistics, and second language teaching, all of which are addressed by all chapters in the volume.

xxxii How to Use This Book

Thompson (pp. 82–91)

- Lexicon

Bacabac (pp. 92–101)

- Syntax
- Discourse
- Lexicon

Pfeiffer (pp. 102–110)

- Lexicon
- Semantics

Schaefer & Darcy (pp. 113–122)

- Phonology

 Lesson Plans and Support Material

Each chapter in this collection includes a lesson plan, whose title and page numbers are provided next. Some chapters also include additional teaching materials called "Support Material" that can be found on the book's companion website (www.routledge.com/9780367644703). Additional teaching materials include handouts, presentation materials, activity suggestions, digital resources, and additional examples and explanations of concepts and strategies described in the volume. Recommended grade levels (and sometimes English language facility) have been provided for each lesson in the book, though readers should note that lessons are adaptable for different student demographics.

Raimondi

This volume (pp. 9–10): "Chutnified—Lexical Innovations in Indian English," designed for the undergraduate and lower postgraduate level, with at least B2 CEFRL competence

Support Material: "Borrowings from Indigenous Languages in Colonial Settings"; "Hybrid Formations"

Morató

This volume (pp. 16–20): "Travel With Words!," designed for college students and pre-service teachers, with at least C1 CEFRL competence

Rahal

This volume (pp. 29–31): "Teaching Local Varieties—South African English as an Example," designed for intermediate and advanced students at the secondary or tertiary levels

How to Use This Book   xxxiii

Kemaloglu-Er

This volume (pp. 39–40): "Exploring Varieties of English Through Translation," designed for intermediate (B1), upper-intermediate (B2), or advanced (C1) level or proficient (C2) college students or secondary students

Yeom

This volume (pp. 49–50): "Using Picture Books for EFL Emergent Bilinguals' Translanguaging," designed for secondary-, college-, and adult-level EFL classes

Pastushenkov, Green-Eneix, & Pavlenko

This volume (p. 59): "Interview Activity," designed for beginner high, intermediate, or advanced middle school/high school/university ELLs

Inci-Kavak & Kırkgöz

This volume (pp. 70–71): "Poetry Circles—Nurturing a Multilingual Ecology and Multilingual Content Mastery," designed for secondary school/language major students (11th & 12th Grades); tertiary level ELL and ELT students (at course level); or students with B1+ level & higher (CEFRL)

Yassine & Panossian

This volume (pp. 79–80): "'The Hidden Face of Eve'—A Non-Fictitious Route to Teaching Arabian Feminist Literature," designed for undergraduate students
Support Material: "'The Story of Zahra'—Student-Oriented Teaching of Arabian Feminist Literature"

Thompson

This volume (pp. 89–90): "Writing About Global Englishes—Selecting an Argumentative Topic," designed for secondary English Language Arts (9th–12th grades)
Support Material: "Global Englishes Resources for Secondary Teachers"

Bacabac

This volume (p. 99): "Exploring Language Diversity and Cross-Cultural Variations," designed for students from the upper-level secondary through intermediate college levels
Support Material: "Global Englishes Resources for the Writing Classroom"

Pfeiffer

This volume (pp. 108–109): "Semantic Feature Analysis—Comparing and Contrasting Features of Words," designed for secondary and tertiary students at the B2 level (CEFRL)
Support Material: "Semantic Mapping to Assist Bi/multilingual Learners in Learning Academic Vocabulary"

Schaefer & Darcy

This volume (pp. 120–121): "Accent Detective—Breaking Accents Down Into Their Components," designed for students at the high school, undergraduate, or graduate level
Support Material: "Resources for Working with Global English Accents"

Boonsuk & Ambele

This volume (pp. 129–130): "Student-Foreigners GELT Exposure Activity," designed for students at the tertiary level

Chan

This volume (pp. 138–139): "Role-Play of Code-Switching in Hong Kong," designed for bilingual senior high school to university students

Ocriciano

This volume (pp. 148–149): "Multimodal Flipped Writing Class," designed for young adults at a B2 level or higher

Norova

This volume (pp. 158–160): "Language Varieties and Linguicism—Empowering Ourselves," designed for high school students or for undergraduate first-year English integrated skills course students
Support Material: "PowerPoint for Language Varieties and Linguicism"

Wahyudi

This volume (pp. 163–173): "Critically Negotiating Monolingual Concepts of Dominant Englishes," designed for upper-level undergraduate students

Devereaux & Palmer

Support Material: "Prescriptive and Descriptive Rules Handout"; "Lesson Plan Template"

Part I
Methods and Strategies

Chapter 1

English Words in the English World

Integrating World Englishes in the Linguistics Classroom

Luca Raimondi

The colonial legacies and racial underpinnings entangled with English instruction have become a crucial concern and a research priority for scholars and educators in the field of English language teaching. Drawing insights from the theoretical framework of coloniality (Mignolo & Walsh, 2018), as well as theorisations of the relationships between race, ethnicity, and language (see, inter alia, Alim et al., 2016), an extensive body of literature has challenged the monoglossic ideology and the racialised hierarchical logics on which English language education is rooted (as revealed, for example, by the conventional use of dichotomous labels such as "standard/non-standard varieties" and "native/non-native speakers"). This scholarship has offered recommendations for "provincialising English" (Motha, 2014) and decolonising pedagogies (Kumaravadivelu, 2016).

In contrast to the abundance of studies focused on English language teaching, especially in the context of TESOL (for an overview, see Hsu, 2017), there has arguably been less attention to how the same dynamics have shaped the disciplinary practice of English linguistics. To be sure, a decolonising approach to the scientific investigation of English language has informed the sub-discipline of World Englishes (WE) since its emergence in the 1980s, thanks to the foundational works of Kachru (1982) and Trudgill and Hannah (1982), among others. At a macro level, however, the "norm-providing" varieties have largely remained those of the "inner circle" (Kachru, 1985, p. 16), that is, British English and (less often) American English, as demonstrated by the choice of phonological, morphological, and syntactical features and examples discussed in general English linguistics coursebooks (e.g., Meyer, 2009; Herbst, 2010). That the aspiration to redress the unequal relations between the varieties of English used across the Anglosphere is not being felt evenly across the core branches of the discipline, but rather in only a few subfields such as WE, raises legitimate concerns about the ideological foundations of English linguistics as a whole. Besides, even WE-oriented approaches should be alert to the perils posed by the standardising logic of the discipline, whereby the "World" gets transformed into the unequal and racialised category of the "non-West" (Motha, 2014, pp. 119–124), to reinforce the dominance of a few normative varieties over others.

Disciplinary decolonisation is, of course, a very complex and multi-layered process that involves both "taking control of the principles and practices of planning, learning and teaching" (Kumaravadivelu, 2003, p. 540) and shifting towards a "postmethod pedagogy" that is responsive to local particularities. Furthermore,

DOI: 10.4324/9781003124665-2

disciplinary decolonisation is based on a context-specific theory of practice aimed at raising the socio-political consciousness of language learners (Kumaravadivelu, 2001). In this chapter, I discuss my experience of designing and teaching a module in English linguistics for second-year undergraduate EFL students specialising in Language Mediation. Inspired by Kumaravadivelu's postmethod pedagogic principles and bringing the decolonising perspective of WE to the study of English morphology, this unit is intended as a step in the direction of rethinking the shape of English linguistics pedagogy, particularly in the global university.

The Educational Context

The module discussed in this chapter was designed and delivered during my two-year tenure at the School of Interpreting and Translation, Fondazione Milano (Milan, Italy). A compulsory core course for students on the bachelor's degree-equivalent Diploma in Language Mediation, it ran over 12 weeks for a total contact time of 24 hours. In line with the education policy of the School, teaching occurred through lectures, as is typical in the Italian academic system, and with English as the medium of instruction (EMI), a regular feature of undergraduate and postgraduate programmes in English language and linguistics in Italy. In my class, all students (approximately 60 total) were EFL learners, with nearly the same level of proficiency (B2 CEFR level) and an English-learning background strongly reliant on the "native speaker model": as a recent study of learners' language attitudes has shown, Italian university students consider standard British or American English as the varieties that should be used in the classroom, surely also as a result of ELT coursebooks and learning materials targeting exclusively "native speaker English norms" and cultural contents (De Bartolo, 2018).

Setting Up the Unit

The decision to incorporate a WE approach in the morphology class stemmed from, on the one hand, a personal awareness of the nativist, mono-varietal bias inherent in the discipline of English linguistics, and on the other hand, the tenets of Kumaravadivelu's postmethod framework (2001). I was especially inspired by the parameter of particularity, according to which pedagogic practice "must be sensitive to a particular group of teachers teaching a particular group of learners pursuing a particular set of goals within a particular institutional context embedded in a particular sociocultural milieu" (p. 538). My assumption when designing the unit was that my students—a group of prospective graduates in Language Mediation who would ideally pursue jobs in translation, interpreting, and intercultural communication—would benefit from understanding the implications of the global spread of English and being able to recognise the most salient morphological features of world Englishes. This would indeed help them develop non-adversarial attitudes towards speakers from any region of the Anglosphere, as well as strategies to avoid domesticating or erasing the cultural values of the different source varieties. Such a unit would also lead to a higher degree of ownership of the English language: awakened to the plurality of English underlying the WE paradigm, students would feel legitimised to inhabit the paradigm, filling it with their own accents, intentions, and semantic creativity (see Aiello, 2018). By extension, they would be encouraged to challenge a certain Italian inclination towards linguistic conservatism, particularly in regard to lexical inventiveness (see the bewildering story of the so-called "petaloso-gate" in Gheno, 2016[1]), breaking conventions to retain in their translations the innovative texture of source varieties.

In view of the peculiarities of the Italian academic context, I decided to incorporate information and examples from world Englishes gradually, while keeping a central emphasis on the norms of the British standard variety. In fact, Italian students "are likely to accept novelty and variety, even if only to a certain extent. What they perceive to be valid and legitimate classroom practices are not easily challenged" (De Bartolo, 2018, p. 164). The teaching material was developed by collecting samples from literary works, online newspapers, films, and YouTube videos, in addition to standard textbooks on morphology (e.g., Carstairs-McCarthy, 2002; Bauer, 2003; Lieber, 2009) and on WE (e.g., Kirkpatrick, 2007; Schneider, 2007; Jenkins, 2009). In order to ensure that the contents of this EMI module would not be lost on students with different levels of EFL competence, I frequently used "self-repairs" (Gotti, 2017, p. 61), pausing after key points to reformulate and clarify the meanings of unfamiliar expressions, or asking students to explain the same ideas in their own words. I also offered local renderings for all the major linguistic concepts, in light of complaints by senior colleagues about the reduction or lack of knowledge of Italian terminology among students since the transition to EMI instruction.

The 12-lesson module was organised in three teaching blocks, with the central one focusing on morphology, in particular on word-formation, and the opening and closing blocks providing a WE-inspired contextual framework (although inputs from the field of WE were punctuated throughout the unit). Each two-hour lesson followed a four-step procedure: (1) introducing the topic and catalysing attention and discussion; (2) frontal teaching (the conventional teaching method in Italian higher education, based on a one-way, lecture-style transfer of knowledge from instructor to students); (3) reflection and/or practice; (4) wrap-up and takeaways. The duration of the four parts varied depending on the topic of the lesson, but all segments would provide opportunities for lecturer-student interaction and impromptu debate. Next, I present an overview of the contents and activities of the three teaching blocks; for reasons of space, I will only sketch out the general outline of the lessons and a few selected examples.

Teaching Block One

This session comprised four lessons aimed at problematising the notion of "English language." The first lesson began with an apparently simple question, "What is English?," to which students instinctively responded by pointing either to its association with

---

1 "Petaloso-gate" refers to the controversy that erupted in 2016 over the alleged approval by the Accademia della Crusca, the most authoritative institution for the regulation and standardisation of the Italian language, of the word *petaloso* ("petalous," having petals), coined by an eight-year-old schoolboy to describe a flower. *Petaloso* quickly became a catchword, but it was also decried by many as pointless and ridiculous, leading to abrasive and disparaging comments questioning the Accademia's authority and lamenting the decline of linguistic standards. In fact, the Accademia merely acknowledged that the word followed standard derivation rules (from *petalo* 'petal' + adjectival suffix *-oso* '-ous'), but that this would not automatically qualify it for inclusion in the common Italian lexicon.

the "native-speaker communities" of the UK, Ireland, the United States, Canada, Australia, and New Zealand, or to its widespread use as a lingua franca across the world. They were then asked to probe the assumptions underlying a number of definitions from a range of sources, from Samuel Johnson's 1755 *Dictionary of the English Language* to Francis Lieber's 1833 *Encyclopaedia Americana*, as well as more contemporary reference works. Noting differences and similarities, students acknowledged that all the descriptions relied on sociolinguistic, rather than purely structural elements, and the most perceptive hinted at the possibility of unpacking the notion of English as a unitary, homogeneous entity.

Taking their cue, I moved from this preliminary activity to expand their conceptual framework and elaborate on their spatial map of the language, introducing key sociolinguistic concepts in the field of WE (e.g., native/nativised/non-native; pidgin/creole/varieties of English; see Kirkpatrick, 2007, pp. 5–15) and describing the spectrum of contexts, functions, and factors behind the existence of English varieties. Leveraging this information, in the third segment of the lesson the students examined four cases of English usage in different settings, through video clips taken from the films *Johnny Mad Dog* (2008, Liberia), *Taare Zameen Par* (2007, India), *The Thin Red Line* (1998, USA, set in the Solomon Islands), and *The Spanish Apartment* (2002, France-Spain). They attempted to locate on a map the varieties of English spoken in the scenes, and to determine their statuses in each country. The lesson concluded with a discussion on a further definition of English, the one offered by Kachru (1982, p. 357), which is pivoted on the concept of "Englishes" to fully acknowledge its "multi-cultural identities." Students were very receptive to this characterisation of the language, to the point of raising broader issues concerning linguistic power, bilingualism, and the disappearance or impoverishment of "local" languages as a danger implicit in the global spread of English and the emergence of new varieties.

Following the same structure and using a variety of resources, including maps, videos, and audio clips, the remaining three lessons in this teaching block were devoted to the following: a country-by-country presentation of the historical background and current linguistic situation of the English language in former colonial territories in America, Africa, Asia, and Oceania (see Crystal, 2005, pp. 29–71); a survey of chronological, biological, and geopolitical models of world Englishes (see McArthur, 1998, pp. 78–101); and a detailed examination of Schneider's dynamic model (see Schneider, 2003, 2007).

Teaching Block Two

After the four-class introduction raised students' awareness of the existence and lineaments of global varieties of English, the second teaching block transitioned to the central theme of the module, i.e., morphology and word-formation. The first two lessons served to provide knowledge of basic concepts in morphology, such as free/bound morphemes, roots, bases, affixes, allomorphy, and productivity. The following three focused on word-formation processes: derivation, conversion, compounding, blending, clipping, abbreviations and acronyms, reduplication, backformation. It is in these lessons that I was able to integrate a WE approach by interspersing instances of lexical innovations in world Englishes among examples from standard British and American English. At this intermediary stage in the module, the goal was not to dissect how word-formation operates in these varieties, but to build on students' growing acceptance of the multiple identities of English beyond the native-speaker model and design teaching material that promotes a more inclusive, egalitarian, and decolonial view of the English language.

In the third segment of these lessons, students participated in in-class work that required analysis of words as the products of previously described word-formation processes. Investigating samples from literary texts, newspapers, and online material, students classified words such as *been-to* (from *The House at Sugar Beach*, a memoir by Liberian-born American journalist Helene Cooper), *barbie* (from an Australian Tourism Commission's television advert featuring Paul Hogan), and *to chargesheet* (from an article in the Indian newspaper *Financial Express*) as a compound, a clipping, and a conversion, respectively, without necessarily understanding at first the sociolinguistic context of their production (e.g., that these were examples from Liberian English, Australian English, and Indian English). At the end of each lesson, I would pick out the words belonging to particular English varieties and clarify their origins. Students recognised that these tokens of lexical creativity from so-called non-standard varieties were, in fact, products of adherence to conventional and even standard word-formation rules, taking opportunities to discuss the standard/non-standard distinction and consider questions of language and power, in light of the notions introduced in the first part of the module.

Teaching Block Three

The final section of the module consisted of three lessons focused on analysing word-formation patterns in different varieties of English. At the beginning of the first lesson, students were asked to identify the origin of a list of words which are now widely accepted in standard English vocabulary but were originally borrowed from local languages in colonial settings (e.g., *thug* from Hindi, *amok* from Malay, *boomerang* from Dharuk Aboriginal language; see Support Material 1: Borrowings). This exercise on loanwords served as a playful introduction to the second segment, where students reviewed the most productive word-formation processes and learnt about hybrid formations—that is, words resulting from mixing English elements with others from local languages. During the practice part of the lesson, several innovative coinages belonging to the vocabulary of new English varieties were examined. Many of these terms were taken from Kachru et al. (2006), Schneider (2007), and Kirkpatrick (2010), but I made sure to supplement evidence of their use in context, drawing on literary works, films, and other cultural texts sourced online. Students were keen on discovering unconventional expressions such as Nigerian English *politrickcian* and Australian English *mozzie*, as well as hybrid words such as *kiasuism* (a derivative with a Hokkien root and an English suffix) and *shamba boy* (a compound with a Kiswahili modifier and an English head) (see Support Material 2: Hybrid Formations). At the end of the lesson, they started to reflect on the interconnectedness between form and function of this linguistic creativity—interrogating, in other words, not only "how" word-formation operates in world Englishes but also "why," what it expresses.

The module concluded with two lessons, each dedicated to a single variety: Australian English and Indian English. For an outline of the latter, see the accompanying lesson plan.

Conclusion

Students' feedback at the end of the module showed that a WE-oriented approach to the topic of morphology and word-formation was successful not only in catalysing their interest in the subject, but also, most importantly, in broadening their view of the English language beyond the stereotypical "native-speaker model." Students reported being more aware of the different varieties of English used by characters in books, films, and TV shows, and feeling encouraged to recognise these not as tokens of "broken English" but as the products of specific historical, cultural, and sociolinguistic circumstances which they were eager to contemplate. Naturally, the realisation of the long-term goal of generating positive impact on their professional practice as language and cultural mediators remains in the future, but it was clear from their responses that the perspective of World Englishes contributed to fostering the idea of English as a language to which they, as EFL learners and speakers in a multilingual world, can also stake legitimate claims to belonging and creativity.

Lesson Plan: Chutnified—Lexical Innovations in Indian English

Recommended Level(s)

Higher-education students (undergraduate/lower postgraduate level) with B2 CEFRL competence.

Context

This lesson is designed to take 1.5–2 hours and enables students to appraise and examine distinctive features of Indian English vocabulary. It is best placed towards the end of an introductory course on morphology and word-formation as a themed lesson inspired by the World Englishes approach, or as part of a module on postcolonial varieties of English. Familiarity with basic linguistics concepts and knowledge of word-formation processes is a prerequisite for analysis.

Objectives

Students will be able to:

- discuss the development of the English language in India, its current role and importance;
- recognise unusual and unattested words in standard British and American varieties as products of creative application of morphological rules in Indian English;
- apply their previous knowledge of word-formation processes to examine hybrid words and other innovative lexical items;
- formulate assumptions about the cultural content of certain Indian English expressions.

Procedures

Step 1: Introduction (20–25 Minutes)

Instruct Students to Read the Following Texts:

- Kamala Das' poem "An introduction," lines 1–23 (in Das, 1965, pp. 59–60);
- Agha Shahid Ali's notes on "chutnification" and "biryanisation" of English (in Mehrotra, 1992, p. 4);
- Macintyre (2007)'s article on Indian English (excerpts).

Encourage students to reflect on the authors' attitudes towards Indian English, inviting them to consider their different geographical and cultural contexts. Are the authors' viewpoints surprising? If so, why? And what is their own reaction to the points raised by the authors? As an ancillary activity, ask students to identify Indian English coinages in the texts and name the word-formation processes by which they are formed.

Step 2: Frontal Teaching (20–30 Minutes)

Provide an overview of the history of the English language in India. Describe its condition in postcolonial India, the development of a standard Indian English variety, and the existence of regional and social sub-varieties. If extra time is available, clarify the difference between Indian English and Hinglish.

Step 3: Guided Practice (30–40 Minutes)

Present students with a range of Indian English material: written texts (see Mehrotra, 1998), extracts from films (e.g., *Monsoon Wedding*, 2001; *Slumdog Millionaire*, 2008), and other audio and video clips available online. Ask them to make a list of innovative coinages and to classify them as products of different word-formation processes. Assist the class in examining these new words and understanding their meanings (especially in the case of hybrid forms).

Students with substantial linguistics knowledge can be guided in a discussion about questions of synonymy and blocking restrictions operating in standard English varieties as opposed to Indian English. EFL learners can be prompted to translate Indian English coinages creatively and to translanguage morphologically, forming hybrids that blend morphemes from English or Indian languages with those in their own home languages.

Step 4: Wrap-Up and Takeaways (20–25 Minutes)

Ask students to think back at the comments on Indian English encountered at the beginning of the lesson. Has their reaction changed? How would they now define their own attitude to this variety of English?

References

Aiello, J. (2018). (Co)constructing use, belonging and legitimacy. A study of English language ownership in Italy. *Lingue e Linguaggi, 26*, 7–25. https://doi.org/10.1285/i22390359v26p7

Alim, H. S., Rickford, J. R., & Ball, A. F. (Eds.). (2016). *Raciolinguistics: How language shapes our ideas about race*. Oxford University Press. https://doi.org/10.1093/acprof:oso/9780190625696.001.0001

Bauer, L. (2003). *Introducing linguistic morphology* (2nd ed.). Edinburg University Press.

Carstairs-McCarthy, A. (2002). *An introduction to English morphology: Words and their structure*. Edinburgh University Press.

Crystal, D. (2005). *English as a global language* (2nd ed.). Cambridge University Press. https://doi.org/10.1017/CBO9781139196970

Das, K. (1965). *Summer in Calcutta: Fifty poems*. Rajinder Paul.

De Bartolo, A. (2018). Learner's awareness and attitude towards ELF: A pilot study in an Italian university context. *Lingue e Linguaggi, 26*, 157–171. https://doi.org/10.1285/i22390359v26p157

Gheno, V. (2016, February 28). *Petaloso-gate, servizio debunking*. BUTAC. www.butac.it/petaloso-gate-servizio-debunking/

Gotti, M. (2017). English as a lingua franca in the academic world: Trends and dilemmas. *Lingue e Linguaggi, 24*, 47–72. https://doi.org/10.1285/i22390359v24p47

Herbst, T. (2010). *English linguistics: A coursebook for students of English*. De Gruyter Mouton. https://doi.org/10.1515/9783110215489

Hsu, F. (2017). Resisting the coloniality of English: A research review of strategies. *CATESOL Journal, 29*(1), 111–132. http://www.catesoljournal.org/wp-content/uploads/2017/06/CJ29.1_hsu.pdf

Jenkins, J. (2009). *World Englishes: A resource book for students* (2nd ed.). Routledge.

Kachru, B. B. (Ed.) (1982). *The other tongue: English across cultures*. University of Illinois Press.

Kachru, B. B. (1985). Standards, codification and sociolinguistic realism: The English language in the outer circle. In R. Quirk & H. G. Widdowson (Eds.), *English in the world: Teaching and learning the language and literatures* (pp. 11–30). Cambridge University Press.

Kachru, B. B., Kachru, Y., & Nelson, C. L. (Eds.). (2006). *The handbook of world Englishes*. Blackwell. https://doi.org/10.1002/9780470757598

Kirkpatrick, A. (2007). *World Englishes: Implications for international communication and English language teaching*. Cambridge University Press.

Kirkpatrick, A. (Ed.). (2010). *The Routledge handbook of world Englishes*. Routledge. https://doi.org/10.4324/9780203849323

Kumaravadivelu, B. (2001). Toward a postmethod pedagogy. *TESOL Quarterly, 35*(4), 537–560. https://doi.org/10.2307/3588427

Kumaravadivelu, B. (2003). A postmethod perspective on English language teaching. *World Englishes, 22*(4), 539–550. https://doi.org/10.1111/j.1467-971X.2003.00317.x

Kumaravadivelu, B. (2016). The decolonial option in English teaching: Can the subaltern act? *TESOL Quarterly, 50*(1), 66–85. https://doi.org/10.1002/tesq.202

Lieber, R. (2009). *Introducing morphology*. Cambridge University Press. https://doi.org/10.1017/CBO9780511808845

Macintyre, B. (2007, March 24). English grows into strange shapes when transplanted into foreign soil. *The Times*, pp. 16, S3.

McArthur, T. (1998). *The English languages*. Cambridge University Press. https://doi.org/10.1017/9780511621048

Mehrotra, A. K. (Ed.). (1992). *The Oxford India anthology of twelve modern Indian poets*. Oxford University Press.

Mehrotra, R. R. (1998). *Indian English: Texts and interpretation*. Benjamins. https://doi.org/10.1075/veaw.t7

Meyer, C. F. (2009). *Introducing English linguistics*. Cambridge University Press. https://doi.org/10.1017/CBO9780511757822

Mignolo, W. D., & Walsh, C. E. (2018). *On decoloniality: Concepts, analytics, praxis*. Duke University Press. https://doi.org/10.1215/9780822371779

Motha, S. (2014). *Race, empire, and English language teaching: Creating responsible and ethical anti-racist practice*. Teachers College Press.

Schneider, E. W. (2003). The dynamics of new Englishes: From identity construction to dialect birth. *Language, 79*(2), 233–281. https://doi.org/10.1353/lan.2003.0136

Schneider, E. W. (2007). *Postcolonial English: Varieties around the world*. Cambridge University Press. https://doi.org/10.1017/CBO9780511618901

Trudgill, P., & Hannah, J. (1982). *International English: A guide to varieties of standard English*. Arnold.

Chapter 2

Using Learning Stations at College
An Introduction to Linguistic Shift and Change for English Proficiency Development

Yolanda Morató

Introduction

The use of "rotation stations," "learning centers," or "station teaching" in classroom settings has been regarded as an efficient procedure to introduce, practice, and review interconnected themes and goals in the teaching of complex topics. It is indeed highly beneficial to cater to individual and collective needs in acquisition, especially those needs addressing "problems related to individual learning styles, wide ability ranges within a class, and enrollment" (Strauber, 1981, p. 31); however, its use is rare. Although pre-service teachers at the college level are commonly trained in Communicative Language Learning and Task-Based Learning approaches, empirical research on learning stations (hereafter referred to as LS) has been conducted for more than half a century (Fehrle & Schulz, 1977). Beyond this, implementing LS shows satisfactory results at different educational stages and disciplines. In the area of language teaching and learning, LS allow a vast range of applications of linguistic and intercultural variation, which also facilitates accommodation to different educational needs. Specifically, in the EFL classroom, Chien (2017) has stressed the opportunities LS offered for interpersonal skills and competence development.

Traditionally considered as a set of activities that may mainly suit younger learners, LS are fundamentally based on divisions and groupings of both content and students: the session materials are divided into several parts, which are then assigned to different places within the classroom (i.e., stations). As a result, this makes students move from one spot to another (i.e., rotations) in order to progressively work on independent activities connected to certain goals or a common theme. Recently, Judson (2019) has pointed out that, despite the ascription of LS to the methodology of elementary schools, their use in college classrooms "prompt student groups to engage with relevant activities and have thoughtful discussions while at the same time allow instructors to monitor and interact with students" (p. 250). As empirical data on cooperative learning have revealed, interaction is linked to improvement in several areas and constitutes a sound foundation for critical thinking and the development of ideas in class. Moreover, vocalizing has been shown to be more strongly related to achievement than listening to other members' opinions (Johnson et al., 1985). In the same vein, Schweitzer (1995) highlighted the notion of meaningful involvement through first-hand participation and stated that LS were "valuable in allowing students to be actively engaged in their learning and to build concepts based on their own experiences" (p. 366).

DOI: 10.4324/9781003124665-3

Planning and Teaching the Lesson

My lesson plan in this chapter describes a project that has been implemented in the University of Seville, Spain, a higher education institution with a population of around 70,000 students. Thanks to its academic agreements with American and European universities and colleges, the international student body at the University of Seville is fairly diverse and lessons are delivered in a multicultural environment. Its geographical location in southern Spain and its long-standing reputation as an institution founded in 1505 also contribute to its international character.

Seminars are numerous, with an average attendance of 30–40 students, so many times practical activities cannot be properly planned, monitored, and assessed. As a result, a traditional approach may be adopted in terms of participation, which tends to be rather limited. To promote increased engagement and participation, this chapter will present the necessary components and strategies to implement LS by using a lesson plan that facilitates student work on global variation in the English language, with a special focus on American and British English.

Before this session was first implemented, none of the participants had ever taken part in this type of activity; this obviously meant extra planning. Nevertheless, this challenge was well worth the effort. One of the reasons for choosing LS to cover the topic of linguistic shift and change had to do with the excessive use of textbooks in the modern language class in Spain. In an academic culture in which they tend to be unavoidable, the goal was, therefore, to leave textbooks behind for, at least, one lesson. Thornbury (2009) pointed out that, in Spain, "it is coursebook series like Headway and Cutting Edge that—more than any other factor—determine and define current teaching practice" (n.p.). Pondering how to distance from traditional materials and class management, I took into consideration—as one of the first factors—a strategic framework for second language teaching.

In one of his seminal articles about the evolving nature of methods, Kumaravadivelu (1994) presented ten macrostrategies that may well summarize the goals of the LS that were designed for this lesson plan:

> (a) maximize learning opportunities, (b) facilitate negotiated interaction, (c) minimize perceptual mismatches, (d) activate intuitive heuristics, (e) foster language awareness, (f) contextualize linguistic input, (g) integrate language skills, (h) promote learner autonomy, (i) raise cultural consciousness, and (j) ensure social relevance.
>
> (p. 32)

Students can learn about linguistic change while interacting and developing awareness about the social and cultural impact of language varieties in different contexts and registers. It must be admitted that arranging stations is far from a conventional procedure in the foreign language class; neither is it common in college subjects. For this reason, I followed three pieces of advice to make LS effective by (1) creating "a problem for the student to solve" at each station, (2) providing a set of activities which could be "fairly straightforward," and (3) emphasizing relevant ideas to "be stated explicitly by the students" (Schweitzer, 1995, p. 366). Consequently, for this lesson plan, linguistic skills and components were put into practice by selecting the most revealing differences between American English and British English and classifying them into five different components (lexicon, morphosyntactic features, spelling, pragmatics, and intercultural competence).

Different tables were accordingly divided into five language dimensions with a variety of tasks introducing all participants to new content (see Lesson Plan at the end of chapter). Students also had the opportunity to activate previous knowledge, such as the concepts of *register* and *language shift*, which were included in their reading packs. Therefore, following Jarrett (2010), the goals of these stations were to "teach concepts, integrate subject matter, build interest, and allow for inquiry" (p. 56). There are, of course, variations on how to apply these strategies depending on students' age and level, lesson content, timeframe and background, teachers' resources together with time of instruction, planning and implementation, and even participants' familiarity with cooperative work and other contexts in which peer interaction is key for students' development. The teacher's role is to provide immediate guidance and feedback on the station activities but, for these non-routine tasks, all materials were designed as straightforwardly as possible.

When drafting this lesson plan based on LS, assessment was also an essential part to consider. Ruiset and Butain (2000) recommended a multistage assessment structure for LS:

> After engaging in all of the small-group activities, the class meets together as a whole group for one or two days, reviewing and discussing what they learned or practiced at the various stations. Each rotation also includes one or more assessments of student learning. Suggested assessment techniques range from closed-book, written tests to teacher or student assessments of a product or products students produced while working at one or more stations.
>
> (p. 23)

Since this was a first attempt and, as reflective practitioners, we ought to take into account a series of factors in classroom practice, "the institutional and cultural contexts" (Zeichner & Liston, 1996, p. 6) among them, assessment was designed to be diagnostic and, more particularly, an assessment for learning. After having completed all stations, participants were asked to fill in a short questionnaire about what they had discovered, what they had enjoyed, and what they thought they would improve in their future assignments (see Appendix 3). Reflection on the activity itself was also included, given the novelty of this approach.

Lesson Plan: Travel With Words!

Recommended Grade Level(s)

College students and pre-service teachers. At least a C1 level according to the Common European Framework of Reference for Languages (CEFRL).

Context

This lesson plan covers aspects of language register and variation through audio-visual and printed materials dealing with familiar and formal language, both in the United States and the United Kingdom. It is designed as a single session, so it can be inserted as a diagnostic lesson (for the purpose of observing students' previous knowledge or basic skills in cooperative work) or as a review lesson on some differences between British and American English and language change.

Objectives

Students will be able to:

- distinguish some regional varieties within their linguistic contexts;
- review language conventions in the United States and the United Kingdom;
- reflect on how we use language and how we may judge other people's uses.

Procedures

When working with small groups, from 25 to 30 students, tables are arranged into five, with different instructional activities, so that students rotate from one table to another every six minutes. Larger groups (e.g., around 35–45 students) require seven tables; this arrangement also means more dynamic, shorter activities.

Step 1: Arranging the Stations and Introducing the Activities (10 Minutes)

Place students at five different tables and remind them of time and place rules. To avoid common organizational problems when working in groups, the following measures were devised:

- Clear rules about how stations and start/stop times work are explained at the beginning of the five-station activity:
    - Each student must complete five different stations today.
    - Maximum time for each table is six minutes.
    - Each table has one activity to complete: students are asked to do activities in groups.
    - A countdown timer projected on the screen will tell students the time they have left.
- The countdown timer (www.online-stopwatch.com/countdown-timer/) is projected on the screen so that six minutes for each table can be easily controlled by both teachers and students. An alarm goes off when time is up.
- Tables have a number, from 1 to 5, in order to be easily registered in students' notepads and on the assessment sheet.

Using Learning Stations at College   17

Step 2: Learning Stations (30 Minutes)

Five activity-based learning stations have been designed to cover the topic of linguistic shift and change. Students will move to a different table every six minutes.

1. **Lexicon (*Travel with words!*).** This is one of the most common topics in textbooks (with examples presented in isolation and opposition, such as *fall/autumn* or *elevator/lift*). However, this station addresses a "translation" of a brief text in which ten British common words are contextualized and need to be rewritten using American English. The text reads:

   At La Guardia Airport

   Kelly has flown from Heathrow Airport, in London, to visit some of her mates from the time she went to uni. Everything seemed to go well: her flight timetable and in-flight meals were pretty decent. But when she arrived, her suitcase was not on the baggage carousel. She went to the toilet thinking it would be there, waiting for her, some minutes later but it wasn't. It had been a smooth flight with no stopovers. . . . Where was her luggage then? All her trousers, jumpers, and best trainers were definitely somewhere else. That evening Kelly went to her friends' flat, where they had something for supper and borrowed some clothes from them.

   This fragment is offered in two versions; the first (shown earlier) can be displayed with or without words in blocks, depending on students' familiarity with this area of language. The second contains the words in blocks to make them aware of their work and provide them with self- or peer-correction opportunities.

   At La Guardia Airport

   Kelly has flown from Heathrow Airport, in London, to visit some of her **buddies** from the time she went to **college**. Everything seemed to go well: her flight **schedule** and in-flight meals were pretty decent. But when she arrived, her suitcase was not on the baggage carousel. She went to the **restrooms** thinking it would be there, waiting for her, some minutes later but it wasn't. It had been a smooth flight with no **layovers**. . . . Where was her luggage then? All her **pants**, **sweaters**, and best **sneakers** were definitely somewhere else. That evening Kelly went to her friends' **apartment**, where they had something for **a light meal/snack** and borrowed some clothes from them.
   ---

2. **Morphosyntactic features (*Is this right or wrong?*).** This table promotes debate on whether uses of traditionally prescribed elements should be deemed "wrong." Topics are displayed in three cards, and the group needs to decide which one of the three they are going to select for their discussion:

Card 1: Ain't

Have Your Say: A teacher has crossed out the word *ain't* in one assignment on the grounds of being grammatically wrong and has included the following note from the *Cambridge English Dictionary*: "This word is not considered to be correct English by many people."
(https://dictionary.cambridge.org/dictionary/english/ain-t)

Discuss with your group the following aspects:

- The importance and relevance of register
- Social class biases in language use
- Usage in the United States and the United Kingdom

Card 2: Data is or Data are

We all change and so does language: Read the handout (see Appendix 1) and decide your views on the use of singular or plural verb forms for the word *data*.

You may explore the following options:

- Language shift and foreign words that end up having their own rules in a different language
- Word evolution and popular acceptance of rules

Card 3: Everyone is doing their part

Read the following excerpt from the *Merriam Webster Dictionary* (www.merriam-webster.com/dictionary/their#usage-1):
   The use of *they, their, them*, and *themselves* as pronouns of indefinite gender and indefinite number is well established in speech and writing, even in literary and formal contexts. In recent years, these pronouns have also been adopted by individuals whose gender identity is nonbinary.

Exchange your ideas on the following aspects:

- Whether you use *his* or singular *their* in oral or written texts
- If you have ever encountered gender-neutral pronouns before

3. **Spelling (*Now you are the editor*).** A text with American spelling and punctuation is provided as a handout and students need to adjust it to British English (z/s, -or/-our, single and double quotation marks/inverted commas). The activity reads:

> *You are launching an American book in the British market and the back cover has a text you need to adjust to British conventions:*
>
> It's Monday, June 3. Susan has passed her exam with flying colors. However, when she gets home, she realizes something is not quite the same. On her neighbor's door a post-it note reads "Back in 5 minutes." Two hours later Susan is still waiting for her. The streets are deserted; her coworkers don't answer back when she calls. Where is everybody? In this thriller, a woman wonders what to do in a world where human beings have suddenly vanished.

They are also provided with the key so that they can self-assess their work:

> It's **Monday 3 June**. Susan has passed her exam with flying **colours**. However, when she gets home, she **realises** something is not quite the same. On her **neighbour's** door a post-it note reads 'Back in 5 minutes.' Two hours later Susan is still waiting for her. The streets are deserted; her **co-workers** don't answer back when she calls. Where is everybody? In this thriller, a woman wonders what to do in a world where human beings have suddenly vanished.

4. **Pragmatics (*Say hello to new expressions*).** Using appropriate conventions in British and American English, students are given a set of ten cards with which to say hello, goodbye, and other expressions in informal UK/US registers. For this purpose, cards are placed face down on the station and by turns each student needs to match a UK/US pair used in the same context on both sides of the Atlantic. See Appendix 2 for cards.

5. **Intercultural competence (*Do you know where I come from?*).** Each student has three post-it notes with words with different origins (*diapers, subways, boomerang, raccoon, mafia, parking lot, tap, faucet, groovy, freeways, moose, blue chip, white collar*). They are asked to exchange their views and to place them on a map.

To check their results, students are asked to watch on a tablet a 1-minute video by The Open University ("American English," *The History of English*, available at https://youtu.be/rbvumrknAKs), detailing the evolution of the English language and its words.

If students have extra time, one of them can read a list of words related to food so that the rest of the group can classify them according to their origin (e.g., *pretzel, squash, coleslaw, cookies, delicatessen*).

Step 3: Reflecting and Sharing (5 Minutes + 10 Minutes of Discussion)

At the end of their rotations, students are given a worksheet and asked to write down what they have learned through the different stations (see Appendix 3). Finally, they share their results and vote for the most useful station(s).

Step 4: Collecting Cards and Texts (5 Minutes)

Extension Activities

- Ask students to write a short essay (around 500 words) on gendered language and whether they think grammatical gender is going to experience a fairly fast evolution towards inclusive language.
- Start the following lesson with reflections from bilingual students on whether they switch from one language to another and if they do it consciously or unconsciously.
- Use this first lesson to lead into a lesson on Global Englishes and the influence of other modern languages.

The provided lesson plan illustrates that LS related to the practice of different Englishes and words from several origins by using cards, post-it notes, and other textual materials are highly popular among students from different backgrounds of English as a foreign language.

References

Cambridge English Dictionary. (n.d.). Ain't. In *Dictionary.cambridge.org dictionary*. Retrieved January 20, 2021, from https://dictionary.cambridge.org/dictionary/english/ain-t

Chien, C. W. (2017). Undergraduates' implementations of learning stations as their service learning among elementary school students. *Education, 45*(2), 209–226. https://doi.org/10.1080/03004279.2015.1074601

Countdown Timer. (2021). *Online-stopwatch*. www.online-stopwatch.com/countdown-timer/

Fehrle, C. C., & Schulz, J. (1977). *Guidelines for learning stations* (ED139415). ERIC. https://eric.ed.gov/?id=ED139415

Jarrett, O. (2010). "Inventive" learning stations. *Science and Children, 47*(5), 56–59.

Johnson, D. W., Johnson, R. T., Roy, P., & Zaidman, B. (1985). Oral interaction in cooperative learning groups: Speaking, listening, and the nature of statements made by high-, medium-, and low-achieving students. *The Journal of Psychology, 119*(4), 303–321. https://doi.org/10.1080/00223980.1985.9915450

Judson, E. (2019). Learning stations in college classrooms. *College Teaching, 67*(4), 250–251. https://doi.org/10.1080/87567555.2019.1650707

Kumaravadivelu, B. (1994). The postmethod condition: (E)merging strategies for second/foreign language teaching. *TESOL Quarterly, 28*(1), 27–48. https://doi.org/10.2307/3587197

Merriam-Webster. (n.d.). Their. In *Merriam-Webster.com dictionary*. Retrieved January 20, 2021, from www.merriam-webster.com/dictionary/their#usage-1

OpenLearn from the Open University. (2011, June 24). American English—the history of English. *Youtube* [Video]. https://youtu.be/rbvumrknAKs

Rogers, S. (2012, July 8). Data are or data is? *The Guardian*. www.theguardian.com/news/datablog/2010/jul/16/data-plural-singular

Ruiset, R. A., & Butain, S. M. (2000). Using teaming, active learning, and technology to improve instruction. *Middle School Journal, 32*(2), 21–29. https://doi.org/10.1080/00940771.2000.11495263

Schweitzer, J. (1995). The use of learning stations as a strategy for teaching concepts by active-learning methods. *Journal of Geological Education, 43*(4), 366–370. https://doi.org/10.5408/0022-1368-43.4.366

Skapinker, M. (2020, March 17). You say criteria, I say criterion. *Financial Times*. www.ft.com/content/b7c23744-676b-11ea-800d-da70cff6e4d3

Strauber, S. K. (1981). Language learning stations. *Foreign Language Annals, 14*, 31–36. https://doi.org/10.1111/j.1944-9720.1981.tb01404.x

Thornbury, S. (2009). Methods, post-method and métodos. *Teaching English, BBC*. www.teachingenglish.org.uk/articles/methods-post-method-m%C3%A9todos

Zeichner, K. M., & Liston, D. P. (1996). *Reflective teaching: An introduction*. Lawrence Erlbaum Associates Publishers. https://doi.org/10.4324/9780203822289

Appendix 1

"Data" in *The Guardian* (Rogers, 2012) and *Financial Times* (Skapinker, 2020)

> In Latin, data is the plural of datum and, historically and in specialized scientific fields, it is also treated as a plural in English, taking a plural verb, as in the data were collected and classified. In modern non-scientific use, however, despite the complaints of traditionalists, it is often not treated as a plural. Instead, it is treated as a mass noun, similar to a word like information, which cannot normally have a plural and which takes a singular verb. Sentences such as data was (as well as data were) collected over a number of years are now widely accepted in standard English.

Figure 2.1   Explanation from the Oxford English Dictionary *(cited in* The Guardian*)*

> @User1 Of course data is plural. And what is wrong with datum for a single item of data?
> @User2 Singular data annoys the same people that find split infinitives objectionable—pedants with no understanding of linguistics.

Figure 2.2   Twitter (cited in The Guardian*)*

> "Data" is in a transitionary state, sometimes singular, sometimes plural. The *Financial Times* style remains plural—"the data are clear"—although no one seems to use the singular "datum" any more.

Figure 2.3   The Financial Times *on the usage of "data"*

Appendix 2

A Variation on Pelmanism: Cards With Greetings and Other Expressions

UK Hiya!	US Hey!
UK Alright, mate?	US What's up, buddy!
UK Cheers!	US Thanks!
UK Ta-ra!	US Bye!
UK Blimey!	US Wow!

Appendix 3

Self-Assessment Questionnaire

Learning Stations
Name at least three things you have discovered in these activities
_____
_____
_____

Tell us your favorite activity or about something you have enjoyed
_____
_____

Think about what you have learned today: How can this help you in future work?
_____
_____

Did you enjoy this lesson?
Yes/No because _____
_____
_____

Chapter 3

Balancing the Focus on Local and Global Varieties of English
Can Teaching Pedagogy Take the Multilingual Turn?

Aicha Rahal

Introduction

The global spread of English has led to the emergence of new forms and varieties of English, meaning that English becomes plural and multilingual (Rahal, 2019a). These varieties are called "Englishes," conveying "the concept of pluralism, of linguistic heterogeneity, of cultural diversity and of different theoretical and methodological foundations for teaching and research in English" (Kachru, 1984, p. 26). Kachru and Smith (1985) also provide the characteristics of this concept:

> "Englishes" symbolizes the functional and formal variation in the language, and its international acculturation, for example, in West Africa, in Southern Africa, in East Africa, in South Asia, in Southeast Asia, in the West Indies, in the Philippines, and in the traditional English using-countries: the USA, the UK, Australia, Canada, and New Zealand. The language now belongs to those who use it as their first language, and to those who use it as an additional language, whether in its standard from or in its localized forms.
>
> (p. 210)

To show the multilingual profile of English, Kachru (1985) further asserts that English consists of "a unique cultural pluralism, and a linguistic heterogeneity and diversity" (p. 14). Metaphorically speaking, English is compared to a ship which is "built in Spain; owned by a Norwegian; registered in Cyprus; managed from Glasgow; chartered by the French; crewed by Russians; flying a Liberian flag; carrying an American cargo; and pouring oil on the Welsh coast" (*The Independent*, 1996, as cited in Graddol, 1997, p. 32).

The global status of English has led to questions around teaching pedagogy. The question being raised here is "can teaching pedagogy take the multilingual turn?" Different research studies point to this issue, but the main problem remains that "most teachers of English are sublimely unaware of the ELF [EIL] debate, which for the most part takes place among a very small group of researchers" (Maley, 2010, p. 38). Matsuda (2003) stresses a real classroom problem: when students have limited exposure to English varieties, being taught in one model variety, they can resist those real varieties outside of the classroom. This problem shows the gap between the reality of English outside the classroom and the type of English introduced in teaching. McKay (2012) lists the features of the traditional paradigm which is still

DOI: 10.4324/9781003124665-4

used: "traditionally L2 pedagogy and research have been dominated by the assumption that the goal of bilingual users of English is to achieve native-like competence in English" (p. 10).

It is evident that the changing role of English from the native language of its speakers to the lingua franca of the world raises questions about the changing of language teaching. Kachru (2003) claims that one of the requirements of the increasing use of English as an international language is the legitimation of non-native varieties. He further adds that there is a need for the recognition of the paradigm shift in the standard norm used in those non-native contexts. Crystal (1997) argues that people would use dialects in their own country but switch into World Standard Spoken English (WSSE) when speaking to people in other countries. Crystal's words reflect the idea that we need to learn both local and international varieties for the purpose of intelligibility and successful communication. Matsuda (2003) also argues that the inclusion of multilingual Englishes provides "a different way of looking at the language, which is more inclusive, pluralistic, and accepting than the traditional, monolithic view of English in which there is one correct, standard way of using English that all speakers must strive for" (p. 727).

The English Language Teaching paradigm, which is based on the ideology of native speakers, needs to be changed to a new paradigm that reflects diversity, relates the language classroom to the world (Pennycook, 2000), and takes into account local varieties of English. Moreover, teaching pedagogy should equip learners with the necessary skills to become international speakers and raise their awareness on the multilingual and diverse linguistic contexts of English. Modiano (2009) supports this idea, stating that "an understanding of the diversity of English, for production as well as for comprehension, makes one a better communicator" (p. 59).

Motivated by the spread of English and the emergence of its varieties, this chapter attempts to create a balance between local and global varieties of English. My suggested classroom activities mainly aim to raise awareness of the need for a paradigm shift that goes away from native language norms and call for developing a bottom-up curriculum to integrate the new philosophy of "World Englishes." Researchers (Rahal, 2019b; Mckay, 2002; Jenkins, 2006; Kirkpatrick, 2002) believe that there is a pressing need to rethink teaching pedagogy in the global English era. Mckay (2002), for example, advocates that "the teaching and learning of an international language must be based on an entirely different set of assumptions than the teaching and learning of any other second and foreign language" (p. 1). Seidlhofer (2011) also argues that there is a mismatch between innovations in the discourse of the teaching of the new varieties of English and the real teaching content (p. 11).

Educational Setting and Objectives

This chapter highlights my experience in teaching one of the varieties of English. It is an attempt "to invent the language we are supposed to teach" (Decke-Cornill, 2002, p. 59) for the purpose of incorporating English varieties into practice. The purpose of my lesson is to raise my students' awareness of the newborn varieties of English and to understand the listening tasks of the Test of English for International Communication (TOEIC). However, my goal is not to teach all varieties of English. Rather, my goal aligns with Kachru's (2005) philosophy:

Learning and teaching world Englishes does not mean learning and teaching of each regional variety to everyone in the Inner Circle classrooms or everyone learning English in Brazil, China, Japan, Saudi Arabia, or Southern Africa. It means making learners aware of the rich variation that exists in English around the world at an appropriate point in their language education in all the three Circles and giving them the tools to educate themselves further about using their English for effective communication across varieties.

(p. 166)

The program in my teaching context includes preparation for TOEIC. This course is a good opportunity to balance the focus between local and global varieties of English at the level of pronunciation. To assist with the listening tasks of the TOEIC test, students can find different accents or different Englishes in various audio recordings. Some researchers propose a number of activities to teach the local varieties of English. Jindapitak and Teo (2012), for example, suggested an activity which includes three steps adapted from Munro et al. (2006):

- Collecting and preparing speech samples from various non-native communities;
- Presenting the selected audios to learners to evaluate the speakers on predetermined dimensions;
- Tallying the results of the evaluations, followed by in-class discussion of the task outcomes.

Farrell and Martin (2009) consider a balanced approach to teaching English varieties. These include the following points:

- Teachers need to carefully consider their teaching context (McKay, 2002).
- After choosing their target of instruction based on that context, teachers should value their learners' current English usage (El-Sayed, 1991).
- Teachers need to prepare learners for future international English encounters by exposing them to other varieties of English (Matsuda, 2003) and by teaching them strategic competence when interacting with speakers who speak other varieties of English.

Students are taught pronunciation to help them understand the different accents and to differentiate among them. Audio recordings provide exposure to native and non-native English pronunciation. They are an awareness-raising activity. Subsequently, the tasks and discussion provide students with an opportunity for deeper reflection regarding the different Englishes encountered. This course took place at the Higher School of Engineers of Gafsa, a city in southwest Tunisia. At this higher school, we teach different levels, including "cycle préparatoire" students in maths and physics, and engineering students in information technology.

In this course, we explored pronunciation differences in spoken English in Tunisia, British English, American English, Indian English, Australian English, and South African English. The related classroom activities (see Lesson Plan) are designed to be highly interactive and funny. They are based on a communicative approach to help students memorize pronunciation differences. This approach incorporates the

"PPP model," a teaching paradigm which stands for Presentation, Practice, and Production. According to Ur (1996), PPP is

> based on behaviorist theory which states that learning a language is just like learning any other skill. The high degree of teacher control which characterizes the first and second stages of this approach lessens as the class proceeds, allowing the learner to gradually move away from the teacher's support towards more automatic production and understanding.
>
> (p. 19)

The instructor and students listened to many recordings and identified different pronunciations while playing games or using flash cards to relate the features to different types of English. Students also performed dialogues and role-plays in which they chose their favorite varieties and tried to imitate them. The role of the teacher was to guide the students to do the role-plays and to perform them imitating the different dialects. The students need to be reminded about the purpose of this task, which is the appreciation of the diversity as a way to communicate in English in this global context rather than imitating these dialects in stereotypical or derogatory ways.

To demonstrate this activity, this chapter concludes with a sample lesson plan illustrating how to integrate World Englishes in the classroom and to use different teaching aids. This lesson plan consists of three stages. The first stage is used to present the target variety of English, in this case, the South African variety of English. The teacher uses videos to listen to South African speakers of English to identify the characteristics of this variety. In the second stage, the teacher creates a controlled practice; she divides the students into groups to prepare a prewritten role-play including the identified characteristics. In the third stage, the students perform their role-plays in the class. It is an opportunity to interact and explore the target variety. This chapter can be a reference for a number of teachers to create a bridge between the different varieties of English in an interactive way.

Lesson Plan: Teaching Local Varieties—South African English as an Example

Recommended Level(s)

Intermediate and advanced students

Context

This lesson can fit many courses, such as phonetics and sociolinguistics. But I used it to prepare students for the TOEIC exam, especially the listening portion. My students were studying second-year engineering in computer science. This lesson is a continuation of other courses in pronunciation, including British and American pronunciation. It can be introduced in the middle of the listening course. I used it to introduce the features of South African English, which was followed by units on other varieties of English such as Indian English, Australian English, Nigerian English, and Cameroon English. It is a learner-centered course in which the teacher functions as a monitor, controller, and feedback-giver. This course is also based on the communicative approach to teaching.

Objectives

Students will be able to:

- identify and discuss the characteristic features of the English variety spoken in South Africa;
- demonstrate awareness of different varieties of English;
- comprehend different varieties of English;
- consider the strengths of English language varieties.

Procedures

Step 1: Warm-Up Activity (5 Minutes)

The teacher starts the lesson by asking questions, including the following:

- Do you speak British or American English?
- Do you think that the English you speak is influenced by your native language and first language?
- Have you faced a difficulty in understanding English spoken in other places?

Step 2: Individual Work (15 Minutes)

In this stage, the teacher presents the materials that the students will use. The materials consist of a number of audio recordings taken from different online open sources, namely "English Accents," "The International Dialects of English Archive," and "Drama: Dialect and Accent Resources." Students are asked to listen to the audio recordings several times and note down pronunciation differences. This is called the "present stage" according to the PPP approach (see chapter). The students work individually.

Step 3: Small Group Discussion (10 Minutes)

After noting down the identified pronunciation differences, the teacher divides the students into small groups and asks them to share what they found. This is a continuation of the previous stage in which the students present the different features of pronunciation. The teacher asks the students to discuss the results and write a summary, which includes the identified pronunciation varieties. The students notice that the characteristics of South African English are different from British and American English. They try to identify a number of features. These include consonant substitution, such as the use of /f/ instead of /θ/, the pronunciation of the sound /h/ as a voiced /ɦ/, etc. This part of the lesson is rather interactive: the students share their feedback with each other. The teacher asks the students to practice saying the new features without ridicule or scorn.

Step 4: Group Work (20 Minutes)

In this stage, the teacher:

- divides students into groups;
- asks them to write a role-play and use the identified features;
- invites them to perform their role-play and imitate the variety.

This stage is a mixture of both product and practice. It includes a practice-based activity with the new varieties introduced in the "present stage." It also includes product-based tasks, such as group work, writing, and role-play. One example of the activities is a role-play between two students who speak different varieties. The first student speaks British or American English and the second student speaks South African English. They perform a role-play about "asking for directions in the street," in which they try to imitate the two varieties and to use the identified features. The students have the opportunity to practice the features of pronunciation in a controlled environment and get comments and feedback from both the teacher and the other students. During this stage, the students practice their communication skills. The goal of these activities is to create a harmony between the different varieties of English and to value diversity. The role of the teacher is to remind the students about the importance of diversity and advise them not to mock or ridicule people who speak non-standard forms.

Step 5: South African Dialect Quiz (10 Minutes)

In this stage, the teacher introduces different activities to check the understanding of the students. These include the following:

1) Test each other on the characteristics of South African English at the level of pronunciation, going different ways:
   a. Say a word in the South African variety and see if your partner can pronounce it in British or American English.
   b. Say a word in British or American pronunciation and see if your partner can pronounce it in the South African variety.

2) The teacher distributes flash cards; some cards have examples of the characteristic features of South African English, British English, and American English. The other cards have the names of the varieties: British, American, or South African. Students are asked to match them.

The role of the teacher is to check the answers of the students, clarify, and correct if there are mistakes. It is noteworthy that the main goal is not to put one variety on a pedestal more than another one. Rather, the goal is to keep the different varieties being taught, as well as students' own Englishes, on equal footing.

References

Crystal, D. (1997). *English as a global language*. Cambridge University Press. https://doi.org/10.21832/9781783095681-004

Decke-Cornill, H. (2002). We would have to invent the language we are supposed to teach: The issues of English as a lingua franca in language education in Germany. In M. Byram & P. Grundy (Eds.), *Context and culture in language teaching and learning* (pp. 59–70). Multilingual Matters. https://doi.org/10.21832/9781853596728-007

Drama: Dialect and Accent Resources. (n.d.). Retrieved February 23, 2021, from https://guides.lib.uw.edu/c.php?g=341386&p=2298558

El-Sayed, A. (1991). Towards an international standard of English in the Arab world: An ethnosociolinguistic perspective. *Indian Journal of Applied Linguistics, XVII*, 155–167.

English Accents. (n.d.). Retrieved February 23, 2021, from www.uv.es/anglotic/accents_of_english/03/index.html

Farrell, T. S., & Martin, S. (2009). To teach standard English or world Englishes? A balanced approach to instruction. *English Teaching Forum, 47*(2), 2–7.

Graddol, D. (1997). *The future of English*. The British Council.

The International Dialects of English Archive. (n.d.). Retrieved February 23, 2021, from www.dialectsarchive.com/

Jenkins, J. (2006). Current perspectives on teaching world Englishes and English as a lingua franca. *TESOL Quarterly, 40*(1), 157–181. https://doi.org/10.2307/40264515

Jindapitak, N., & Teo, A. (2012). Thai tertiary English majors attitudes towards and awareness of world Englishes. *Journal of English Studies, 7*, 74–116.

Kachru, B. B. (1984). World Englishes and the teaching of English to non-native speakers: Contexts, attitudes and concerns. *TESOL Newsletter, 18*(22), 1–211.

Kachru, B. B. (1985). Standards, codification and sociolinguistics realism: The English language in the outer circle. In R. Quirk & H. G. Widdowson (Eds.), *English in the world: Teaching and learning the language and literatures* (pp. 11–30). Cambridge: Cambridge University Press. https://doi.org/10.2307/326771

Kachru, B. B. & Smith, L. (1985). Editorial. *World Englishes, 4*, 209–212.

Kachru, B. B. (2003). Liberation linguistics and the quirk concern. In B. Seidlhofer (Ed.), *Controversies in applied linguistics* (pp. 19–33). Oxford: Oxford University Press.

Kachru, Y. (2005). Teaching and learning of world Englishes. In E. Hinkel (Ed.), *Handbook of research in second language teaching and learning* (pp. 155–173). Lawrence Erlbaum. https://doi.org/10.4324/9781410612700-28

Kirkpatrick, A. (2002). ASEAN and Asian culture and models: Implications for the ELT curriculum and for teacher selection. In A. Kirkpatrick (Ed.), *Englishes in Asia* (pp. 213–224). Language Australia Ltd.

Maley, A. (2010). The reality of EIL and the myth of ELF. In C. Cagliardi & A. Maley (Eds.), *EIL, ELF, global English: Teaching and learning issues* (pp. 235–264). Peter Lang, Routledge. https://doi.org/10.3726/978-3-0351-0061-7/3

Matsuda, A. (2003). The ownership of English in Japanese secondary schools. *World Englishes, 22*(4), 483–496. https://doi.org/10.1111/j.1467-971x.2003.00314.x

Mckay, S. L. (2002). *Teaching English as an international language: Rethinking goals and Approaches*. Oxford University Press.

McKay, S. L. (2012). Principles of teaching English as an international language. In L. Alsagoff, S. L. McKay, G. Hu, & W. A. Renandya (Eds.), *Principles and practices for teaching English as an international language* (pp. 28–46). Routledge. https://doi.org/10.1111/weng.12043

Modiano, M. (2009). EIL, native-speakersim and the failure of European ELT. In F. Sharifian (Ed.), *English as an international language: Perspectives and pedagogical issues* (pp. 58–77). Multilingual Matters. https://doi.org/10.21832/9781847691231

Munro, M. J., Derwing, T. M., & Sato, K. (2006). Salient accents, covert attitudes: Consciousness-raising for pre-service second language teachers. *Prospect*, *21*(1), 67–79.

Pennycook, A. (2000). English in the world/the world in English. In A. Burns & C. Coffin (Eds.), *Analysing English in a global context: A reader* (pp. 78–89). Routledge. https://doi.org/10.1075/eww.24.1.15boo

Rahal, A. (2019a). English or Englishes? A question of multilingual reality. In B. Christiansen, & E. Turkina (Eds.), *Applied psycholinguistics and multilingual cognition in human creativity* (pp. 83–102). IGI Global. https://doi.org/10.4018/978-1-5225-6992-3.ch004

Rahal, A. (2019b). Transdisciplinary approach to linguistic diversity: Can we co-exist without "one English"? In V. X. Wang (Ed.), *Handbook of research on transdisciplinary knowledge generation* (pp. 383–396). IGI Global. https://doi.org/10.4018/978-1-5225-9531-1.ch026

Seidlhofer, B. (2011). *Understanding English as a lingua Franca*. Oxford University Press.

Ur, P. (1996). *A course in language teaching: Practice and theory*. Cambridge University Press.

Chapter 4

Translation as an Asset to Raise Global Englishes Awareness in the English Classroom

Elif Kemaloglu-Er

As multicompetent beings, learners of English have an important asset, which distinguishes them from a monolingual native speaker of English. This asset is their native language (L1), with the aid of which they can make translations (Cook, 2002). In the pedagogy of English as a Lingua Franca (ELF), L1 is deemed to be a vital part of a non-native speaker, and moderate use of L1 in the English classroom is seen as an egalitarian and humanitarian way of embracing non-native users of English with their own backgrounds and characteristics (Kemaloglu-Er & Bayyurt, 2018, 2019, 2020). Also in Global Englishes teaching, L1 is defined to be a resource that impacts diverse varieties of English spoken by interlocutors with multivariate L1 backgrounds and acts as a vehicle to understand and be informed about such profoundness (Galloway & Rose, 2015, 2018).

Integrating students' L1 into English classes can take place in the form of translation activities. Despite the use and ubiquity of translation in the global world, this bilingual activity has long been ignored in the field of ELT. However, scholars propose its incorporation into English classes, arguing that it can act as a valuable strategy that can help L2 learners comparatively and profoundly analyze the source and the target languages and, furthermore, discover the in-depth meanings of texts and reflect on them (e.g., Cook, 2010; Pym, 2018; Widdowson, 2016). Translation for pedagogical purposes or "pedagogical translation" fulfills primarily an instrumental function as a tool for improving the language learner's foreign language proficiency (Klaudy, 2003; Koletnik, 2013). In this context, translation is principally implemented as a means of awareness raising as well as language practicing.

Translation helps learners extend vocabulary and grammar knowledge; become aware of sociocultural aspects and multiple meanings of words and phrases; pay attention to the coherence and contextualization of texts; strengthen reading, listening, writing, and speaking, as well as analytical and critical thinking skills; and test fully that a text has been completely understood (Auerbach, 1993; Calis & Dikilitas, 2012). As stated by Stulajterova (2008), translation is a communicative activity, naturally involving speculation, discussion, expression, and negotiation of meaning. Through this task, the teacher can help learners raise awareness of the issues of the text being studied and overcome the difficulties they have in L2 learning and communication by having them analyze the links and usages in their L1. Schäffner (1998) also maintains that translation could be a beneficial tool in foreign language learning to improve verbal agility, expand students' vocabulary in L2, consolidate L2 structures for active use, monitor and improve the comprehension of L2, and

DOI: 10.4324/9781003124665-5

develop their understanding of how languages work. According to Canga-Alonso and Rubio-Goitia (2016), translation assists second language acquisition because it uses authentic materials, is interactive- and learner-centered, and promotes learner autonomy as it makes learners active participants responsible for their own learning.

This chapter argues that translation is an invaluable asset of the bilingual speaker-hearer that can be pedagogically useful in raising awareness of the multifaceted aspects of Global Englishes. To illustrate the value of translation in the multilingual classroom, a translation activity intended to raise learners' awareness of Global Englishes will be introduced. The activity can be applied in an ESL or EFL environment with learners of English at the intermediate (B1) level or above. The context where this activity was practiced was an advanced (C1) level English class in the School of Foreign Languages at an English-medium state university in Turkey. It was a preparatory English class where the students received intensive English education to get ready for their majors. In this program, students receive general English education through a series of coursebooks and skills-based courses where they are expected to improve their reading, writing, listening, and speaking. The L1 of all the learners and the teacher was Turkish.

The activity was applied in four phases: First, there was a theoretical phase where the learners were introduced to the concept of "Global Englishes" via explicit instruction through videos, readings, critical reflections, and reflective interactions, as elaborated in Kemaloglu-Er and Bayyurt (2018, 2019, 2020). In this theory-based phase, the students were also informed about Kachru's (1985, 1992) Three Circle Model of World Englishes depicting a global diversity of English. The model describes the spread of English in terms of three concentric circles: the Inner Circle, the Outer Circle, and the Expanding Circle, which represent "the type of spread, the patterns of acquisition and the functional domains in which English is used across cultures and languages" (Kachru, 1985, p. 12). The Inner Circle includes countries where English is spoken as the native language of a substantial majority of the population. The United States and the United Kingdom can be given as examples. The Outer Circle primarily comprises countries where English has a colonial history and fulfills significant institutionalized roles as the language of administration and education or often as an explicitly announced "official language." Some examples are India, Pakistan, Singapore, or the Philippines. Finally, Expanding Circle comprises countries which have no colonial history and where English is used and spreads as a foreign language. Turkey, Italy, Spain, and Japan are examples of Expanding Circle countries.

Although Kachru's (1985, 1992) model has been criticized for being more centered on geography and history than linguistic features (Jenkins, 2015), it can act as a precise and practical way to show the rationale behind Global Englishes teaching to students. That is, a great majority of English users are now within the Outer Circle and Expanding Circle, and English is no longer used exclusively by Inner Circle English users (i.e., among native English speakers or in native English-speaking settings). Thus, it seems increasingly irrelevant for language learners to be intensely exposed to a monolingual native model, and it becomes significant to integrate varieties of Englishes from all circles into the English classroom (Cameron & Galloway, 2019).

After the theoretical phase in which students were introduced to the concept of Global Englishes and its rationale, they were assigned to select and watch videos of speakers from Kachru's three circles, analyze the qualities of the varieties, and reflect on their perceptions about them. Then, after the assignments were assessed by the teacher and students' peers, the class moved on to an in-class practice involving a translation activity within groups. Each group was told to translate from English to Turkish (their native language) one of the three videos of three English speakers, each of whom was from one of Kachru's circles. The activity in our context involved a British, an Indian, and a Spanish speaker representing the Inner, Outer, and Expanding Circles, respectively. The British speaker, Gordon Ramsey, is a chef giving practical recipes to the audience. The interviews with Amir Khan, an Indian actor from the Outer Circle, and Pedro Alonso, another famous actor from Spain, were chosen to inspire the students to speak English confidently with their own varieties. The purpose of the translation was also defined to the students in accordance with Skopos Theory, which maintains that the basic principle which determines the process of translation is the purpose (skopos) of the translational action (Vermeer, 1996). Accordingly, the assumed purpose was that the students were to translate the videos for a magazine issued in Turkey addressing young adult university students.

The groups translated the audiovisual texts of the speakers into Turkish. Then, in the third phase, the students were asked to reflect on the variety of English they worked on (namely, its linguistic and cultural qualities), the specific aspects that facilitate or hinder intelligibility, and their perceptions about these varieties and their specific features. In the final phase of the activity, the learners shared their translations and reflections with their teacher and classmates; evaluated the learning gains as well as the challenges of the translations and how they addressed them; and received feedback (see the lesson plan at the end of this chapter for a sample implementation).

There are certain points to take into consideration in arranging and applying this activity. First, before it begins, students should be informed about Global Englishes and Kachru's circles via *explicit* ways (Kemaloglu-Er & Bayyurt, 2018, 2019, 2020). This can be done through lectures, displays of videos where speakers with different varieties talk and interact, and critical reflection and discussion activities on the features of varieties. Furthermore, instructors can acknowledge non-native use and users of English, with their own linguistic and cultural qualities, rather than assessing them against a native speaker benchmark.

Second, Kachru's concentric circles can refer to broadly defined categories, meaning it may take time and energy to select the appropriate speakers with different varieties for the in-class translation activity. It is recommended that the teacher carefully choose speakers that represent linguistic and cultural diversity. For instance, it may be better to include Outer and Expanding Circle varieties that show salient deviations from Standard English, allowing students to experiment with the concept of diversity in a more realistic sense. As for the choice of videos or video segments, they can be selected by the teacher, or students can be given an assignment before the lesson asking them to choose videos of speakers from each of the three circles. Then, the teacher can opt for the most appropriate ones for the classroom activity. The criteria for appropriateness may involve, among other possibilities, linguistic and cultural diversity; gender, race, and age diversity; and relevance and diversity of topics or themes. The teacher should also make sure to pick a variety of students' suggestions so that each student can feel like they contributed.

Third, it would be better to do some translation practice with students before the activity so that the class can more easily accommodate to the process. For instance, prior to the activity, students can be assigned to choose a speaker from one of the circles and translate their short video, commenting on the features of the English variety and the translation process. This can then be evaluated by the teacher and/or the students' peers. In contexts where the teacher and the students share the same native language, before this activity there can also be some preparatory in-class practices where the videos of speakers with different English varieties are translated into the native language.

It is necessary to define the aim of the translation activity in contexts teaching ESL or EFL. Translation in this EFL context was used as a pedagogical means to make in-depth analyses of the audiovisual source texts so that the students could pay close attention to and possibly gain deep insights into the linguistic and cultural diversity of English through the use of their L1. Since the type of translation intended was pedagogical translation, students should at least be given some basic guidelines. A sample set of guidelines is presented next:

1. Students should be told to make a detailed search of the vocabulary and phrases by using not one bilingual dictionary, but a variety of quality bilingual and monolingual dictionaries, as well as other relevant sources to ensure appropriate equivalence.
2. Students should be advised to avoid mechanical translations and make translated statements sound as "natural" as possible in the target language.
3. It would be useful to tell students to transfer the *meanings* of the statements intended by speakers to the target language/s rather than strict "mot-a-mot" (word-for-word) adherence to forms. The aim of this translation is to speculate, discuss, express, and negotiate the meanings intended to be conveyed by a broad range of users of Global Englishes.

Another issue to consider is the native language/s of the learners and the teacher. If the whole class and the teacher share the same native language, the translations and the opinion exchanges would be done as a whole-class activity. If there are a variety of native languages in the class and they are not spoken by the teacher, then the students with the same native languages would be grouped together. They would comment on each other's translation into the shared native language and reflect, elaborate on, and interact about the process in their L2 (which is English in this case). Herein, it is essential to remind teachers that they don't need to be anxious about not being knowledgeable about the native languages of their students or not being fully fluent in them. They can learn from their students—e.g., whenever it's helpful in the classroom, they can ask students to teach them words or phrases from their home languages and how those map onto or are different from English words and phrases. Also, when teachers interact in English with students using languages or dialects that they don't speak, they should try to make their own speech/teacher-talk as intelligible as possible, opting for a slow pace, a use of common words, and/or a clarification of meaning when they deem it is necessary.

The in-class time allocated to the translation activity is also important. Since students are expected to transcribe the video and then translate it in an effort to understand and decipher the Englishes of different people, this dual responsibility may take a great deal of time. Therefore, it is better to choose short (e.g., 8–10 minute) and meaningful audiovisual texts. Then, the teacher should adjust the duration of class time based on the anticipated difficulty and students' expected performance.

When engaged in the activities described in this chapter, learners experienced varying levels of difficulty in understanding the words or statements uttered by the speakers, so they listened to the recordings again and again. If they still could not understand a word, they made reasonable predictions. The participants were content to find out that they were not alone in having difficulty understanding Englishes spoken in diverse ways by different interlocutors. Although they had challenges in understanding the varieties, they had positive perceptions about them and found this diversity an inseparable part of Global Englishes communication. Overall, the learners said the activity was effective in teaching them about different aspects of Global Englishes. These findings highlight the fact that translation along with critical reflections can be utilized as a potentially impactful asset of the bilingual learner in Global Englishes pedagogy.

Lesson Plan: Exploring Varieties of English Through Translation

Recommended Grade Level(s)

Intermediate (B1), upper-intermediate (B2), or advanced (C1) level or proficient (C2) college students or secondary students

Context

The current lesson was implemented in an advanced (C1) level EFL preparatory class at the tertiary level in Turkey, yet the activity can be applied to ESL or EFL classes at the secondary or college level aiming to raise Global English awareness. Since translation is a major part of the activity, a certain level of proficiency in English is required, so the level of the students should be intermediate (B1) and above.

Objectives

Students will be able to:

- analyze varieties from Kachru's three circles, namely Inner, Outer, and Expanding Circles;
- translate audiovisual source texts reflecting varieties of Global Englishes into their native language;
- reflect on and discuss characteristics of varieties (e.g., linguistic and cultural features, intelligibility, and communication strategies) and their perceptions about them;
- evaluate learning gains and challenges of translations with regard to Global Englishes.

Procedures

Step 1: Warm-Up and Instructions (5–7 Minutes)

Having introduced the term *Global Englishes* to students with lectures, videos, and discussions, use this lesson as the practice-based phase of internalizing the subject matter. Remind students of the term *Global Englishes* and Kachru's circles and tell them that they are going to watch and analyze videos of speakers from the three concentric circles. They will then translate these audiovisual texts into their native language.

Divide the class into three groups, each responsible for translating the given audiovisual text representing one of the three circles. Then divide these groups into sub-groups sharing the same native language. Tell students that each group is expected to watch the given video carefully, analyze the English statements, translate each of them into their native language, and reflect on the characteristics of the variety. Send the links of the videos to the students through an online classroom communication platform and have them work via their mobile devices or the computers of the school.

Step 2: Translation Activity (25 Minutes)

Tell students to transcribe and analyze each statement, translate it into their native language, and write the translated versions one by one after the source statements. Walk around the class and answer their questions if they need help.

Step 3: Reflection and Discussion Within Group Work (10–15 Minutes)

When they finish the translation, tell groups to reflect on and discuss the characteristics of the given variety and how they perceive them. After this, tell groups that it is time to reflect now on their translation and tell them to discuss the benefits, learning gains, and challenges of their translations and how they addressed them.

Step 4: Whole Class Interaction (10 Minutes)

Ask each Circle group if they liked the activity and why. Ask each group to state at least one deviation from Standard English that attracted their attention, one learning gain, one challenge of the translation activity with regard to the English variety, and how they addressed this challenge. If more time is needed, these reports can be carried over to the next class.

Extension Activity

In the lesson discussed, each student had the opportunity to closely analyze and translate one variety from one circle. Now to get them to have a more intense and diverse experience, have each student translate a video from another circle and comment on the features of the varieties, how they feel about them, and the learning gains and challenges of the translation process. Finally, have them consider solutions for the challenges.

References

Auerbach, E. R. (1993). Reexamining English only in the ESL classroom. *TESOL Quarterly, 27*(1), 9–32. https://doi.org/ 10.2307/3586949

Calis, E., & Dikilitas, K. (2012). The use of translation in EFL classes as L2 learning practice. *Procedia—Social and Behavioral Sciences, 46*, 5079–5084. https://doi.org/10.1016/j.sbspro.2012.06.389

Cameron, D., & Galloway, N. (2019). Local thoughts on global ideas: Pre- and in-service TESOL practitioners' attitudes to the pedagogical implications of the globalization of English. *RELC Journal, 50*(1), 149–163. https://doi.org/10.1177/0033688218822853

Canga-Alonso, A., & Rubio-Goitia, A. (2016). Students' reflections on pedagogical translation in Spanish as a foreign language. *Tejuelo, 23*, 132–157. https://doi.org/10.17398/1988-8430.23.1.132

Cook, G. (2010). *Translation in language teaching*. Oxford University Press. https://doi.org/10.1093/applin/ams005

Cook, V. J. (2002). Background to the L2 user. In V. J. Cook (Ed.), *Portraits of the L2 user* (pp. 1–28). Multilingual Matters. https://doi.org/10.21832/9781853595851

Galloway, N., & Rose, H. (2015). *Introducing global Englishes*. Routledge. https://doi.org/10.1017/9781316678343

Galloway, N., & Rose, H. (2018). Incorporating global Englishes into the English classroom. *ELT Journal, 72*(1), 3–14. https://doi.org/10.1093/elt/ccx010

Jenkins, J. (2015). *Global Englishes*. Routledge. https://doi.org/10.4324/9781315761596

Kachru, B. (1985). Standards, codification and sociolinguistic realism: The English language in the outer circle. In R. Quirk & H. Widdowson (Eds.), *English in the world: Teaching and learning the language and literatures* (pp. 11–36). Cambridge University Press.

Kachru, B. (1992). *The other tongue: English across cultures*. University of Illinois Press.

Kemaloglu-Er, E., & Bayyurt, Y. (2018). ELF-aware pre-service teacher education: Teaching practices and reflections from Turkey. In L. Cavalheiro (Ed.), *Preparing English language teachers for today's globalized world* (pp. 47–63). Húmus.

Kemaloglu-Er, E., & Bayyurt, Y. (2019). ELF-awareness in teaching and teacher education: Explicit and implicit ways of integrating ELF into the English language classroom. In N. C. Sifakis & N. Tsantila (Eds.), *English as a lingua franca for EFL contexts* (pp. 147–163). Multilingual Matters. https://doi.org/10.21832/9781788921770

Kemaloglu-Er, E., & Bayyurt, Y. (2020). Project-based and ELF-aware pre-service teacher education in Turkey: Sample cases of discovery, creativity, interaction and multicultural diversity. In A. Gras-Velazquez (Ed.), *Project-based learning in second language acquisition: Building communities of practice in higher education* (pp. 82–97). Routledge. https://doi.org/10.4324/9780429457432

Klaudy, K. (2003). *Languages in translation*. Scholastica.

Koletnik, M. (2013). Translation in foreign language teaching. In N. Kocijančič-Pokorn & K. Koskinen (Eds.), *New horizons in translation research and education* (pp. 61–71). Publications of the University of Eastern Finland.

Pym, A. (2018). Where translation studies lost the plot: Relations with language teaching. *Translation and Translanguaging in Multilingual Contexts, 4*(2), 203–222. https://doi.org/10.1075/ttmc.00010.pym

Schäffner, C. (1998). Qualification for professional translators—translation in language teaching versus teaching translation. In K. Malmkjær (Ed.), *Translation and language teaching: Language teaching and translation* (pp. 117–133). St. Jerome Publishing.

Stulajterova, A. (2008). The place of translation in English language teaching. *Humanising Language Teaching, 10*(6). https://old.hltmag.co.uk/dec08/sart01.htm

Vermeer, H. J. (1996). *A skopos theory of translation: Some arguments for and against*. Wissenschaft.

Widdowson, H. G. (2016). The role of translation in language learning and teaching. In J. House (Ed.), *Translation: A multidisciplinary approach* (pp. 224–240). Palgrave Macmillan. https://doi.org/10.1057/9781137025487

Chapter 5

Practical Suggestions for Integrating Translanguaging in Secondary EFL
Using a Wordless Picture Book and Book Club Discussions

Eun Young Yeom

Introduction: Translanguaging and Multimodality

In current society, secondary-level emergent bilingual students in EFL (English as a Foreign Language), who are also known as English learners, are exposed to superdiverse, multimodal, and multilingual communications (Blommaert, 2013). Many people are engaged with multiple SNS (Social Networking Services) platforms and YouTube videos, which integrate multiple languages and semiotic modes simultaneously (Androutsopoulos, 2013; Zhao & Zappavigna, 2018). In this sense, it could be argued that secondary emergent bilinguals in EFL, especially teenagers who grow up with various Internet resources in their daily lives, can fluidly move between different named languages and semiotic repertoires. Hence, more flexible approaches to language teaching and learning, such as translanguaging, have gained popularity (García & Li, 2014; Pennycook, 2017). A translanguaging lens posits that languages, modes, and cultural repertoires exist in one interconnected continuum, in which multilinguals, including emergent bilinguals, fluidly traverse (García & Li, 2014). During English learning, therefore, emergent bilinguals concurrently integrate their diverse linguistic resources (their home languages and English), as well as multimodal and cultural repertoires (García & Li, 2014). In the process of English learning, which is ongoing and includes dynamic social practices (Li, 2018), EFL learners can also be assumed to become emergent bilinguals within dynamic bilingualism (García, 2009), who can integrate linguistic, multimodal, and cultural resources of two different languages, i.e., their respective home language(s) and English.

Secondary EFL Teaching and Learning in South Korea

Instead of integrating the fluid nature of translanguaging into English teaching (Turnbull, 2016), language separation and monoglossic ideology dominate English teaching in many EFL contexts (Escobar, 2019), including South Korean EFL. In score-oriented secondary EFL classrooms in South Korea, students' diverse linguistic, multimodal, and cultural repertoires are not valued for the sake of teacher-centered

DOI: 10.4324/9781003124665-6

and lecture-based English teaching and learning based on Grammar Translation Methods (GTM)[1] (Ryu & Boggs, 2016).

Due to the immense focus on word-to-word translation based on GTM, it is highly likely that Korean emergent bilinguals in Korean EFL cannot fully enjoy the process of dynamic and active meaning-making by incorporating and traversing linguistic, cultural, and semiotic repertoires, as the combination of *trans+languaging* denotes. It must be mentioned, however, that English classrooms, including after-school programs, can be a translanguaging space for emergent bilinguals. Li Wei (2011) conceptualized a translanguaging space as a place where languages and various semiotic resources interact and co-create meanings. In the classroom as a translanguaging space, emergent bilinguals' L1 repertoires can be integrated into English (L2) speaking and writing and vice versa, thereby generating what-looks-to-be ungrammatical English expressions, such as Konglish (Korean and English). Also, with the use of readily available multimodal resources like picture books, emergent bilinguals can incorporate their semiotic repertoires to make meanings and transfer these meanings into written or spoken forms of languages.

This chapter will illustrate how I, as a previous in-service English teacher at a local middle school in South Korea, created a translanguaging space for EFL emergent bilinguals through after-school book club discussions using a wordless picture book, *Flotsam* (Wiesner, 2006). I will show how the book club discussions appreciated EFL emergent bilinguals' linguistic repertoires while not pushing them to use standardized English. Furthermore, I will demonstrate how appreciating their Korean repertoires led them to use more creative multimodal meaning-making and how the co-created meanings were incorporated into subsequent writing activities.

Classroom Background

The translanguaging pedagogy and related activities shared in this chapter are based on the weekly afterschool book club discussions that I organized and managed in 2016. In this space, I recommended that the book club members use both Korean and English for discussions and subsequent writing activities. They were not penalized for non-standardized usage of English sentences or Korean ways of using English (Konglish). The 15 book club members, who were eighth- and ninth-grade South Korean students, gathered every Monday after school, discussed the weekly assigned readings of English young adult literature using both Korean and English, and wrote their final thoughts in both Korean and English.

This chapter shares how three ninth-grade focal students discussed visual images of the picture book and wrote about *Flotsam*, which is about the imagination and exploration of the mystery of the deep ocean. The focal students' names are Jin, Bum, and Hyun, pseudonyms to protect their identity. The particular weekly book club discussions regarding this picture book took place for six weeks (one meeting per week) from August 22 to September 26, 2016.

---

[1] Practices applying the Grammar Translation Method are characterized by teachers presenting language structures, which are practiced in the form of speaking and writing exercises by language learners (Chang, 2011).

Book Club Discussion and Subsequent Writing

Each session started with the silent individual reading of six pages of the wordless picture book for five to ten minutes; 36 pages were read in total over the six sessions. The book club members carefully read, observed, and appreciated each visual image individually. Then, the teacher-facilitated discussion on each visual image began, which simultaneously incorporated Korean and English. The discussion started from a factual question and moved into more in-depth questions. I initiated the conversation by asking, "What is going on in this picture?" Students shared their own observations and thoughts, and I pushed them to think further with the question "Could you tell me why?" As each session proceeded, book club members' answers became more sophisticated and more detailed with the use of more refined observations, imaginations, and opinions. Regarding their peers' observations and opinions, other book club members sometimes jumped in to add their own thoughts. Then, I added another question, "Could you tell me if there are other opinions and questions? And could you tell me if we missed anything in this picture?" If the book club members said that there were no other things to be added, we moved on to the next visual image in the book.

During discussions, I tried to show my students how two languages can coexist to make meanings. When asking them the aforementioned questions, I spoke in Korean first and then said the same sentence in English to send the message early on that Korean language is neither an inferior language nor a mere translation tool when learning English. Moreover, when facilitating and responding to students' questions, I mixed English and Korean without translating in a one-to-one fashion. Although encouraged to use both Korean and English in speaking and writing, use of Korean language dominated peer-to-peer spoken interactions probably because the book club members were socialized into monolingualism (Korean only) within South Korean society, or they thought that they were not proficient enough to produce "perfect" English sentences during interactions. After each discussion, the participants were engaged with individual subsequent writing, during which time they could use both Korean and English. However, all subsequent writings were written in English presumably because they were not used to mixing two languages in writing, and because using Korean language for English learning, including English writing, was not promoted in English classes (Rabbidge, 2019).

Discussion Transcript

The following transcript is a part of the first session when we covered the first six pages of *Flotsam*. Right after the discussion, book club members engaged with a follow-up writing exercise, in which they wrote down thoughts they had during the discussion. This excerpt covers page three of the picture book, in which the main character is curiously observing a small crab at the beach. Students spoke solely in Korean, which has been translated into English in the third column. Teachers' sentences with quotation marks were originally spoken solely in English or in both Korean and English. Right after the discussion, each student wrote their final thoughts on the paper.

Table 5.1 Book club discussion original transcript and translation

Speaker	Original transcript	Transcript translated in English
Teacher:	"Ok, 이 그림에서 무엇이 보이나요? could you tell me what you can see in this picture?" "진, 너가 먼저해볼래? Jin, would you go first?"	Ok, could you tell me what you can see in this picture? Jin, would you go first?
Jin:	아, 네. 음, 한 남자아이가 돋보기로 가재를 보고 있어요.	Yes, sure. Um, a boy is looking at a crab with a magnifying glass.
Teacher:	"Ok, 다른 의견있어요? Anyone who wants to add to Jin's observation?"	Ok, anyone who wants to add to Jin's observation?
Bum:	바스켓 안에 미역이 잔뜩 있고, 상자 안에는 문어가 있어요.	There is a bucket filled with seaweed, and a box that has an octopus in it.
Teacher:	이 그림에서 "seaweed and probably an octopus" 가 보이네요. 현, 다른 의견 있니?	We can see "seaweed and probably an octopus" within the image. Hyun, would you like to add anything?
Hyun:	음 . . . 남자아이 뒤에 하얀 모래성이 있어요.	Um, there is a white sandcastle behind him.
Teacher:	그럼, 이제, 왜 이 남자아이가 돋보기로 가재를 관찰할까요? "이 남자아이가 어떤 아이일까요? What can we guess about this boy?"	Okay, then, why do you think he observes this little crab with a magnifying glass? What can we guess about this boy?
Bum:	호기심이 많은 아이?	He is a very curious boy?
Jin:	아니면 해양생물에 관심이 많을 수도 있어요. 그래서 부모님이 아이를 데리고 해변에 왔을거에요.	Or he is passionate about marine life. And that is why their parents brought him to this beach.
Teacher:	"왜 그렇게 생각해? What makes you say that?"	What makes you say that?
Jin:	이전 장면에서, 두 사람이 부모님 같아 보였어요. 그리고 파라솔 밑에서 책을 읽었어요. 옆에 도구가 많이 있었는데도요.	In the previous page, the other two people seemed to be the boy's parents, and they were just reading books under the parasol, although there were many gadgets beside them.
Teacher:	잘 관찰했어요. "또 무엇을 볼 수 있어요? 다른 의견 있어요? What else can we find in this picture? Any opinions?"	Nice observation. What else can we find in this picture? Any opinions?
Students:	아니요.	Nope.
Teacher:	"Ok, then, let's move onto the next page."	

Table 5.2 Jin's subsequent English writing for the first session (page 1—page 6 of the picture book)

Page 1	I think someone watching thing which can see in water, but I don't know who he or she is.
Page 2	In the book, there was two person, but I don't think one of them is the person who has the eye before this page.
Page 3	(*the page discussed in the excerpt*) He is the guy who has the eye in the first page. I think they are his parents and they went sea because of him. So they were reading book to fill in the time. He likes observing organism that live in sea and he likes collecting too because the box next to him filled with something alive.
Page 4	After observing, he sent another place to serve something new and found crab so he started observing crab.
Page 5	Because of watching crab, he didn't know the big wave was coming to him. So he was pushed by wave with crab.
Page 6	After he pushed by wave, he was really wet and the crab was gone with his collections which had gathered. He looked really disappointed, but some people can think he looked something special.

Because of limited space in this chapter, only Jin's writing has been shared. His written response, based on the teacher-facilitated book club discussion, demonstrates how translanguaging can be promoted and enacted in a secondary EFL classroom. Jin traversed between visual (the picture book), speaking, and writing modes, as well as between two different languages while conversing with his peers and his teacher. When moving between different modes to make meanings, his own visual and verbal repertoires intermingled with other peers' repertoires, which were articulated in their verbal responses in Korean. Subsequently, the meanings that he made in Korean during the spoken interactions were integrated into his English writing. For example, Jin guessed about the characters based on evidential reasoning, as seen in the excerpt, which was transferred to subsequent writing. Incorporating his experiential knowledge, he thought the two other characters in the visual image were the main character's parents, who generously brought him to the beach, based on the visual evidence signifying that the two other characters were grown-ups and were indifferent to their surroundings. Jin considered that the young boy might not have been able to visit and explore the beach without adult supervision, and the adults who would sacrifice their time for the boy must be his parents. Presumably, on the basis of his experiential knowledge, he might have thought that the boy's parents read books to spend time at the beach while waiting for the boy. Jin also guessed the boy was enthusiastic about marine life based on visual cues, including the gadgets and the boy's collection of living creatures in the box. And he wrote about his speculation as seen in the subsequent writing.

Moreover, Jin's written response shows his emerging English repertoire, which does not seem to be as proficient as his Korean language. It should be noted that verbally producing his own sophisticated thinking process might not have been possible if he was asked to speak only in English. Using Korean language enabled him to generate more refined thinking, which was reflected in his English writing. His English writing showed grammar mistakes and awkward expressions if seen from a monoglossic point of view, which is geared toward native-like English proficiency. However, he tried his best to communicate meanings by taking risks and his intended meanings were delivered in English. His attempts were appreciated by both the teacher and the book club members, who did not measure his English for "correctness" based on idealized standards. His English was not judged or corrected in the supportive and acceptive translanguaging space of this after-school book club.

Conclusion and Implications

The book club activities shared in this chapter showed the promising aspects of translanguaging pedagogy in EFL. The translanguaging activities enabled the secondary EFL emergent bilinguals to fluidly traverse between different named languages and modes. While crossing between visual, spoken, and written modes, and moving between Korean and English, the secondary EFL emergent bilinguals in this book club had the opportunity to improve their linguistic and semiotic repertoires. They incorporated their Korean linguistic repertoires to read and analyze the messages within visual images, mixed their own interpretations with other peers' thoughts to create another meaning, and transferred these meanings onto the paper in English. Particularly, Jin's language experiences show that these students were meaning-making agents, who can integrate various semiotic resources, including visuals and traditional spoken and written languages. The effectiveness of this approach has been demonstrated in other recent studies, in which young emergent bilinguals have shown aptitude in mixing multiple semiotic resources and named languages simultaneously (Zhao & Flewitt, 2020).

More importantly, through sociocultural book club activities using a wordless picture book, the classroom became a translanguaging space, where dynamic multimodal and bilingual communication took place. A translanguaging space can be defined as "a space for the act of translanguaging as well as a space created through translanguaging" (Li, 2011, p. 1222). That is, the book club discussion provided a space for the secondary EFL emergent bilinguals to experience translanguaging as well as to create a sociocultural space through translanguaging. While socioculturally negotiating meanings with their peers, the participants crossed and moved between the boundaries of languages and modes, which used to be separated in their regular curricular English classrooms. In this regard, Escobar (2019) contends that "language separation in EFL programs is so deep-rooted that any translanguaging that takes place in the classroom is clandestine and ignored as a tool through which learners can foster ownership and pride of their emergent bilingual skills" (p. 291). In the translanguaging space created for and through book club activities, the secondary EFL emergent bilinguals did not have to feel ashamed of using their home language, which instead proffered them rich linguistic repertoires to think and write. Moreover, they were able to learn that foreign language learning did not have to be print-centric with word-to-word translation and a sole focus on target language acquisition. EFL emergent bilinguals' linguistic and semiotic repertoires should be acknowledged and valued more, since they serve as beneficial resources for English teaching and learning.

Lesson Plan: Using Picture Books for EFL Emergent Bilinguals' Translanguaging

Recommended Grade Level(s)

From secondary- to college-level and adult EFL classes. If picture books are incorporated for college-level EFL emergent bilinguals, more profound social issues embedded in picture books could be integrated into discussions. For example, the teacher can bring up environmental issues in *Flotsam* when discussions cover the visual images of the deep ocean polluted by waste disposal.

Context

This lesson plan, which uses picture books written in English or wordless picture books for secondary EFL students' multimodal meaning-making and translanguaging, was initially employed in afterschool book club discussions. Discussions based on picture books can also be incorporated into English classes to foster emergent bilingual EFL students' reading activities, peer-peer interactions, critical thinking skills, multimodal meaning-making, and translanguaging. The lesson plan was first used by students who all shared the same home language. Even so, in a classroom context in which students speak different home languages, picture book discussions can still reap benefits since they provide various ways for EFL emergent bilinguals to make meanings.

Objectives

Students will be able to:

- interpret the visuals along with verbal components of a selected picture book;
- support peers' meaning-making processes and co-create meanings out of visuals and verbal components;
- make meanings with the combined use of home language(s) and English.

Procedures

Step 1: Individual Reading (5 Minutes)

Students read the visual images and verbal components (if present) of a picture book individually.

Step 2: Questions About the Messages (10–15 Minutes)

The teacher can model translanguaging during the discussion by traversing between their home language(s) and English. The teacher initiates the discussion with questions: "What do you see in this picture? What is happening in this picture and the concurrent texts?" After students answer by mixing their home language(s) and English, the teacher goes deeper into the image and the concurrent texts by asking, "What more can we find in the picture and the text?" The point here is promoting the students' flexible language uses, not the teacher's knowing all of the students' diverse home languages.

Step 3: Facilitate Sociocultural Interactions and Critical Thinking (15–20 Minutes)

As students produce more interpretive responses, the teacher asks, "What makes you say that?" Responses to students should be open-ended, such as "Yes, this can be A and this can be interpreted as B. Are there any other opinions?" The teacher can allow EFL emergent bilinguals to interact in their home languages and English, and the teacher facilitates in their home language(s) and English. If students are not used to translanguaging, the teacher can model translanguaging for them.

Step 4: Writing Time (15–20 Minutes)

Students write their thoughts and opinions that they had during the discussion using both their home language(s) and English. For their written responses, EFL emergent bilinguals can also incorporate visuals to express their meanings and opinions.

References

Androutsopoulos, J. (2013). Networked multilingualism: Some language practices on Facebook and their implications. *International Journal of Bilingualism*, *19*(2), 185–205. https://doi.org/10.1177/1367006913489198

Blommaert, J. (2013). *Ethnography, superdiversity and linguistic landscapes: Chronicles of complexity*. Multilingual Matters.

Chang, S. C. (2011). A contrastive study of Grammar translation method and communicative approach in teaching English grammar. *English Language Teaching*, *4*(2), 13–24. https://doi.org/10.5539/elt.v4n2p13

Escobar, C. F. (2019). Translanguaging by design in EFL classrooms. *Classroom Discourse*, *10*(3–4), 290–305. https://doi.org/10.1080/19463014.2019.1628789

García, O. (2009). *Bilingual education in the 21st century: A global perspective*. Wiley-Blackwell.

García, O., & Li, W. (2014). *Translanguaging: Language, bilingualism, and education*. Palgrave Macmillan.

Li, W. (2011). Moment analysis and translanguaging space: Discursive construction of identities by multilingual Chinese youth in Britain. *Journal of Pragmatics*, *43*(5), 1222–1235. https://doi.org/10.1016/j.pragma.2010.07.035

Li, W. (2018). Translanguaging as a practical theory of language. *Applied Linguistics*, *391*, 9–30. https://doi.org/10.1093/applin/amx039

Pennycook, A. (2017). Translanguaging and semiotic assemblages. *International Journal of Multilingualism*, *14*(3), 269–282. https://doi.org/10.1080/14790718.2017.1315810

Rabbidge, M. (2019). *Translanguaging in EFL contexts: A call for change*. Routledge.

Ryu, J., & Boggs, G. (2016). Teachers' perceptions about teaching multimodal composition: The case study of Korean English teachers at secondary schools. *English Language Teaching*, *9*(6), 52–60. http://doi.org/10.5539/elt.v9n6p52

Turnbull, B. (2016). Reframing foreign language learning as bilingual education: Epistemological changes towards the emergent bilingual. *International Journal of Bilingual Education and Bilingualism*, 1–8. https://doi.org/10.1080/13670050.2016.1238866

Wiesner, D. (2006). *Flotsam*. Clarion Books.

Zhao, S., & Flewitt, R. (2020). Young Chinese immigrant children's language and literacy practices on social media: A translanguaging perspective. *Language and Education*, *34*(3), 267–285. https://doi.org/10.1080/09500782.2019.1656738

Zhao, S., & Zappavigna, M. (2018). The interplay of (semiotic) technologies and genre: The case of the selfie. *Social Semiotics*, *28*(5), 665–682. https://doi.org/10.1080/10350330.2018.1504724

Chapter 6

L1 Use and Translanguaging in ELL Peer Interaction
A Problem or a Useful Tool?

Dmitrii Pastushenkov, Curtis A. Green-Eneix and Olesia Pavlenko

Many communicative and task-based language teaching (TBLT) classrooms have adopted peer-interactive tasks to facilitate second language (L2) use (Loewen & Sato, 2018). Such oriented tasks have been shown to benefit learning and to lower students' anxiety levels of using the L2 compared to interacting with their teacher (Sato & Ballinger, 2016). Yet, teachers often encounter a pressing question concerning language use: should students use their first language (L1) to facilitate task-based peer interaction? With the idea of *translanguaging*—the intermixing of languages, linguistic registers, and repertoires (García et al., 2016)—coming into the spotlight, many English language teachers may be hesitant or unsure how a lesson can include the use of multiple languages within the classroom.

This chapter sets out to show that English does not need to be the only medium of peer interaction. We discuss how prior research has shown that L1 use can be beneficial in scaffolding (Macaro & Lee, 2013) and supporting students academically, linguistically, and socially (Lialikhova, 2019). Following the benefits of incorporating translanguaging in L2 classrooms, we talk about a study we have conducted that examines adult ESL students from the United States (Pastushenkov et al., 2021). In understanding how and why students may use their L1, we will describe peer-interactive tasks that tap into students' translanguaging abilities using examples from previous research and our own work in the areas of English as a second (ESL) (Pastushenkov & Pavlenko, 2020) foreign language (EFL), and Russian as a Foreign Language (Pastushenkov, forthcoming): consensus task, conversation, and spot-the-difference tasks, an interview activity, and the role-playing game "Mafia." The chapter concludes with a lesson plan based on the interview activity.

Translanguaging

As teachers instruct students with different linguistic backgrounds, questions concerning mode of communication come up no matter the material being taught. This has been widely debated among language teachers and researchers, with scholars proposing the idea of *translanguaging* (García et al., 2016; Kayi-Aydar & Green-Eneix, 2019). Translanguaging suggests that both teachers and students use their entire repertoire to learn both the L2 and the course content (García & Kleyn, 2016). This idea highlights that language is open: individuals can use, for instance, Spanish resources (e.g., vocabulary, grammar, phrases, and idioms) to understand

DOI: 10.4324/9781003124665-7

content taught in English. This allows students and teachers to tap into all their resources, spanning from their linguistic background to their personal history and knowledge acquired at home, to where they can produce meaningful communication with their peers to deepen their understanding (García et al., 2016). For example, Kayi-Aydar & Green-Eneix (2019) found their teacher participant, Mr. Armendarez, used translanguaging to teach Mariachi, a musical genre that originates in Mexico. Mr. Armendarez used both English and Spanish to teach his students to be mariachi performers by helping them learn to sing in Spanish as well as develop their emerging bilingual repertoire.

Translanguaging appears to allow students to engage in collaborative dialogue with their peers to co-construct or come to a deeper understanding of the content being taught (García & Kleyn, 2016). For example, Lialikhova (2019) found that Norwegian ninth graders in a content-integrated, language-learning classroom used translanguaging. Specifically, ninth graders intermixed their available linguistic resources as they engaged in peer-collaborative tasks; translanguaging thus allowed them to better understand the content through acts of corrective feedback, scaffolding each other's understanding, and to participate in knowledge co-construction. Lialikhova's (2019) findings support the idea that translanguaging is a support tool for students to learn both the content and language as they complete classroom activities. The caveat to these findings, importantly, is that teachers need to be open to the use of multiple languages within the classroom as part of their pedagogical practices and instructional efforts to "respond to individual children's [or adult's] language repertoires" (García & Kleyn, 2016, p. 23). In noting the potential benefits of students and teachers using L1, we shift to consider how translanguaging occurs during peer interaction.

L1 Use in ELL Peer Interaction: Prior Research

In L2 classes, some teachers and administrators impose strict policies regarding L1 use, while others let their students switch between languages and fully use their linguistic repertoire (Macaro & Lee, 2013). Despite teachers' concerns regarding their students' L1 use in peer interaction (e.g., going off task), L1 can be a useful tool to assist learners at different proficiency levels. Studies have shown that in communicative peer interaction, students often stayed on task when switching between languages to better understand the vocabulary and grammar (Azkarai & Mayo, 2015; Sato & Angulo, 2020) and for task management (Pastushenkov et al., 2021). It is important to note that students' L1 use in peer interaction may depend on the task type. For example, speaking tasks that include a writing component may involve more L1 production than speaking-only tasks (Azkarai & Mayo, 2015).

To address some of the questions we had as English teachers, we conducted a study of ESL pair interactions at a large Midwestern university in the United States (Pastushenkov et al., 2021). The purpose of our study was to investigate the effects of having the same or different L1 background in a pair, the amount of L1 use in the same-L1 pairs, and peer familiarity in interactive pair work to understand how using L1 influenced learners' task scores and language-related episodes (LREs)—language used to discuss the language they produced. Additionally, we set out to acquire a better understanding as to why students may switch to their L1s.

As ESL teachers, we often did not speak the L1s of our students. For example, none of the authors of this article spoke the following languages of our participants who were part of our study (except for Russian): Arabic, Chinese Mandarin, Gujarati, Korean, and Spanish. As part of the study, we recruited 42 intermediate students who were then placed into different types of groups based on their L1 and how familiar they were with the other participant: same-L1/familiar, same-L1/unfamiliar, different-L1/familiar, and different-L1/unfamiliar. We did not observe any clear differences between the same-L1 and different-L1 groups with regard to task completion and production of LREs. With the help of our colleagues, we translated the Arabic and Chinese Mandarin L1 segments and found that the pairs stayed on task the entire time and only used their L1s for task management or vocabulary deliberations.

The study's findings were promising, as one of the main concerns of many ESL teachers (including us) was whether students stayed on task when they switched to their L1s. Based on our findings, L1 can be used for scaffolding to learn and clarify vocabulary, as well as move the task along. However, despite its benefits, we suggested that L1 use may be limited in short interactive tasks, as we also found a negative relationship between the amount of L1 use and both task scores and LREs. Here are some examples of students' interactions **(the L1 segments are presented in bold, translated into English for clarity)**. The subjects were engaged in an activity called *spot-the-difference*, which will be discussed in the next section of the chapter.

Example 1. Same-L1 Arabic Dyad (Pastushenkov et al., 2021).

A: Here. the mic is . . . like fish
B: **Really?** Light and fish.
A: **And here are the** shoes. Here they are orange and here they are not.
B: Shoes?
A: Yes, and the book . . . **Like this.** Check the color of the pants . . .
B: Yellow . . . on the left . . .

In this example, the students used Arabic to ask a question (express doubt). Student A also used some Arabic to move the task along. Some of these sentences may have been easier to say in Arabic (even though the student repeated a similar sentence in English in one of the instances).

Here is another example that shows that L1 use can potentially help learn new vocabulary:

Example 2. Same-L1 Chinese Mandarin Dyad (Pastushenkov et al., 2021).

A: **What is the color of pants?**
B: Blue.
A: **And this is** yellow. **How to say that?**
B: Something yellow. How to say, **'next to something?'**
A: Next to . . .

In this example, one of the interlocutors did not know how to say "next to something" in English and switched to Chinese Mandarin to learn new vocabulary. This benefit of L1 use in peer interaction has also been discussed in previous research (e.g., Azkarai & Mayo, 2015; Sato & Angulo, 2020).

L1 Use in ELL Peer Interaction: Tasks and Examples of Interactions

In this part of the chapter, we will talk about five communicative tasks that we used in our teaching and research in the areas of ESL, EFL, and Russian as a Foreign Language: consensus, conversation, spot-the-difference, interview, and the role-playing game "Mafia." The examples of interactions for the three tasks (consensus, conversation, and spot-the-difference) were recorded for one of our current projects. These examples illustrate how communicative activities can be used to tap into learners' translanguaging abilities. The consensus, conversation, and spot-the-difference tasks were adapted from studies by Loewen and Wolff (2016) and Loewen and Isbell (2017). A lesson plan built around the interview activity appears at the end of this chapter.

Consensus Task

In consensus tasks, students receive different pieces of information; they must discuss the different information and come up with a solution. For example, in the following task, the students (two Russian-speaking English learners) received information about three candidates for a fellowship to study in the United States (for the instructions, see Loewen & Isbell, 2017 or IRIS[1]). Each candidate has their strengths and weaknesses. In Example 3, students D and G were in the middle of a discussion about the candidates.

Example 3. **Consensus Task**

D: . . . current level of spoken English—good. **It's difficult, I don't understand everything** . . .
G: Don't be afraid. Let's tell something.
D: Julia . . . very **crap, how do I say 'low?' Here I just need to say, how do you say 'low level'** . . . **I just** . . .
G: Less level, than . . .
D: **Ahh, here it is.** So, thank you, thank you. Less level of IQ is a 85. That's little. Little level.
G: **Uh-huh.**
D: . . . of . . . of . . . **crap.**
G: I think, that Julia is better because her father is diplomat and . . . aaa . . . he could help her to travel and . . . and . . . and . . . **How do you say 'acquire'?**

---

1 A free and publicly available digital repository of instruments, materials, and stimuli for L2 research (Marsden et al., 2016).

D: **That's a difficult word.** Your . . . **oups** . . . her . . . her current of spoken English is upper-intermediate is a best current level of . . . of all candidates.
G: But I see that she failed the class because she's parting . . . and has a difficult childhood. A . . . she not reliable than Julia. Albert—I don't know. She has level of spoken English, than Gina. And . . .

Like in Examples 1 and 2, the learners in Example 3 used L1 to move the task along and ask each other words that they did not know. In line with our previous study, the students stayed on task the entire time.

Conversation Task

The conversation task also comes from Loewen and Wolff (2016) and Loewen and Isbell (2017). The task is called "Favorite Things." In this activity, learners ask each other questions about several familiar topics (favorite book, actor, movie, cuisine, etc.). The teacher can pick topics based on the syllabus. Then the students discuss what they have in common and what is different. Example 4 illustrates how Russian learners of English accomplish this activity.

Example 4. Conversation Task

L: Uh . . . my favorite book . . . um . . . you know I like books about love and it's . . . I can't translate . . . uh . . . the name of this book . . . prediction and . . . uh **gosh, Pride and Prejudice . . . I don't remember how to translate it** . . . this book because . . . because it is about love, really love, strong love and what is your favorite movie?
J: My fav . . . I love **The Matrix** because Keanu Reeves is actor of this film. And what's your favorite movie?
L: Um . . . my favorite movie . . . I like a lot of movies, but my favorite movie is Titanic. Because it's a very nice story about love. And what is uh your favorite childhood memory?
J: It's very hard question. I think it's simple memory about my . . . about spend my time with my parents anywhere: home, we. . . **'Nature' how? Gosh, I forgot.**
L: Nature?
J: Nature. Yeah. That's all and you favorite childhood memory?

Like in Example 3, the speakers here used L1 for vocabulary deliberations. Interestingly, they did not translate the titles (*Pride and Prejudice* and *The Matrix*). Overall, they mostly used English and stayed on task the entire time even though the researcher collecting the data (Olesia Pavlenko) did not intervene in their discussion. This highlights the importance of allowing students moments to interact and translanguage with one another as they work through the task without teacher intervention. If teachers do want to facilitate translanguaging in the classroom, they can do so by reviewing task expectations, answering students' questions, and modeling translanguaging in their own teacher-talk.

Spot-the-Difference Task

Even though spot-the-difference tasks are sometimes perceived as less authentic than other communicative tasks, they effectively promote peer interaction and thus have been widely used in interaction research (e.g., Loewen & Isbell, 2017; Pastushenkov et al., 2021). In spot-the-difference tasks, learners are given two similar, but slightly different pictures. The interlocutors need to communicate to find the differences.

The following is an example of peer interaction during a spot-the-difference task (pictures available on the IRIS repository, www.iris-database.org/). Such tasks can also tap into learners' translanguaging abilities and promote vocabulary learning. Upon completion of the task, the teacher can go over the differences that the learners have found.

Example 5. Spot-the-Difference Task

A: O! just a second . . . One, two, three, four, five, six, seven, eight, nine, ten, eleven, twelve **and I don't remember what's next . . .**
IK: No, no, no, not flowers. Trees, trees.
A: **These are tourists, yes?**
IK: **No, trees.**
A: A! Trees! Oh, my God! fu . . . two . . . two palms.
IK: Two, ho, I have three.
A: I have two . . .
IK: Ok. Maybe, you have also three trees. Can you see behind the children, how to say it, ok, . . . Do you see swings, yeah? Left side . . .
A: **Could you repeat that?**
IK: Swings. **Swings.** Do you have . . . do you see? Do you see left side girl?

Interview Task

This task was originally developed for use in STARTALK Russian immersion programs (Pastushenkov, forthcoming). This activity will be discussed in detail in the next section of the chapter (Lesson Plan). Unlike the other tasks from this chapter, the interview activity includes speaking and writing, as well as interactions with both peers and guests (interviewees). The teacher invites three interviewees (advanced speakers of the L2; maybe, of different age groups). The interviews are conducted in-person or via online conferencing. During the lesson, the students work in groups (3–5 students) and prepare questions for the interviews (which could be related to the topic of the lesson). Then each team interviews one guest at a time. The teams switch, so they could interview each guest. Upon completion of the interviews, the students prepare a presentation/written report about their guests. Optionally, the students can vote for the best team/interviewer.

The Role-Playing Game "Mafia"

We adapted "Mafia," a popular Russian role-playing game, for our English classes (see Pastushenkov & Pavlenko, 2020). Unlike the other activities from this chapter,

"Mafia" can be played in large groups (10–15 students) with the teacher acting as the host of the game. It has the following roles: Mafia (three students), Doctor (one student), Detective (one student), Other Civilians (the other students in a class), and Host (the teacher). The game has two stages: Day and Night. During the day, the students need to interact and try to figure out who is in the Mafia. The Mafia are the informed minority (they know who the other Mafia members are; they greet each other during the first night).[2]

Conclusion

Peer interaction is a platform for experimenting with linguistic resources, including in the form of translanguaging. The communicative tasks described in this chapter tap into learners' abilities to intermix their languages as a form of support and scaffold one another to develop in the target language. Supported by teachers' own examples and modeling (e.g., using multiple languages to understand the target vocabulary and grammar), such tasks allow learners to fully use their linguistic repertoire and enhance their language-learning experiences to see that learning a language does not require "starting over." Rather, learning another language is achieved by expanding their linguistic home to add another room.

---

2 For the full procedure, see Pastushenkov and Pavlenko (2020).

Lesson Plan: Interview Activity

Recommended Grade Level(s)
Beginner high, intermediate, or advanced middle school/high school/university ELLs.

Context
This lesson can be adapted for different courses. For example, it can be used in advanced ESL speaking classes. Depending on the students' proficiency, they may require varying levels of support from teachers. It may be helpful to focus on specific topics and give more examples with beginner learners. The activity can also be implemented using online conferencing.

Objectives
The students will be able to:

- participate in spontaneous spoken conversations on familiar topics and practice note-taking during interactions;
- prepare a presentation/written report based on a series of interactions on familiar topics.

Procedures

Step 1: Group Placement and Question Preparation (10–15 Minutes)

The teacher places the students randomly into groups of three to five students (depending on the number of interviewees/guests). For each interviewee, there should be one team of interviewers, so that the students can interview one guest at a time. Upon placement, the students interact and prepare questions for the interviewees. These questions may be related to the theme/topic of the lesson/week/module. The teacher helps the students prepare questions if necessary.

Step 2: Interviews (10 Minutes per Interviewee; Three Interviewees = 30 Minutes)

The teams interview one guest at a time. After ten minutes, they switch, so the teams could interview every guest.

Step 3: Presentation Preparation (10 Minutes)

Upon completion of the interviews, the teams prepare a short report (a presentation) about the interviewees. Each can prepare a written report about the interviewees as a homework assignment. The teacher can create a prompt for the writing assignment (e.g., what music genres do different generations of Americans like?).

Step 4: Presentation (10 Minutes)

Each team gives a short presentation about the interviewees. The students can optionally vote for the best team/interviewer.

References

Azkarai, A., & Mayo, M. P. G. (2015). Task-modality and L1 use in EFL oral interaction. *Language Teaching Research, 19*(5), 550–571. https://doi.org/10.1177/1362168814541717

García, O., Johnson, J., & Seltzer, K. (2016). *The translanguaging classroom: Leveraging student bilingualism for learning*. Caslon.

García, O., & Kleyn, T. (2016). *Translanguaging with multilingual students: Learning from classroom moments*. Routledge.

Kayi-Aydar, H., & Green-Eneix, C. A. (2019). Shared identities through translanguaging practices in the multilingual mariachi classroom. *TESOL Journal, 10*(4), 1–17. https://doi.org/10.1002/tesj.502

Lialikhova, D. (2019). "We can do it together!"—But can they? How Norwegian ninth graders co-constructed content and language knowledge through peer interaction in CLIL. *Linguistics and Education, 54*, 1–19. https://doi.org/10.1016/j.linged.2019.100764

Loewen, S., & Isbell, D. R. (2017). Pronunciation in face-to-face and audio-only synchronous computer-mediated learner interactions. *Studies in Second Language Acquisition, 39*(2), 225–256. https://doi.org/10.1017/s0272263116000449

Loewen, S., & Sato, M. (2018). Interaction and instructed second language acquisition. *Language Teaching, 51*(3), 285–329. https://doi.org/10.1017/s0261444818000125

Loewen, S., & Wolff, D. (2016). Peer interaction in F2F and CMC contexts. In M. Sato & S. Ballinger (Eds.), *Peer interaction and second language learning: Pedagogical potential and research agenda* (pp. 162–184). Amsterdam, the Netherlands: John Benjamins.

Macaro, E., & Lee, J. H. (2013). Teacher language background, codeswitching, and English-only instruction: Does age make a difference to learners' attitudes? *TESOL Quarterly, 47*(4), 717–742. https://doi.org/10.1002/tesq.74

Marsden, E., Mackey, A., & Plonsky, L. (2016). The IRIS repository: Advancing research practice and methodology. In A. Mackey & E. Marsden (Eds.), *Advancing methodology and practice: The IRIS repository of instruments for research into second languages* (pp. 1–21). Routledge.

Pastushenkov, D. (forthcoming). Task-based peer interaction in Russian as a second/foreign language classes. In S. Nuss & W. Martel (Eds.), *Task-based instruction for teaching Russian as a foreign language*. Routledge.

Pastushenkov, D., Camp, C., Zhuchenko, I., & Pavlenko, O. (2021). Shared and different L1 background, L1 use, and peer familiarity as factors in ESL pair interaction. *TESOL Journal, 12*(2), 1–15. https://doi.org/10.1002/tesj.538

Pastushenkov, D., & Pavlenko, O. (2020). Mafia: A role-playing game promoting peer interaction. In U. Nurmukhamedov & R. W. Sadler (Eds.), *New ways in teaching with games* (pp. 149–151). TESOL Press.

Sato, M., & Angulo, I. (2020). The role of L1 use by high-proficiency learners in L2 vocabulary development. In W. Suzuki & N. Storch (Eds.), *Languaging in language learning and teaching: A collection of empirical studies* (pp. 42–66). Benjamins.

Sato, M., & Ballinger, S. (2016). Understanding peer interaction: Research synthesis and directions. In M. Sato & S. Ballinger (Eds.), *Peer interaction and second language learning: Pedagogical potential and research agenda* (pp. 1–30). Benjamins.

Part 2
Literature and Writing

Chapter 7

A Conversation-Analytic Approach to Translanguaging Practices in Literature Courses in Turkish Higher Education

Vildan Inci-Kavak and Yasemin Kırkgöz

Introduction

There has been a dramatic rise in the number of bilingual and multilingual education programmes as an outcome of globalisation and internationalisation of university education. Following the trend, a select number of state and private universities in Turkey have adopted English as the medium of instruction (EMI) since they see this policy as a major tenet of academic prestige, and they have been increasingly aware of the rising competition among international higher education institutions. Whilst the language of everyday communication in Turkey is Turkish, the official language of instruction at universities tends to vary from one department to the other, particularly considering that departments such as engineering, medicine, and English studies necessitate an English-medium learning environment to ensure the up-to-datedness of course contents, qualifications of students, and competitiveness of the programmes. Nevertheless, even at universities where educational policies explicitly state that English is the medium of instruction, the governing bodies have partial or limited control of the actual in-class practices.

This chapter looks at content-based classrooms—an English literature class in this case—in terms of how, when, and why students employ their linguistic repertoires for different purposes. The chapter argues that focusing on learners' language uses in the classroom would benefit learners by raising their awareness of their own language practices and benefit lecturers by encouraging a reflective approach to their students' speech habits.

Translanguaging

One currently recommended strategy for encouraging a focus on learners' language in the classroom involves *translanguaging*, though researchers have offered various competing terms that cover similar grounds. Garcia (2009) defines *translanguaging* as

> an approach to bilingualism that is centered not on languages as has often been the case, but on the practices of bilinguals that are readily observable. These worldwide translanguaging practices are seen here not as marked or unusual, but rather taken for what they are, namely the normal mode of communication that, with some exceptions in some monolingual enclaves, characterizes communities throughout the world.

(p. 44)

Garcia and Leiva (2013) see language as "an ongoing process that only exists as languaging" (p. 204). Languaging thus not only does shape but is also shaped by people as a constant and complex interaction that generates social, cultural, political, and linguistic meanings and implications. In this context, terms such as *code-switching*, *code-mixing*, and *borrowing* have lost their past popularity because languages are less likely to be seen as completely separate, identifiable, and distinct systems today. The main focus of translanguaging is thus not on "codes" or established patterns anymore. Translanguaging is a natural and essential element of bilingual and multilingual meaning-making processes in social interactions, in which language is entangled with other semiotic aspects, not merely the language code (Lin, 2019; Hawkins & Mori, 2018). Translanguaging, in this sense, comprises fluid verbal and linguistic performances in diverse and interwoven social and cultural exchanges.

Translanguaging has blurred and challenged the limitations of conventional discourse on languages. Otheguy et al. (2015) suggest that while bilingual or multilingual speakers are in the process of talking, they do not obey the social and political rules and boundaries of the named languages. Likewise, Garcia (2009) puts special emphasis on the dynamic nature of translanguaging and makes an analogy between translanguaging and a banyan tree which "does not only grow vertically but horizontally as well" (Garcia, 2009, p. 143).

Classroom Translanguaging

Translanguaging occurs in numerous EMI classrooms at universities at different levels. It is a common practice in classrooms where students' mother tongue is not the language of instruction and, furthermore, encourages learners to "participate, elaborate and raise questions" by scaffolding (Lewis et al., 2012, p. 645). This practice also "increases the inclusion, participation, and understandings of pupils in the learning processes; developing less formal relationships between participants; conveying ideas more easily; and accomplishing lessons" (Ellis & McCartney, 2011, p. 189). In other words, translanguaging pedagogy stresses "linguistics of participation" (Li, 2018, p. 17) because teachers and students often have to cooperate in the co-construction of knowledge (Garcia, 2019). Maillat and Serra (2009) also state that if students use their L1 in tandem with L2 strategically, their language skills and content mastery will improve simultaneously. Garcia and Kleifgen (2010) claim that there are several strategical translanguaging practices such as the following:

- using a text that is in one language and discussion that is in another language;
- moving from a text in one language to another text in another language;
- discussing in one language, checking understanding in another language;
- reading in one language, writing in another language or vice versa;
- discussing in one language, writing in another language or vice versa;
- integrating students' entire linguistic resources; and
- using both (or all) languages flexibly in micro-alternation mode (Esquinca et al., 2014, p. 167).

The Context

Our study of a translanguaging approach in a literature classroom was conducted at Gaziantep University (GAUN), which is one of the prestigious universities in Turkey that adopts English as a medium of instruction. It offers courses in a range of undergraduate and postgraduate programmes in English.

Research Design

The data obtained through audio recordings, interviews, observations, and field notes were taken during the 2018–2019 spring semester. The post-colonial literature class, which consisted of three teaching hours a week, was recorded and observed regularly during class discussions for two months. While the first half of the lesson was dedicated to post-colonial literary theory, the second half featured a novel entitled *Kehinde* written by Buchi Emecheta. Eight teaching hours were transcribed meticulously by using Jeffersonian transcription codes for conversation analysis (Jefferson, 1984). The data, along with complementary information from interviews and notes, were examined to identify the functions of classroom translanguaging practices.

Data Analysis

The Analysis of the Sample Extracts

Although the complete recordings last about 277 minutes, only the most representative sampling extracts are presented here. Background information is provided before each analysis to illustrate the various ways different aspects of translanguaging facilitate language learning and literary interpretation.[1]

Excerpt 1: Introducing the Topic, Generating Motivation, Checking Comprehension, Scaffolding

The chosen literature class begins with a discussion about race and ethnicity. The participants follow a book called *Beginning Postcolonialism* by John McLeod. The lecturer reads excerpts from the book and then initiates a class discussion.

---

1 The transcription symbols used here are common to conversation analytic research and the system of transcription is a slightly adapted version of Jefferson's (1984). The common conventions are as follows:
    L   lecturer
    Sx   identified student
    ↑   rise in intonation
    :   lengthening of sound
    =   no gap between turns
    (.)   micropause
    (.2)   a pause of .2 seconds
    tr   translation

1 Lecturer: huh uh yes ↑ok in a way do you ↑think that races are necessary
to↑divide certain people in a group ↑to exclude others? (0.2)
2 °acaba°öyle ↑kaçınılmaz bir taraf mı oluyor birilerini kabul
3 ederken birilerini dışlamak işte bunun bir yolu da ırkçılık oluyor
4 peki ırkçılığa bir bakalım
[tr: is there an inevitable part of it, while it is including some, it
is also excluding, ok, let's look at racialisation.]
5 racialisation ↑last paragraph u::hhh ↑second sentence uhh ((L starts
6 reading aloud)) race as a category is the result of this social and historical
7 process which we can call ↑racialisation ((L stops reading))umm ↑yani
8 kitap bu şey ırk meselesini tamamen ↑reddediyor etnik olmasının
9 haricinde ↑sosyal °ve°↑tarihsel bir yapılandırma olup bununda aslında
10 ırkÇILIĞIN bir sonucu olduğu üzerinden tartışıyor oraya bir bakalım
[tr: I mean, the book rejects this racialisation, it discusses that
apart from its relation with ethnicity, this is a social and historical
construction, which is the conclusion of racialization, let's look
at that part.]
11 ((T continues reading aloud)) raCISM is the ideology that upholds the
12 discrimination against certain people on the grounds of perceived racial
13 difference (.) and claims these constructions of racial identity are true or
14 natural ((L stops reading)) ↑race is used in quotation marks in the book
15 ((L continues reads)) emphasising existence as a ↑HISTORICAL
16 CONSTRUCT and not a biological given ((T stops reading)) what do
17 you think I think this is very important I was ↑also thinking that race is
18 something related with biology as a ↑scientific fact ↑whereas it is like the
19 ↑manipulative tool of the western countries do you ↑think ↑Eastern
20 societies are devising these concepts racialisation
21 Student: ok race is about ↑how we perceive the ↑other race related with the
22 ideology of others
23 Lecturer: huh uh when we say ↑others ↑who do we ↑mean

The lecturer begins with a question to initiate a classroom discussion. After a two-second silence, s/he delivers the same question in the mother tongue to invite students into brainstorming and discussion. This seems to be a strategy to present what the class will explore and interpret in the lesson. The lecturer introduces the subject matter and familiarises the students with it by inviting them to reflect upon it in both languages. In this way, the students are incorporated and their attention is attracted to the content of the lesson regardless of their proficiency levels. In Line 4, the lecturer delivers all the terminology in English, but literary expressions and the relevant jargon (i.e., "racialisation," "postcolonialism") are introduced in the target language. Line 7 shows that classroom texts are English, but the debate on the text is in both languages (Williams, cited in Baker, 2006), which can be called an example of "transliteracy" (Baker, 2006). While translation is practised in the classroom, students try to reproduce an utterance that is already produced in one language in another one (Creese et al., 2016). Although translation is a practice under translanguaging, both have a similar function such as crossing boundaries. They both "stress the permeability of boundaries" (Creese et al., 2016, pp. 4–5) as social and linguistic notions.

In Line 10, the lecturer uses discourse markers such as "oraya bir bakalım" (tr: "Let's look at it") to hold the students' attention on the topic of "race" and "racialisation." As it is the very beginning of the lesson, the students need to be encouraged about the topic. In Line 16, the lecturer reiterates what is written in the book, but s/he does not prefer to read the whole excerpt of the book as this could result in students' losing their attention. Between Lines 17 and 20, the lecturer comments on a statement in the book and highlights a misconception about the definition of "race" and "racialisation." S/he ends with a question aimed at figuring out whether the students have comprehended her/his comments or not. In Line 21, a student nominates himself to summarise the concept, which is appreciated by the lecturer with a discourse marker "uh huh" (Line 23). S/he encourages the student to bring in more details on the concept of "others," which is a critical term in the discussion of "race."

Excerpt 2: Discussing Culturally and Religiously Taboo Topics, Giving Suggestions, Elaboration

The novel *Kehinde* is reviewed again for the second half of the Postcolonial Literature course on Thursday afternoon. The students volunteer to read some extracts from the novel, and the reader is asked to stop from time to time to comment on the text. There is a part where a detailed description of Albert and his second wife having a sexual relationship is described, which attracts comments from the students.

```
1 Lecturer:    istersen ↑İngilizce konuş ↑ Türkçede daha ↑şey olabilir ((laughter)) ben
2              bu durumlarda ↑ingilizceye dönüyorum ((laughter))
               [tr: you can speak in English if you like, I would switch to
               English in these kind of cases]
3 Student 6    =↑ok u:mmmm=
4 Lecturer     ya ↑sen bilirsin nasıl istersen [tr: as you like it, whichever you like.]
```

```
5  Student 6   two people come together and (.)↑united u:mm
6  Lecturer    ↑United Kingdom ((laughter))
7  Student 6   ↑sexually united I think this is not only ↑human suffer actually this is not
8              ↑woman's fault [regarding this having children or a baby in this case
9  Lecturer                   [yes
10 Lecturer    =we should BLAME ↑Albert ((laughter)) send him ↑back to ↑Nijeria
11 Student 6   yani burada bir ↑force var zaten conservatism düşünülmeden erkeğe
12             biçilmiş bir davranış var bu da Albert'in isteği ile gelişen bir şey bu
13             konuda yapacak bir şey ↑yok yani burada bir ↑patriarchal domination
14             var çünkü hani böyle bir ↑arz talep meselesi gibi bir durum var yani
               [tr: I mean, here there is a force, there is conservatism, there are
               roles shaped by (the society) without thinking. These happen
               with Albert's consent, there is nothing we can do about it, and
               it is also about patriarchal domination because it is like supply
               and demand curve.]
```

Student 6 self-nominates to comment on the extract, but the students are supposed to put their ideas into words in an appropriate manner. The lecturer interjects with a suggestion in the form of translanguaging. Here is a unique example of the lecturer asking students to use L2, not L1, in the form of L1, so s/he continues to hold the floor with the discourse marker "ummm." L2 is considered to be more appropriate and acceptable for sexual topics since sex is seen as taboo, and it would not be possible for the students to discuss it in their L1 openly. It is evidenced in the data that the lecturer especially suggests L2 be used for these kinds of culturally inappropriate cases. This allows speakers to put some distance between the participants and the topic. Cultural and religious values prevent them from discussing this topic in their native language.

In Lines 7 and 8, a student comments on the extract in L2, and it gets positive feedback with a "yes" from the lecturer. Student 6 makes a contribution in L2 just after the lecturer's utterance in L1. This representative extract shows that the students do not use translanguaging because they have a deficiency in their bilingual skills. Rather, they prove that—as is the case in this particular extract, too—they can deploy all of their linguistic repertoires and skills masterfully to discuss a complex and challenging topic such as sexuality by translanguaging purposefully and strategically.

After s/he attempts to contribute fully in L2, in the second run, Student 6 attempts to translanguage. S/he starts with "yani," which Eldridge (1996) describes in his study at a Turkish secondary school. He makes an analogy between the Liverpudlian "like" and the Turkish "yani," as neither carries any conversational value in regard to the content being delivered. Here, it has a function of elaboration and clarification as a common discourse marker. In the last four lines, Student 6 gives her/his opinion about the topic, which showcases how the students challenge the monolingual policy (Makoni & Pennycook, 2005) when they interrupt the flow of L2 hegemony and dominance in the class (Rosa, 2016).

These lines reveal how students take ownership of their language skills. All the keywords such as "force" and "patriarchal domination" are kept in L2 while the conversation around the topic is kept in L1 for elaboration. Here, a clear function of translanguaging is to discuss taboo topics and avoid cultural condemnation from the audience. The lecturer and students are aware that they can easily alienate themselves from the topic to make their comments more appropriate and acceptable in the class, which represents the general public culturally and linguistically.

Conclusion

The study concludes that translanguaging practices are ubiquitous in the academic setting. Common practices—such as (1) the consistent use of key terminology in L2, (2) the discussion of L2 resources in L1, (3) reiteration, (4) the use of addressee words in L2, and (5) the adoption of L2 for non-existent words in L1—have been identified by Inci Kavak (2021) as effective methods for delivering course content. These serve various pedagogical functions such as introducing the topic, generating motivation, checking comprehension, scaffolding, discussing culturally and religiously taboo topics, giving suggestions, and elaboration. It could be stressed that lecturers and students in literature classes use language not only as a means to unpack the meaning of a text or topic but also as an end in itself since they aim to get better at this language when they complete their university programme. (See lesson plan in the next section for an additional example involving literary analysis and writing.) Also, as a context-sensitive practice, some courses require students and lecturers to use translanguaging more frequently during delivery and interactions due to the specific nature of some courses such as translation, poetry, and linguistics.

Another important point is that classroom translanguaging should be given more attention as it gives lecturers and students an opportunity to explore and reflect on their language habits (see Appendix 1 for examples of interactional patterns that teachers can use to foster classroom translanguaging). By being translanguaging-conscious, both students and lecturers would become aware of how much, how often, and for what purposes they use language. This awareness of languaging can help the lecturer redesign the course for a planned, structured, and purposeful translanguaging practice, which can address students' needs and generate richer interactions. Knowing students' speech habits can educate the lecturer to become aware of the interactional and pedagogical dynamics of the classroom, which can accordingly feed into the course objectives and activities. In brief, this study carries implications for different stakeholders in the content classroom, by encouraging practitioners to reconsider how translanguaging practices could be integrated into current curricula as an effective and essential learning and teaching tool in content-based bilingual courses.

Lesson Plan: Poetry Circles—Nurturing a Multilingual Ecology and Multilingual Content Mastery

Recommended Level(s)

Secondary school/language major students (11th and 12th grades); tertiary level ELL and ELT students (at course level); students with B1+ level & higher (CEFRL)

Context

In this course, students collaborate in a poetry analysis and creative writing task. As this course discusses the choices people (might) make, it has the potential to generate opportunities for rich bilingual discussions.

Objectives

Students will be able to

- read, analyse, comprehend and translate the poem "The Road not Taken" by Robert Frost (2002);
- compare and contrast the two versions of poems in L1 and L2;
- develop creative writing skills and achieve bilingual content mastery.

Procedures

Step 1: Lead-in (15–20 Minutes)

Before students are introduced to the poem, a picture of a forked road and the title of the poem are shown on a slide, and the lecturer encourages students to make predictions about the picture in L1 and L2. Once a satisfactory number of answers are produced and a preparatory bilingual discussion is achieved, the poem is read aloud by the lecturer and comprehension questions are answered by the students.

Step 2: Analysis of the Poem (15–20 Minutes)

The poem is analysed structurally in terms of rhyme, meter, and poetic devices. Students' contributions are encouraged, no matter if they are in the target language or not. Inferences and interpretations are made regarding why the poet might have used certain keywords such as "diverge," "trodden," or "undergrowth."

Step 3: Poetry Circles: Write Your Own Poem (15–20 Minutes)

The students are put into groups of four to five to translate the poem into their mother tongue. The lecturer walks around, monitors, and encourages students to come up with various translations. They can translate the poem from English to their L1 with their personal touches. Thus, they are expected to write, check, edit, revise, and produce the final draft. In this way, the students and lecturer are encouraged to use their whole linguistic repertoire in L1 and L2 in any combination in order to analyse a literary text, translate it, and write their own versions.

Step 4: Microreflection Session (20–25 Minutes)

The lecturer asks each group to nominate a volunteer for class recitation and reflect on which parts they are happy with, which parts could have been improved, and what other words they might have used and why. The same questions are asked to other students, and they are encouraged to give suggestions to each other. In this way, their linguistic knowledge is expanded with each group's contribution. The lecturer here aims to increase the students' metalinguistic awareness by spotting the nuances between similar-looking content words both in L1 and in L2.

Extension Activities

1. Ask students to write a short essay on their choices and their outcomes in English.
2. Take this lesson as an introductory course and study other poems by Robert Frost.
3. Organise a competition to write creative poems in L1 and translate them into L2.

References

Baker, C. (2006). *Foundations of bilingual education and bilingualism*. Multilingual Matters.
Creese, A., Blackledge, A., & Hu, R. (2016). Noticing and commenting on social difference: A translanguaging and translation perspective. Translation and Translanguaging Project.
Eldridge, J. (1996). Code-switching in a Turkish secondary school. *ELT Journal, 50*(4), 303–311.
Ellis, S., & McCartney, E. (Eds.). (2011). *Applied linguistics and primary school teaching*. Cambridge University Press.
Esquinca, A., Araujo, B., & Piedra, M. T. (2014). Meaning making and translanguaging in a two-way dual-language program on the U.S.-Mexico border. *Bilingual Research Journal, 37*(2), 164–181. https://doi.org/10.1080/15235882.2014.934970.
Frost, R. (2002). *The road not taken: A selection of Robert Frost's poems*. Palgrave Macmillan.
Garcia, O. (2009). *Bilingual education in the 21st century: A global perspective*. Wiley-Blackwell.
Garcia, O. (2019). Translanguaging: A coda to the code? *Classroom Discourse, 10*(3–4), 369–373. https://doi.org/10.1080/19463014.2019.1638277
Garcia, O., & Kleifgen, J. (2010). *Educating emergent bilinguals: Policies, programs, and practices for English language learners*. Teachers College Press.
Garcia, O., & Leiva, C. (2013). Theorizing and enacting translanguaging for social justice. In A. Cresse & A. Blackledge (Eds.), *Heteroglossia as practice and pedagogy* (pp. 199–216). Springer.
Hawkins, M. R., & Mori, J. (2018). Considering "trans-" perspectives in language theories and practices. *Applied Linguistics, 39*(1), 1–8. https://doi.org/10.1093/applin/amx056
Inci Kavak, V. (2021). *A functional analysis of translanguaging practices in engineering and literature courses in an English medium higher education context in Turkey* (Unpublished doctoral dissertation, Çukurova University).
Jefferson, G. (1984). Transcription conventions. *Structures of Social Action*, 9–16.
Lewis, G., Jones, B., & Baker, C. (2012). Translanguaging: Developing its conceptualisation and contextualisation. *Educational Research and Evaluation, 18*(7), 655–670. https://doi.org/10.1080/13803611.2012.718490
Li, W. (2018). Translanguaging as a practical theory of language. *Applied Linguistics, 39*(1), 9–30. https://doi.org/10.1093/applin/amx039
Lin, A. M. Y. (2019). Theories of trans/languaging and trans-semiotizing: Implications for content-based education classrooms. *International Journal of Bilingual Education and Bilingualism, 22*(1), 5–16. https://doi.org/10.1080/13670050.2018.1515175
Maillat, D., & Serra, C. (2009). Immersion education and cognitive strategies: Can the obstacle be the advantage in a multilingual society? *International Journal of Multilingualism, 6*(2), 186–206. https://doi.org/10.1080/14790710902846731
Makoni, S., & Pennycook, A. (2005). Disinventing and (re) constituting languages. *Critical Inquiry in Language Studies: An International Journal, 2*(3), 137–156. https://doi.org/10.1207/s15427595cils0203_1
Otheguy, R., Garcia, O., & Reid, W. (2015). Clarifying translanguaging and deconstructing named languages: A perspective from linguistics. *Applied Linguistics Review, 6*, 281–307. https://doi.org/10.1515/applirev-2015-0014
Rosa, H. (2016). *Resonanz: Eine Soziologie der Weltbeziehung*. Suhrkamp verlag.
Simpson, J. (2014, September 8–10). *Empowering teachers by helping legitimise translanguaging practices in Rwandan classrooms, British association of international and comparative education*. 2014 Conference, University of Bath.

Appendix 1

Interactional Patterns to Foster Classroom Translanguaging

Here are some **interactional patterns** that can be used by lecturers:

- "In English we say xxx, in [your home language], we say yyy."
- "How do you say xxx in [your home language]?"
- "What [home language] words do you know for this topic?"
- "Work in pairs. One student says the word in English, the other in [their home language]. Then you switch."
- "I'm going to ask the questions in English. You can tell me the answer in [your home language]."
- "You can start in [your home language], then move to English."
- "You can use [your home language] to discuss this topic in your pairs [or groups], and then report it back to the class in English."
- "Now we have some time for questions in [your home language]."
- "Make a list of new words in your notebook. Write the English word on the left and the [home language] equivalent on the right." (Adapted from Simpson, 2014)

When teachers employ these sorts of interactional cues, students will have the opportunity to:

- translate between languages;
- compare and be playful with different languages;
- mix words and expressions from different languages in the same spoken or written utterance;
- use the home language in one part of an activity and the target language in another part.

Chapter 8

The Subtle Case of Beirut
Translingualism in the English-Medium Undergraduate Literature Classroom

Salma Yassine and Vicky Panossian

Historical Overview

Contemporary Beirut has its own dynamic educational milieu. Looking at it from a historical perspective, Beirut was considered to be the educational capital of the Ottoman Empire (Abou-Hodeib, 2017). However, due to its prominent Christian population, by the 19th century, Beirut became a harbor for a multitude of foreign missionaries (Ferguson, 2018). These missionaries established schools and universities, offering an unprecedented opportunity for the attainment of education, particularly for women (Auji, 2016). During the collapse of the Ottoman Empire and the establishment of the French Mandate, Beirut was exposed to a plethora of European languages, which were effortlessly adopted and internalized. Scholarly research has demonstrated that the people of Beirut perceived Latin-based and heavily Latin-influenced languages as a symbol of social prestige (Akar & Albrecht, 2017). Thus, it became a privilege to use French and English in one's everyday life. The Mandate brought about the utilization of French as the second official language of the country. Consequently, it became a major part of Lebanese people's life and identity. The variations of Arabic that were otherwise spoken and learnt within the educational setting were gradually replaced by foreign languages—first French and, later on, English (Baki, 2013).

Arabic is still the initial official language, as it is the language of religious sects, the law, and formal societal affairs. However, it is not necessarily the only means of communication, even for the "uneducated" masses; it is common to find Latin-based languages being spoken by blue-collar workers or those with less formal education (Shuayb, 2016). On the other hand, institutions of higher-level education have grown accustomed to choosing a particular foreign language as their official language of administration and education. Lebanon harbors a handful of universities that are Arabic based; however, universities in Beirut may be broken down into two subsets: English-medium and French-medium universities. The language of instruction also dictates the teaching method, as well as the strategy of courses that are offered.

In this chapter, we will focus on the English-medium classroom in universities located across Beirut due to its critical geopolitical position. Beirut is a melting point of differing sectarian, religious, and political ideologies. Consequently, a theoretical educational research analysis of Beirut may also be adjusted to serve its neighboring regions and nations. Beirut's diversity also resembles that of contemporary international Middle Eastern refugee camps. Therefore, this interdisciplinary translingual approach may also serve refugee educators who are striving to enhance class interactions and combat sociocultural prejudices.

The Classroom

Before venturing into the teaching strategy at hand and the theoretical framework explained throughout this chapter, it is important to comprehend the nature of English-medium undergraduate classrooms in Beirut, particularly ones that focus on literature. It is notable that existing studies of Lebanese undergraduates' perception of foreign/second languages are relatively scarce, particularly within the past decade.

There are two main variations of teaching Arabian literature in the Lebanese English-medium undergraduate setting: the first includes Arabic literature written in its original language, while the second utilizes English translations of Arabic literature. Consequently, all students are required to attain passing grades in an English- as well as an Arabic-language or literature course in order to complete their undergraduate requirements from any English-medium university across Beirut, with the exception of a few cases. Therefore, the resultant classrooms become a meeting point for students of a variety of undergraduate disciplines (Diab, 2006).

This chapter focuses on the English-medium literature classrooms and methods that enable student interaction and enhance students' understanding of the material. Since most of these students have acquired English as a second or third language, it is important to understand that teaching strategies are quite challenging (Diab, 2005). Nonetheless, as per our research experience and personal narratives, acknowledging as well as promoting a translingual approach not only enables students' interaction with the material but also improves their overall perception of literature courses.

Cultural Accommodation

As per contemporary research done on curriculum design in the Middle East, it is fundamental to take into account the cultural diversity of the students. Beirut is a highly sectarian city, with each ideological group having its own set of values and principles (Womack, 2012). Hence, teaching these students the literary works of an entirely foreign setting, such as a European or American one, would not be as engaging as teaching them an Arabian work that they can relate to. The strategy discussed in this chapter utilizes works that emphasize scenarios and cultural aspects, which students in Beirut can largely connect with through their past experiences (Mermier, 2013).

Although some researchers might argue that it is ideal for students to take on international literature in order to broaden their horizons and witness various cultural perspectives (Arnold, 2016), our experience with international literature in Beirut classrooms resulted in decreased student engagement, particularly in undergraduate-level courses, where students are offered a culturally foreign literary reality. Thus, the optimal strategy for preserving an active teaching method and maintaining maximum student engagement has resulted from using works that were originally written in Arabic and later translated into English.

Teaching Strategy

Since most of the literary works covered in the classroom setting are originally written in Arabic, it is ideal that the instructor encourages students to read in whichever language they prefer—be it Arabic or English. The teaching strategy at hand applies to both languages, since it promotes a multilingual approach to education by enabling pedagogical translingualism.

There are variations of translingualism that have been tested in various international classroom settings; however, the primary principle is the acknowledgement that students who come from culturally diverse backgrounds, who have their own dialects, languages, proverbs as well as value systems, ought to be encouraged to bring their cultures into classroom discussions (Canagarajah, 2013). Consequently, classroom discussion becomes a mosaic of different voices of minority groups of various sects, who have their own perception of the debated thematic constituents of the literary piece.

The translingual approach is a theoretical framework that is oftentimes mistaken for classroom bilingualism or the promotion of code-switching (Canagarajah, 2013). However, translingualism in the international classroom setting is not merely limited to the accommodation of a few languages in a singular utterance but rather it is the promotion of students incorporating their value systems into the discussion (Arnold, 2016). It may include the translation of cultural proverbs and sayings, religious references, utilizing varying languages as well as incorporating the grammatical and linguistic patterns of students' own language into English. Our research argues that an undergraduate literature classroom is not a means to learn a language but rather to learn how to tolerate, understand, perceive, and listen to one another's thoughts and ideas. Therefore, acknowledging the acceptance and practice of classroom diversity promotes a generational multilingual educational environment that encourages conversation and debate.

Arabic Language Variations

The Arabic language encompasses different variations, thereby rendering the use of translingualism as a vital strategy. Arabic is divided into two major subsets: Modern Standard Arabic (*fusha*) and Colloquial Arabic (*aamiya*) (Albirini & Chakrani, 2017). Modern Standard Arabic is the written form of the language, which is officially adopted in almost all forms of written manuscripts, ranging from academic books to official paperwork. It is also utilized in the news, some talk shows, and seminars. However, Colloquial Arabic is the dominant subset of the language, which is used as the main means of communication on a day-to-day basis. It is notable to mention that there exist different dialects of Colloquial Arabic, each of them unique to an Arabic-speaking country (Albirini & Chakrani, 2017). Arab countries that are neighbored at a close geographic proximity often share very similar linguistic features, such as North African countries, or Levantine ones (Zaidan & Callison-Burch, 2014); Lebanon belongs to the

Levantine parasol, Beirut mirroring the core of Arabian progressive ideologies. Each Arabic-speaking country also harbors a diverse set of accents pertaining to its colloquial variations. In particular, Lebanon's intricate identity brings forth an array of accents that are not only geographically but also socioeconomically, religiously, and sectarianly specific (Al Merabi, 2011). This phenomenon creates a diverse linguistic collision in the English-medium Lebanese classroom in general and the undergraduate one in particular. Thus, the translingual process is rendered richer when hybrid linguistic and sociocultural exchanges occur. The latter rely on Standard English, Modern Standard Arabic derived from texts at hand, and discussions that are inclusive of spoken accent variations of Colloquial Arabic stemming from different Lebanese regions and backgrounds.

Arabian Perception of Feminisms and Taboos

Within contemporary conservative Arab nations, be it in a public, social, political, or familial setting, performing progressive feminist ideologies is often unwelcomed and frowned upon. This sociocultural phenomenon is linked to the Arab world being heavily reliant on traditional cultural and religious teachings that lack a feminist nature (Makdisi et al., 2014). Such Arab features endorse a cis-heteronormative patriarchal structure, which is praised as the pivotal norm. Any deviation from this standard model would be automatically outcast by society (Abadeer, 2015). This lack of feminist representation is mirrored in the literature of the Arab region, since literary works often are a by-product of their environment. Arab women's struggles, therefore, are often disregarded in mainstream Arabic society. This does not imply that women's issues such as sexism and oppression are undocumented; yet, canonical Arabian feminist novels did not emerge until the mid-20th century (Hanna, 2016). Despite the Beirut-oriented proliferation of the feminist Arab novel in contemporary times, many of these works still receive backlash, because they are thought to be transgressing taboo lines. The concept of taboo (*muharram*), when interwoven with the notion of shame (*aayb*), is widespread in the Arab realm (Abadeer, 2015). It bespeaks of any deviances that disturb the sociocultural and religious status quos. Zooming into a woman's place in the Arab world, unveiling the concealed, be it sexual organs and activities, domestic violence, Female Genital Mutilation (FGM), falls under the parasol of taboo and shame. Such matters are rarely discussed, and they are considered challenging when referred to, because their scientific jargon is unfamiliar. For instance, due to the scarcity and tainted usage of the Arabic term, undergraduate students in Beirut have resorted to utilizing *clitoris* as a widely acceptable English alternative to the Arabic word (*bathar*). Therefore, while discussing FGM with students in Beirut, particularly those with bilingual or multilingual proficiency, it is advisable to encourage them to adopt a translingual approach to ease their expression.

Feminist Inclusivity in Undergraduate English-Medium Curricula

Despite the marginalization of feminist-inclusive literature in Lebanon, which is part of the Arab world, the English-medium undergraduate classroom is an exception. Unlike the majority of Lebanese high school students, whose perceptions are highly influenced by their socioeconomic, sectarian, religious, and familial backgrounds (Mortimer, 2001), many undergraduate students in Beirut are granted the opportunity to shape their own ideological stances. This phenomenon tends to be more common in English-medium classrooms, which are based on Western-accredited curricula (Mortimer, 2001). It paves the way for students enrolled in these classrooms to be acquainted with Arabian works of literature that are considered relatively progressive in terms of their content; these fictitious and non-fictitious manuscripts can be read in their original language, or a translated version of them can be borrowed. Syllabi of these classrooms often encompass readings that are inclusive of feminist and gender theories.

This chapter is built on the notion that even when Arabic literary works are read in their original language in an English-medium classroom that allows a multilingual discourse, selected sections are sometimes discussed in English. These sections often bespeak of topics related to sexism and feminism, as well as gender and sexuality. There lingers a variety of reasons behind the commonality of this translingual practice. On the linguistic end, students find the urge to code-switch from Arabic to English, and in rare cases, to French, simply because Arabic lacks the diversity in and preciseness of jargon that may be perceived as critical and/or taboo from an Arabian lens.

Jargon related to the field of gender and sexuality is culturally and religiously tainted, which renders its utilization uncomfortable in classroom discussions. Some Arabic terms may be problematic, for they convey sexist or homophobic meanings; therefore, replacing them with English alternatives would be a radical solution. For instance, the Arabic term for queerness is often referred to as *shuthuth*, which signifies 'perversion' or 'anomaly.' However, a modern and more literal translation of the term evolved into *mithliya*, which simply means 'homosexuality.' As an aftermath, English is rendered a safer alternative, which explicitly preserves and delivers feminist and sexual connotations as they are, devoid from hateful and "shameful" predispositions.

Conclusion

This chapter argues that translingualism may be used as a gateway for teachers who would otherwise abstain from engaging in discussions that revolve around taboo subjects. Translingualism is not merely restricted to the subtle case of Beirut, but it also combats the geopolitical and sociocultural constraints that hinder explicit feminist expression. On this book's companion website, we have provided a lesson plan that looks into an example of translingualism being implemented to promote feminist discussions in an English-medium undergraduate literature classroom (see Support Material). An additional lesson plan concludes this chapter; it illustrates one translingual strategy for engaging with Arabian literature, in which students are asked to merge literary analysis with creative nonfiction writing skills.

Lesson Plan: "The Hidden Face of Eve"—A Non-Fictitious Route to Teaching Arabian Feminist Literature

Recommended Grade Level(s)

Undergraduate

Context

This lesson is designed for multilingual Arab undergraduate students in any literature classroom. Although this lesson is designed on the basis of teaching practices in Beirut, it may be adjusted to serve either multilingual Arabs in other Levantine countries or Arabic-speaking refugee communities. This lesson is not designed to advance the students' linguistic abilities but rather to promote class discussions about otherwise silenced feminist social issues.

Objectives

Students will be able to:

- use various languages at their disposal to express their views regarding taboo subjects;
- debate their own culturally specific feminist narratives rather than adopting foreign ones;
- show tolerance of other students' means of expression as well as ideological stances;
- demonstrate their ability to transform the personal into the interpersonal through merging literature with the writing of creative nonfiction.

Procedures

Step 1: Prompt-Based Writing Exercise (15 Minutes)

The instructor begins the session with a writing application, by incorporating *The Hidden Face of Eve: Women in the Arab World* (1980), a canonical Arabian novel written by Nawal El Saadawi, a leading Arab feminist. It encompasses fictitious and non-fictitious accounts of women's oppression in the Arab world. Students are asked to extract an excerpt from the novel and to write a reflection, a personal anecdote, or a creative nonfiction piece, in which they produce a collision between the literary work at hand and a personal experience. As an alternative, this exercise could also be given as an assignment, to be discussed and/or workshopped in class within the same duration of time. Translingualism should be maintained throughout the exercise, meaning Modern Standard Arabic, Standard English, and Standard French, if chosen by the student, should be utilized in written and spoken forms.

Step 2: Evaluation (10 Minutes)

Students are asked to track and reflect on the instances of code-switching between Modern Standard Arabic and Standard English, as well as the intermarriages between different Eastern and Western ideologies in their written content. This evaluation will allow them to derive linguistic and conceptual interpretations regarding the expressions that they felt challenged their mode of expression and the underlying reasons behind using translingualism in an academic setting.

Step 3: Alternate Story/Hybrid Form Writing Exercise (15 Minutes)

The instructor gives the students another writing exercise that grants them the agency to create a parallel narrative for the protagonist in *The Hidden Face of Eve* (1980). A suggested passage to be recreated could be the one that tackles El Saadawi's memory of undergoing Female Genital Mutilation. Students are encouraged to use a translingual approach that combines Standard English and the unclassical Colloquial end of the Arabic language spectrum (see discussion of Colloquial Arabic in the "Arabic Language Variations" section earlier in this chapter).

Step 4: Evaluation (10 Minutes)

Students are asked to reflect on the Colloquial Arabic choices they made, those which urged them to express themselves in the language they use to communicate on a daily basis. This renders the process of incorporating critical terms pertaining to feminism in general and female sexual organs in particular taboo-free. After this evaluation, translingualism becomes a gateway for students to not only find comfort in using the colloquial form of their L1 but also question and thus alter particular ideologies in which they've been indoctrinated.

References

Abadeer, A. S. Z. (2015). *Norms and gender discrimination in the Arab world*. Palgrave Macmillan. https://doi.org/10.1057/9781137395283

Abou-Hodeib, T. (2017). *A taste for home: The modern middle class in Ottoman Beirut*. Stanford University Press.

Akar, B., & Albrecht, M. (2017). Influences of nationalisms on citizenship education: Revealing a "dark side" in Lebanon. *Nations and Nationalism*, 23(3), 547–570. https://doi.org/10.1111/nana.12316

Albirini, A., & Chakrani, B. (2017). Switching codes and registers: An analysis of heritage Arabic speakers' sociolinguistic competence. *International Journal of Bilingualism*, 21(3), 317–339. https://doi.org/10.1177/1367006915626587

Al Merabi, D. (2011). *The economy of standardization and dialect variability in Arabic*. ProQuest Dissertations Publishing.

Arnold, L. R. (2016). "This is a field that's open, not closed": Multilingual and international writing faculty respond to composition theory. *Composition Studies*, 44(1), 72–88.

Auji, H. (2016). *Printing Arab modernity: Visual culture and the American press in nineteenth-century Beirut*. Brill.

Baki, R. A. (2013). Bilingual design layout systems: Cases from Beirut. *Visible Language*, 47(1), 38–64.

Canagarajah, S. (2013). *Literacy as translingual practice: Between communities and classrooms*. Taylor and Francis. https://doi.org/10.4324/9780203120293

Diab, R. L. (2005). Teachers' and students' beliefs about responding to ESL writing: A case study. *TESL Canada Journal*, 23(1), 28–43. https://doi.org/10.18806/tesl.v23i1.76

Diab, R. L. (2006). University students' beliefs about learning English and French in Lebanon. *System (Linköping)*, 34(1), 80–96. https://doi.org/10.1016/j.system.2005.06.014

Ferguson, S. (2018). "A fever for an education": Pedagogical thought and social transformation in Beirut and Mount Lebanon, 1861–1914. *Arab Studies Journal*, 26(1), 59–84.

Hanna, K. (2016). *Feminism and Avant-Garde aesthetics in the Levantine novel: Feminism, nationalism, and the Arabic novel*. Palgrave Macmillan.

Makdisi, J. S., Bayoumi, N., Sidawi, R. R., Khoury, E., Centre for Arab Unity Studies (Beirut, Lebanon), & Lebanese Association of Women Researchers. (2014). *Arab feminisms: Gender and equality in the Middle East*. I.B. Tauris.

Mermier, F. (2013). The frontiers of Beirut: Some anthropological observations. *Mediterranean Politics*, 18(3), 376–393. https://doi.org/10.1080/13629395.2013.834563

Mortimer, K. J. (2001). *Common errors of English in Lebanon: A guide for teachers & students in an Arabic- & French-speaking milieu*. NDU Press.

Saadawi, N. E. (1980). *The hidden face of Eve: Women in the Arab world*. ZED Books.

Shaykh, H. (1994). *The story of Zahra* (1st Anchor Books hardcover ed.). Anchor Books.

Shuayb, M. (2016). Education for social cohesion attempts in Lebanon: Reflections on the 1994 and 2010 education reforms. *Education as Change*, 20(3), 225–242. https://doi.org/10.17159/1947-9417/2016/1531

Womack, D. F. (2012). Lubrani, libanais, Lebanese: Missionary education, language policy and identity formation in modern Lebanon. *Studies in World Christianity*, 18(1), 4–20. https://doi.org/10.3366/swc.2012.0003

Zaidan, O. F., & Callison-Burch, C. (2014). Arabic dialect identification. *Computational Linguistics—Association for Computational Linguistics*, 40(1), 171–202. https://doi.org/10.1162/coli_a_00169

Chapter 9

Integrating Global Englishes Into Literature and Writing Units
Advice for Secondary Teachers

Victoria E. Thompson

Introduction

Despite a history of standardization efforts, language is not an immutable construct. As English teachers well know, this both complicates and invigorates the instructional process, particularly in the secondary classroom, where the evolution and intermingling of English varieties occur in real-time. Discussing these nuances of language—whether it be register-shifting, dialectal variations, or sociocultural implications—provides an opportunity for a richer, critical understanding of the English language, its influence, and its relevance (Devereaux & Palmer, 2019).

In particular, investigating English through a global lens prepares knowledgeable, responsible, and global-minded students with empathy and critical self-awareness (Devereaux et al., 2021). Furthermore, the examining and embracing of English language varieties in literary texts and writing assignments enable students to observe and "play" with language: for example, by noting and discussing different voices when they read, and by reflecting on and experimenting with different variations of language, particularly their own varieties, when they write. Such instruction invites nuanced understanding of language conventions and encourages creative output from English students, from beginning English language learners to speakers whose first language is English, by empowering them to leverage and represent their personal language variations in the classroom (Rosenhan & Galloway, 2019).

This chapter features Global Englishes (GE) content taught virtually in an American tenth-grade ELA curriculum during the COVID-19 pandemic in March, April, and May of 2020. Teaching the unit in this unprecedented learning environment was not part of the plan, of course, but the notable increase in participation along with student comprehension and insight from the GE lesson content (Devereaux et al., 2021, pp. 238–242) made it well worth the venture. Since integrating any unfamiliar content can be daunting, this chapter provides teacher recommendations, ELA standard skillset alignments, educator resources, and an example lesson plan. Most importantly, it also illustrates several rewarding *ah-ha!* moments that my collaborators, Chris C. Palmer and Michelle D. Devereaux, and I experienced while exploring GE topics with secondary students.

DOI: 10.4324/9781003124665-11

Introducing GE to Students

The success of the GE unit, despite remote learning, is due, in part, to an introduction of GE-adjacent language topics earlier in the school year. Students engaged with several sociolinguistic concepts during a previous *Othello* unit, including the power of naming and the importance of examining historical and modern perspectives on language variation. Beyond this, warm-ups and lesson extension activities consistently prompted students to consider American language variations and standardized-language ideologies, as well as showcase their unique language expertise (Crystal, 2003). For example, students were encouraged to use the language of their home and community, including social media vernacular, in their class assignments. Establishing their own language expertise was especially beneficial for struggling students (in participation and comprehension of general ELA content) because it increased confidence and engagement with some of the complex material they encountered in GE lessons (Curzan, 2019). These early lessons and activities around language variation built an inclusive community of reciprocal learning.

Although I had introduced sociolinguistic concepts to students before the GE-centered content, I now recognize that even earlier integrations could provide an easier transition and stronger foundation for World Englishes (WE), English as a Lingua Franca (ELF), and Global English Language Teaching (GELT) topics. Therefore, structurally speaking, I encourage educators to think flexibly about where GE content can fit into curriculum objectives for overall unit design and daily lesson planning. Since March 2020 was my first attempt at integrating GE content into my curriculum, I made it a dedicated final unit of the school year, but the relevant content of GE is easy to embed within any curriculum structure. For instance, teachers who want to introduce GE content, but do not want to dedicate an entire unit to the material, can condense GE lesson material down to a mini-unit that leads to a larger unit on postcolonial literature or, perhaps, coursework that features multilingual authors.

Selecting Relevant GE Texts

Throughout students' virtual GE curriculum, they engaged with informational, argumentative, and literary multimodal texts[1] from diverse global regions to support different learning styles and to increase comprehension and engagement (Jones & Hafner, 2012). Each of the texts (regardless of format or genre) provided varying global perspectives on GE, WE, GELT, and ELF advantages (e.g., social connection, international business, scientific collaboration, technology, and artistic progress) as well as detrimental ramifications of GE and ELF (e.g., social justice/equity issues, colonization, miscommunication, and the effects on cultural heritage for multilingual English speakers). These texts offered gateways to critical conversations about Global Englishes and human society.

---

1 *Multimodal* in this chapter refers to the various types of mediums in which information can be communicated, including paper and digitally printed, video, audio, and stationary or moving-image texts.

Many of the texts were selected specifically due to their GE-specific content and relevance to ELA CCSS (Common Core Standard Skills[2]). Students interacted with multimodal texts featuring American, Australian, British, Chinese, Irish, Korean, and Malaysian speakers, as well as writers who introduced them to dialectal distinctions among World Englishes. My students particularly enjoyed the phonology and dialectal morphology/lexicon instruction provided primarily via videos, featuring diverse English speakers showcasing their own regional Englishes in a humorous, inclusive manner (see Support Material). While studying GE concepts such as the evolution and spread of the English language and other ELF concepts, students read, annotated, and reported on what they learned from informational and opinionated articles that met ELA CCSS requirements. Several of these multimodal texts (see Support Material) allowed students to explore various dialects of English and to reflect on both language authorities (those who determine "standard" vocabulary and grammar conventions) and social justice issues (such as assumptions/prejudices/stereotypes about race, economic status, and intelligence). In addition to learning and applying relevant vocabulary from sociolinguistics (e.g., *dialects* and *accent*), students discussed important elements of lexical variation within different dialects of English (e.g., American English versus Irish English versus Malaysian English) and excitedly referenced their observations about these dialect distinctions in discussion and in their work (e.g., producing TikTok videos describing experiences and connections with dialect variations such as Australian English *chips* versus American English *fries*).

As the unit progressed, additional texts were selected on the basis of student discussions and journal responses regarding current events and personal connections. For example, a small-group discussion in which my students connected Amy Tan's essay "Mother Tongue" (1990) to current linguistic prejudices against Asian Americans, such as some speakers naming COVID-19 "the China Virus" or "the Chinese Virus," inspired me to dedicate more time towards topics and literature portraying both the power of naming and Asian American experiences to leverage the interest and empathy students had on these issues. In particular, the slam poem "What Kind of Asian are You?" by Alex Dang (2014) and the poem "money for your english" by Khairani Barokka (2018) resonated with students and were referenced thoughtfully and frequently in their informal writing. These texts, alongside other Asian American perspectives in the lesson material, engaged critical and empathetic thinking in students' work and led to students even citing relevant current events in their informal writing.[3]

While learning about WE, students also reflected on other GE topics such as GELT and English as a lingua franca. The chosen multimodal texts featured topics on English education, its usage, its history, and its future implications, including argumentative and informative videos such as the 2009 Ted Talk, "Jay Walker: The world's English mania," and a satirical comedic clip by Trevor Noah on the ramifications of British colonization in South Africa and India (Noah, 2016). Additionally, students observed and responded to individual perspectives on English education;

---

2 *Common Core* refers to an American education system set of standards that specifies academic content area skills students need to master each year: www.corestandards.org/ELA-Literacy/RL/9-10/
3 For an in-depth analysis of student responses to these lesson materials, see Devereaux et al., 2021.

they discussed internal, cultural, and familial conflict in personal narratives, such as an interview with Nigerian author and activist Chimamanda Ngozi Adichie (2020). Responses to these topics often demonstrated both cognitive dissonance and critical thinking as they contended with English-language-learning experiences that conflicted with English-centric narratives popular in American culture and with education that promotes ideologies such as "The American Dream." Students grappled with narratives and informational texts that described the opportunities afforded by English language learning and usage alongside global perspectives on the cultural and social oppression associated with English as a lingua franca:

> Some of the advantages that Adiche had was the he was able to learn English from a young age and have many more opportunities as he grew up, which many people do not have. But he also had against that it was not having the opportunity to learn his own language to perfections since although they taught him more important it was to learn English. This story also has a connection to world English. Because Adichie learned English from a very young age and that made it possible for her to express herself with her story in English to the world and reach more people who probably would not have arrived with her other language so learning English gave her more opportunities now as a writer.
>
> (Liliana, ELL[4] Latina Student[5])

Poetry was included throughout the curriculum as it seemed to incite impassioned responses from students as well as maintain their analytical skills with complex literary texts previously taught in the *Othello* unit. For example, after viewing Alex Dang's performance of "What Kind of Asian Are You?" alongside a close-reading of Khairani Barokka's "money for your english," students were able to identify theme, draw parallels between poems and personal experience, and arrive at conclusions related to GE topics such as culture erasure:

> In the video the young man spoke feely and strongly about being asian and what difficulties A lot of asians face . . . I think his key points were explaining how Asians are not tapping into their true oots anymore because they are afraid of what others might think of them. The poem talks about how throughout life we are taught the history of others while losing the history of our own. Erasing our culture to prepare for a culture that was given to us instead of embracing the one that is a part of us.
>
> (Kiara, Black student)

For teachers who want additional literary material in this curriculum, consider including passages from novels by the authors Chimamanda Ngozi Adichie and Amy Tan (e.g., *Americanah* and *Saving Fish from Drowning*) since students are already engaging with these authors' nonfiction narratives about their English language

---

4 English Language Learner.
5 All students referenced throughout this chapter have been provided with pseudonyms alongside ethnic and education-level descriptors.

experiences. Inclusion of these texts would be seamless and logical, encouraging students to identify figurative language while applying literary criticism with a GE-focused lens. Additionally, it would be interesting to observe how embedding poetry and short stories from regions featured in the WE-specific texts could affect student engagement with and comprehension of literary analysis practices.

Designing Effective GE and ELA Assessments

On the basis of the curriculum's placement at the end of the year, my students needed to demonstrate growth in specific ELA skills: informational reading comprehension and argumentative writing skills (see lesson plan at the end of this chapter). To help prepare students for success, I informed them at the beginning of the unit that the final major assessment was an argumentative essay about one of the GE topics (students were given choices for differentiation and engagement purposes). Each lesson required that students produce several things in writing or in preparation for writing—most of the time informal in nature—that would strengthen the comprehension skills and confidence necessary for success on the unit's major assessment, including multimodal journal reflections and warm-up responses (e.g., writing, GIFs, TikTok videos), guided reading/viewing questions, graphic organizers, and multimodal discussion responses (e.g., written discussion threads and Flipgrid[6] videos).

Regardless of structural flow and assessment preferences, I recommend that teachers provide informal writing tasks throughout the curriculum to build student confidence with some of the more complex GE material. Such writing proves especially beneficial when teaching classes where differentiation is necessary for student success (e.g., English Language Learners and students in need of specialized instruction due to a learning disability). For example, during a small-group tutorial, I was able to reference a student's informal notes as support for an argumentative paragraph. The student, who typically struggled with formal writing and classroom participation, leapt into the conversation to help create the paragraph with unprecedented confidence—producing higher quality writing as a result.

Teaching the Content

The GE-unit daily lessons encouraged student metacognition, where students looked outside themselves at the world and then flipped the lens back to examine themselves. For example, many lessons began with multimodal texts depicting an unfamiliar dialect or a unique perspective on the English language and then ended with a reflection that tied perspectives from the lesson material to their own experiences. By the end of the unit, these reflections proved to be a helpful note-taking resource for their more formal writing.

Since this unit was first taught during the beginning of the COVID pandemic, the structure looked different than traditional schooling. However, many of these adaptations still proved useful during the 2020–2021 school year when many

---

6 An educator platform that enables students to post creative video presentations in a secure environment.

classrooms, including mine, were set up with simultaneous face-to-face instruction and virtual instruction. For example, I began, and continue to begin, each lesson with an agenda that includes a list of the lesson tasks and assessments (formative or summative), as well as a recorded Zoom video, where I give an overview of the agenda with helpful reminders and tips for success, including where students can find additional resources. The agendas and recorded videos are posted in the same place the night before each lesson, and they save me a great deal of time and energy. Also, I have noticed that this modification has been beneficial for students who have formerly had low participation in my class due to busy or stressful home lives and work schedules, as well as for students who are reluctant to ask questions.

Prior to the pandemic, each lesson began with a warm-up, and I maintained this structure throughout remote learning. Students watched a short video on GE topics related to each lesson and responded to a short prompt (see Support Material). Although these warm-ups were rarely graded, they were conspicuously connected to future graded assignments. It helped that the videos I selected were those I knew most of my students would find funny or interesting, with relatable speakers and topics (e.g., animated WE phonology videos and a comedy skit by Trevor Noah).

My pedagogical preference is to stray away from direct instruction because I have found that the best way for students to sharpen their reading comprehension and writing skills is to practice active reading and writing. That being said, I did have to provide some direct instruction reviewing general ELA skills such as reading and vocabulary comprehension strategies, creating a thesis statement, and building a body paragraph. To reinforce these concepts and help struggling students, I posted recordings where I modeled annotation and textual evidence gathering strategies for some of the more difficult GE articles (Gallagher, 2009). I also met with small groups during work sessions as well as outside of official class time to answer general questions about assignments, facilitate discussions about GE topics, gauge student interest, and model tasks in real time (e.g., writing a thesis statement, finding relevant quotes, embedding a citation, constructing a paragraph). This dedicated time provided additional instructional support for students struggling with GE material and/or needing mastery of the necessary ELA skills; it also gave me vital insight into how students were responding to and connecting with GE concepts.

Outside of brief instances of direct instruction, students learned the GE material through the guided instruction woven into lesson assignments. For example, students completed graphic organizers (e.g., charts where students outlined the pros and cons of English as a lingua franca). Although I taught and modeled how to best use an organizer, students had to read and annotate each article and categorize their annotations (e.g., either for or against English as a lingua franca). This process helped students critically consider and organize ideas, and it prepared them to identify their strongest argument with textual evidence.

To help develop student argumentative skills even further, I had students write opinions on topics informally in their journal alongside completing their guided graphic organizers and discussion responses. Once students had completed their rough drafts, I provided a checklist for them to reference as they revised and polished their writing. Had we not been in remote learning, students would have participated in a peer-review session with these checklists. Since this wasn't a feasible option at the time, I recorded myself referencing student examples as well as modeling revision of my own writing.

Conclusion: Global Englishes Resources and Relevance

Considering the depth and breadth of our digital worlds, relevant and engaging GE resources are easily accessible. As teachers work through their own integration of GE, including resources that connect to current events and real-world examples of language variation on a global scale is especially vital for content engagement and relevance. Such resources also help students connect, interact, and empathize with English speakers across the globe with a respectful, inquiring mindset.

Because of their accessibility and relevance to students' lives, GE materials provide teachers with new and exciting avenues to both engage and challenge students while meeting the literature and writing objectives of their existing lessons and units. As the following lesson plan illustrates, integrating Global Englishes content into English Language Arts at the secondary level allows for a creative pragmatism that will not overpack a standard curriculum.

Lesson Plan: Writing About Global Englishes—Selecting an Argumentative Topic

Recommend Grade Level(s)

Secondary ELA (9th through 12th grade)

Context

This lesson is designed to help students identify an argumentative topic about Global Englishes (GE). Prior to the lesson, students have been annotating, note-taking, analyzing, discussing, and writing about GE texts informally in preparation for their final formal argumentative writing assignment. To select an argumentative topic and position about GE, students will need to review all informal writing assignments to gauge where their interest and passion lie and where they have the most support for an argument. This lesson provides time for some general argumentative writing instruction to prepare students for more in-depth writing requirements.

Objectives[7]

Students will be able to:

- demonstrate comprehension of GE texts, topics, and vocabulary in a peer-response, informal written reflection, and a GE survey;
- identify and justify evidence in support of an argumentative stance on their selected GE topic.

Procedures

Step 1: Peer Response to Informative Article Insights (Warm-Up & Review) (15 Minutes)

Students will respond to two peer discussion threads about the article "25 maps that explain the English language" (Nelson, 2015) from the previous lesson. Responses can be written (respond directly on the discussion post prompt) or provided verbally via a Flipgrid video post. Each response must reference a specific connection, additional insight, or an open-ended question.

Step 2: Structured Practice and Application (Formative Assessment) (15 Minutes)

Students will write a reflective response that forms and explains an opinion about a Global Englishes topic that they find topical and thought-provoking. Students should review previous notes for this task.

Step 3: Instruction (15 Minutes)

Students will take guided notes on argumentative writing tips and tricks (see Support Material).

---

7 See CCSS-specific objectives in Support Material.

Step 4: Structured Practice and Application (Formative Assessment) (10 Minutes)

After students have chosen their GE topic for the argumentative paper, they will use their notes to identify and justify examples of evidence for their paper.

Step 5: Closing (5 Minutes)

Students will complete a GE mid-curriculum survey (see Support Material) to demonstrate comprehension and insights of GE unit vocabulary and concepts relevant to their argumentative informal and formal writing assessments.

References

Adichie, C. (2020). In the shadow of Biafra: Chimamanda Ngozi Adichie—language and memory. *YouTube*. www.youtube.com/watch?v=HWBsfN_LNxI

Barokka, K. (2018). *money for your english*. The Transpacific Literary Project. ASEAN at 50: Poem from Across Southeast Asia. Asian American Writers' Workshop. http://aaww.org/asean-at-50-poems-from-across-southeast-asia/

Crystal, D. (2003). *English as a global language* (2nd ed.). Cambridge University Press. https://doi.org/10.1017/CBO9780511486999

Curzan, A. (2019). Foreword. In M. D. Devereaux & C. C. Palmer (Eds.), *Teaching language variation in the classroom* (pp. xi–xiii). Routledge.

Dang, A. (2014). Alex Dang—What Kind of Asian Are You? *YouTube, Button Poetry*. www.youtube.com/watch?v=VoP0ox_Jw_w

Devereaux, M. D., & Palmer, C. C. (Eds.). (2019). *Introduction to teaching language variation in the classroom* (pp. xv–xxiv). Routledge.

Devereaux, M. D., Palmer, C. C., & Thompson, V. E. (2021). Pandialectal learning: Teaching global Englishes in a tenth-grade class. *American Speech*. https://doi.org/10.1215/00031283-9089613

Gallagher, K. (2009). *Readicide: How schools are killing reading and what you can do about it*. Stenhouse.

Jones, R. H., & Hafner, C. A. (2012). *Understanding digital literacies: A practical introduction*. Taylor and Francis. https://doi.org/10.4324/9780203095317

Nelson, L. (2015). 25 maps that explain the English language. *Vox*. www.vox.com/2015/3/3/8053521/25-maps-that-explain-english

Noah, T. D. K. (2016). Trevor Noah on the British colonization—India & South Africa. *YouTube* [Video]. www.youtube.com/watch?v=xyl1kVz1ynI

Rosenhan, C., & Galloway, N. (2019). Creativity, self-reflection and subversion: Poetry writing for global Englishes awareness rising. *System*, *84*, 1–13. https://doi.org/10.1016/j.system.2019.04.005

Tan, A. (1990). Mother Tongue. *The Threepenny Review*, *43*, 7–8. Retrieved May 10, 2021, from www.jstor.org/stable/4383908

Walker, J. (2009, February). Jay Walker: *The world's English mania*. TED. www.ted.com/talks/jay_walker_the_world_s_english_mania

Chapter 10

Language Diversity, Cross-Cultural Awareness, and Digital Media in the Writing Classroom

Florence Elizabeth Bacabac

Introduction

The Conference on College Composition and Communication (2017) states that writing teachers must respond to globalization by exploring pedagogies that promote "a wide range of sociocultural and linguistic experiences and practices" (para. 1). This statement, while addressed to collegiate writing, is also applicable to secondary language arts courses that help students acquire academic writing skills. Many students bring multiple literacies to our classes, and we need to accommodate those literacies to maximize learning. I propose using digital media and technology to promote Global English variation and cross-cultural awareness in the writing classroom.

The ubiquity of multimodal resources cultivates language variety, plural voices, and nonlinearity (Archer & Breuer, 2015; Wysocki et al., 2019); writing teachers should maximize students' digital exposure to enhance awareness of and sensitivity towards international audiences on a global scale. By accessing online sources, student writers may acquire language competency through examining linguistic features as well as rhetorical intent and strategies. Students may also evaluate digital texts to study variations of rhetorical forms based on Connor's (2001) redefinition of Kaplan's (2001, 1966) contrastive rhetoric. Another approach may be to adopt principles on discourse negotiation by Matsuda and Matsuda (2010) that involve writers judging the appropriateness of usage, intentionality of variation, and distinction of stylistic conventions. The possibilities for technology-based writing pedagogies are endless—in fact, I noticed my classroom activities that advocate effective communication with international readers were more productive with the application of digital media. This chapter presents such possibilities from the standpoint of language diversity and intercultural awareness.

Educational Setting

I teach writing courses (i.e., first-year writing, business writing, and professional/technical writing) in an open-enrollment, regional southwestern university in the United States with a diverse student population, including international students and returning adult learners who were Latter-Day Saints (LDS) missionaries in other countries. From this context, incorporating material on Global English variation in writing programs contributes to the institution's internationalization and

DOI: 10.4324/9781003124665-12

globalization efforts and benefits student writers across the curriculum. The lesson plan at the end of this chapter may be applied not only to college-level writing but also to secondary language arts courses interested in advancing Global English through the teaching of writing.

Design

Following Matsuda and Matsuda (2010), I discuss how teachers can "fully embrace the complexity of English and facilitate the development of global literacy" (p. 373) through digital media in order to help students write adequately and cross-culturally. Students are given more options to understand rhetorical contrasts in cross-cultural texts by examining the linguistic and cultural differences of target discourse communities. This design focuses on applications of digital research and contrastive analysis to highlight distinct rhetorical practices and exposure to language variation.

Teaching Strategies

Any teaching strategy should be adjusted according to the requirements of course context and student needs. The strategies discussed here may be applied towards effective communication for an international audience with research practices that involve global perspectives. Taking a more inclusive model of Global Englishes with diverse forms (Rose & Galloway, 2019), I cover the need for understanding (1) linguistic variations and (2) cultural variations through the use of digital media in the classroom.

As teachers, we must give students the opportunity to recognize language variations, honor cultural differences, and increase digital literacy in a networked world (NCTE, 2019, 2005a). Such an approach requires critical engagement across a variety of texts where students explore not only structural varieties but also contrastive cultures using online platforms. Our writing classrooms are important sites of learning where we embrace and impart techniques for negotiating intercultural communication. When assigning reflective exercises, students tend to draw from their own backgrounds or individual rhetorics (Scoggins, 2001) but move on to wider applications. The notion that different contexts have different conventions, customs, and language use becomes more compelling with new access to global information over the internet (e.g., websites, social media, videos, other machine-readable formats). Writing teachers should take advantage of electronic sources to introduce students to diverse linguistic and cultural codes. Thus, I posit that digital research helps facilitate comparisons of textual features (e.g., topic, purpose, language use, cultural norms, codes) across diverse contexts.

The scope of topical content that our students can access online is remarkable. For instructors who are interested in language diversity, cross-cultural awareness, and digital media, I designed teaching strategies based on a conceptual framework (see Figure 10.1) with descriptions of each strategy in parallel stages.

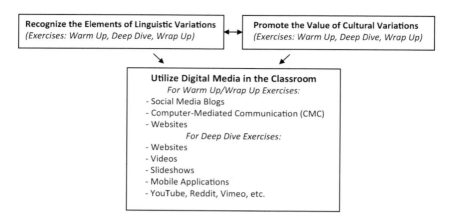

Figure 10.1 Conceptual framework of teaching strategies with digital media

Recognize the Elements of Linguistic Variations

The purpose of this strategy is to enhance linguistic variations by recognizing the different types of writing and language use, identifying surface-level structures and plotting their comparisons, and reflecting how these variations emphasize language diversity as a whole.

Warm Up

To preface an understanding of language variety across distinct genres, a possible opening task is to have students describe the kinds of writing they usually do in school (e.g., English, lab, history) and those they will do (or might have done) at work (e.g., reports, memos, business letters). This description may also focus on the aspects of discursive language entailed in each genre (e.g., organization, sentence structure, word choice, grammar/spelling, applicable rules on mechanics/figures/citations). I usually ask students to start thinking about their own writing of autobiographies, juxtaposing academic and workplace writing with lists or descriptions, while analyzing these genres' similarities and differences to create awareness of the concept of variation. Social media blogs or computer-mediated communication (CMC) forums would work well for posting these thoughts. Other comparisons of writing practices may also work here, such as revisiting their private writing (e.g., journaling) versus transactional writing (e.g., emails) and so on. This initial activity introduces insights for students as they attempt to articulate the distinction between each type of writing, realize how diverse the forms and language use are for each genre, and discern how rhetorical contexts influence linguistic nuances and eligibility. A short summary would be useful afterward, especially with examples illustrating stylistic characteristics to understand what is meant by "varieties of language" (Glenn & Goldthwaite, 2014, p. 222). The accessibility of this topic is ideal in most writing classes as students become more attentive to the role of language diversity across the disciplines.

Deep Dive

After examining writing variations either in school versus work or privately versus transactionally, students should recognize the dominant and non-dominant codes and conventions of discourse communities (Matsuda & Matsuda, 2010) and apply contrastive analysis to varieties of American, British, Canadian, Australian, and/or New Zealand Englishes as well as non-native varieties of English (Connor, 1996). Students may refer to digital media such as websites, videos, slideshows, and so on to research important linguistic features in the process (see Support Material). First, a good exercise might be to assign selected texts and introduce the linguistic variables in the areas of vocabulary, usage, sentence forms, dictional levels, paragraph types, logical organizations, and shared systems/rules. These surface-level structures may cover words and sentences, including prepositions, regularization of suffixes, extension of progressive aspect usage (Jenkins, 2015); jargons, idioms, terminologies (Kolin, 2015); or acronyms, figures (i.e., dates, times, measures), keywords for contrasting rhetorics (Woolever, 2001). Using flipped videos (virtual demos), reference notes, or mini-lessons would help students understand these concepts, along with practice worksheets, mentor sentences, or writing/editing tasks. For example, to review word choice (i.e., abstract versus concrete, colloquial/slang/idioms, formal versus informal), students may be given samples that illustrate the role of rhetorical purpose; to review grammar, mechanics, and punctuation, they may be provided with a checklist on the patterns of dominant versus non-dominant forms of writing; to review sentence structures (i.e., simple, compound, complex, compound-complex), mini-lessons may be incorporated to help them identify subjects and verbs; to review logical organizations, genre analysis may be used to understand the relevance of rhetorical purpose, context, and audience.

Next, to enhance linguistic contrasts, students may then plot significant patterns of elements in a T-chart, a tool for contrastive analysis that contains columns with "one for each language variety being contrasted" (Devereaux & Wheeler, 2012, p. 94). For example, a teacher can demonstrate through a T-chart how some words may vary and ask students to draw from online research to fill in the blanks. To illustrate, Table 10.1 and Table 10.2 may be used to show contrasts in vocabulary

Table 10.1 T-chart exercise on vocabulary

American English	British English
pants	____
____	biscuit
mail	____

Table 10.2 Completed T-chart on vocabulary

American English	British English
pants	trousers
cookie	biscuit
mail	post

between American English and British English (see Support Material for more examples).

Students may also be given sample texts and pre-assigned elements for analysis using T-charts to appreciate language variants in the context of writing. Exposing students to texts that signal the varieties of English with the help of digital research and having them visually dissect comparisons through T-charts allow them to recognize dominant/non-dominant forms as rule-governed systems. In addition, the types of texts we choose for our students to analyze increase their ability "to see the English language in all its variant splendor" (Marshall, 2018, p. 55).

Wrap Up

To close this lesson, students may be directed to reflect on what they've learned about Global Englishes. One possibility is to have them respond to thinking points about language issues or the role of language in their lives (NCTE, 2005b). Another might be to assign an article/chapter about English varieties from selected sources (e.g., Kachru et al., 2009; and/or Davies, 2005) and ask students to reflect on relevant points. Another option might be to ask them the significance of these varieties and what can be deduced from their linguistic comparisons (e.g., acceptable usage across contexts, common types of form and function). Still, other reflective tasks may be implemented to revisit surface-level structures and instill awareness of language diversity. Social media blogs or CMC forums would work well for these reflective posts.

Promote the Value of Cultural Variations

With language variety comes cultural diversity. Moving beyond textual coding means investigating significant representations of culture, identifying deep-level structures and plotting their comparisons, and reflecting how intercultural variations contribute toward effective communication.

Warm Up

To increase awareness of language and cultural diversity, students can draw from personal experiences that connect language patterns to cultural influences. For instance, asking students to identify words or phrases in their own vocabulary that others have either "questioned, laughed at, commented on, or not understood" (Glenn & Goldthwaite, 2014) might serve as an icebreaker for the ways different groups have unique varieties of Englishes. However, this activity may be skipped altogether if a teacher has no experience handling difficult discussions since it can also trigger painful experiences from some students. Instead, students might brainstorm how they learned certain terms or phrases from peer groups, and their possible regional or cultural influences, sharing those thoughts in social media blogs or CMC forums. This exploratory activity will enhance the concept of diversity in our daily speech and writing, and knowing various cultures will help us recognize appropriate usage for specific contexts.

At times, I struggle with how much instruction on standard English should be spent in the classroom versus how much latitude should be given to students using their own language(s) and dialect(s) in class activities and assignments. Such conflict can be resolved with warm-up activities like these that disclose the cultural/regional influences of distinct rhetorical and linguistic patterns, causing students to build on their repertoires, access effective frames of reference, and elicit effective communication. To this end, we can both meet our obligation to study standard English and honor the language varieties in our classrooms.

Deep Dive

Understanding cultural differences is necessary to communicate appropriately in multiple contexts. More than language translation, this next strategy involves close investigations of cultural practices using digital media such as websites, videos, slideshows, etc. (see Support Material). For example, teachers might assign students to research inherent customary practices (e.g., business, religious/spiritual, governance) of two different countries (e.g., United States and Japan) to grasp essential ideas for cross-cultural communication. Another technique might be to go over the guidelines for communicating with international readers, focus on one aspect of the protocol (e.g., cultural sensitivity on the use of visuals/graphics), provide (in)appropriate scenarios (e.g., image of a string tied around an index finger), and have students discuss their propriety in two countries based on research. These contrasts bolster our students' ability to identify culture-driven behaviors that affect communicative practices as each scenario approves or flouts conventions. In the process, they develop intercultural flexibility and competence.

Next, students may then plot these cultural patterns in a T-chart to highlight their contextual differences. To illustrate, Table 10.3 contrasts some business practices in the United States and Japan.

Teachers might need to conduct focused discussions on important rhetorical conventions in "high-context" versus "low-context" cultures (Kraft, 2019; Woolever, 2001). Students should be taught that "high-context" cultures, such as Japan, rely on implicit nuances and the way the message is delivered, while "low-context" cultures, such as the United States, depend on explicit written and oral

Table 10.3 T-Chart on business customary practices

	United States	Japan
Greeting	handshake, kiss on the cheek, hug	bow, nod
Communication	direct, not afraid to speak one's mind	indirect, subtle when expressing opinion
Decision-making	fast, based on available information	slower and done in stages

messages. Knowing these cultural filters would help writing students use appropriate communication styles accordingly. The researched examples on Japanese culture cited earlier connote "high-context" messaging in which participants need special attention to traditions and subtleties for goodwill (e.g., the Japanese bow with several types representing different emotions; indirect, non-verbal communication as legitimate styles; and a slower, discrete approach to decision-making for minimal errors). Identifying culture-driven behaviors through digital research will maximize our students' ability to engage in other cultures, even if these new concepts may seem awkward. Of course, this activity may also focus on other cultural features that affect rhetoric, including religious/spiritual practices, governance/political orientations, and so on (see Support Material for more examples).

Wrap Up

The completion of this lesson may be two-pronged: a reading annotation exercise and a digital mini-research assignment on the history of diverse cultural practices/rituals. Social media blogs, CMC forums, and websites would work well for these tasks. The first task might ask students to read a foreign country's tourism article, noting any questions they want to know about that part of the world. The second task might require students to conduct brief digital research about the history of that country, its cultural practices, and its government orientation. These exercises will drive students to explore the world with curiosity, develop global competence (Moton, 2019), and gain new perspectives for cross-cultural communication (Kachru, 1982).

Conclusion

It is important to note that the strategies listed here are not exhaustive and may include other uses of digital media. The main purpose in teaching writing and/or language arts is not solely to utilize digital media *per se*, but to stress language diversity, cross-cultural awareness, and prevention of stereotypes through digital research and contrastive analysis. As we capitalize on new technologies to conduct our classes, we need to drive our students toward crossing national/international borders in search of "contextual and other text-external factors . . . [to recognize] pluricentric or multi-norms in world Englishes" (Bhatia, 2019, pp. 30–31). This goal improves intercultural competence and constructive interaction, with a deeper understanding of language and rhetoric. We also transform our pedagogies by teaching students to negotiate rhetorical contrasts in cross-cultural communication as a potent tool of language and culture (Wheeler & Swords, 2004). On the whole, the time is rife with possibilities to incorporate linguistic and cultural literacies in a variety of courses, from secondary language arts to first-year or advanced writing, as well as to present a global depiction of the English language among student writers.

Lesson Plan: Exploring Language Diversity and Cross-Cultural Variations

Recommended Grade Level(s)

From upper-level secondary students to intermediate college students

Context

This lesson explores language diversity and cross-cultural variations through online research and contrastive analysis. It works best with a unit on how to communicate effectively with international readers; it can also be adapted to align with other content on language diversity.

Before this lesson, students are introduced to linguistic and cultural variations discussed in this chapter. The teacher should allot at least one week each for the linguistic and cultural variation lessons in order to go through their respective warm-up, deep-dive, and wrap-up exercises.

Objectives

Students will be able to:

- recognize the elements of language variety and cross-cultural variations;
- use online research and contrastive analysis to evaluate a digital text.

Procedures

Step 1: Preliminary Activity (10 Minutes)

Review important notes on contrastive analysis from previous sessions to highlight the linguistic and cultural variations of Global Englishes. The instructor might want to revisit the main ideas of the "Deep Dive" exercises as presented in this chapter.

Step 2: Digital Text Analysis (30 Minutes)

Ask students to compare two online reports from two different countries on a global topic (e.g., the COVID-19 pandemic). More specifically, have them explore the linguistic and cultural variations of both international news articles in English using online research and T-charts for contrastive analysis. The digital texts or online reports may be pre-selected for this particular activity. (See Support Material for a list of global news sources.)

Step 3: Small Group Discussion (10 Minutes)

Have students share their linguistic and cultural T-charts with peers in small groups. How and why do these digital sources have different representations in global mass media? What are their diverse contexts, cultures, and rhetorical situations? (See Support Material for Extension Activities.)

References

Archer, A., & Breuer, E. (2015). Methodological and pedagogical approaches to multimodality in writing. In A. Archer & E. Breuer (Eds.), *Multimodality in writing: The state of the art in theory, methodology and pedagogy* (pp. 1–16). Brill.

Bhatia, V. K. (2019). World English in professional communication. *World Englishes, 38*(1–2), 20–40. https://doi.org/10.1111/weng.12362

Conference on College Composition and Communication. (2017, November). *Statement on globalization in writing studies pedagogy and research*. https://cccc.ncte.org/cccc/resources/positions/globalization

Connor, U. (1996). *Contrastive rhetoric: Cross-cultural aspects of second-language writing*. Cambridge University Press.

Connor, U. (2001). Contrastive rhetoric redefined. In C. G. Panetta (Ed.), *Contrastive rhetoric revisited and redefined* (pp. 75–78). Lawrence Erlbaum.

Davies, D. (2005). *Varieties of modern English: An introduction*. Pearson Education Ltd.

Devereaux, M. D., & Wheeler, R. (2012). Code-switching and language ideologies: Exploring identity, power, and society in dialectically diverse literature. *English Journal, 102*(2), 93–100.

Glenn, C., & Goldthwaite, M. A. (2014). *The St. Martin's guide to teaching writing* (7th ed.). St. Martin's.

Jenkins, J. (2015). *Global Englishes: A resource book for students* (3rd ed.). Routledge.

Kachru, B. B. (1982). Meaning in deviation: Toward understanding non-native English texts. In B. B. Kachru (Ed.), *The other tongue: English across cultures* (pp. 325–50). University of Illinois Press.

Kachru, B. B., Kachru, Y., & Nelson, C. L. (Eds.). (2009). *The handbook of world Englishes*. Wiley-Blackwell.

Kaplan, R. B. (1966). Cultural thought patterns in intercultural education. *Language Learning, 16*, 1–20.

Kaplan, R. B. (2001). Foreword: What in the world is contrastive rhetoric? In C. G. Panetta (Ed.), *Contrastive rhetoric revisited and redefined* (pp. vii–xx). Lawrence Erlbaum.

Kolin, P. C. (2015). *Successful writing at work* (Concise 4th ed.). Cengage Learning.

Kraft, D. B. (2019). Contrastive analysis and contrastive rhetoric in the legal writing classroom. *New Mexico Law Review, 49*(1), 35–58.

Marshall, T. R. (2018). To correct or not correct: Confronting decisions about African American students' use of language varieties in the English classroom. *English Journal, 107*(5), 51–56.

Matsuda, A., & Matsuda, P. K. (2010). World Englishes and the teaching of writing. *TESOL Quarterly, 4*(2), 369–374. https://doi.org/10.5054/tq.2010.222222

Moton, K. (2019, August 16). *Establishing a framework with global competencies*. National Council of Teachers of English. https://ncte.org/blog/2019/08/establishing-a-framework-with-global-competencies/

National Council of Teachers of English [NCTE]. (2005a, November). *Statement on multimodal literacies*. https://ncte.org/statement/multimodalliteracies/

National Council of Teachers of English [NCTE]. (2005b, July). *Supporting linguistically and culturally diverse learners in English education*. https://ncte.org/statement/diverselearnersinee/

National Council of Teachers of English [NCTE]. (2019, November). *Definition of literacy in a digital age*. https://ncte.org/statement/nctes-definition-literacy-digital-age/

Rose, H., & Galloway, N. (2019). *Global Englishes for language teaching*. Cambridge University Press.

Scoggins, D. (2001). Contrastive rhetoric theory in an electronic medium: Teaching ESL writers to become *bricoleurs* in a computer-assisted classroom. In C. G. Panetta (Ed.), *Contrastive rhetoric revisited and redefined* (pp. 65–74). Lawrence Erlbaum.

Wheeler, R. S., & Swords, R. (2004). Codeswitching: Tools of language and culture transform the dialectically diverse classroom. *Language Arts*, *81*(6), 470–480.

Woolever, K. R. (2001). Doing global business in the information age: Rhetorical contrasts in the business and technical professions. In C. G. Panetta (Ed.), *Contrastive rhetoric revisited and redefined* (pp. 47–64). Lawrence Erlbaum.

Wysocki, R., Udelson, J., Ray, C. E., Newman, J. S. B., Matravers, L. S., Kumari, A., Gordon, L. M. P., Scott, K. L., Day, M., Baumann, M., Alvarez, S. P., & DeVoss, D. N. (2019). On multimodality: A manifesto. In S. Khadka & J. C. Lee (Eds.), *Bridging the multimodal gap: From theory to practice* (pp. 17–29). Utah State University Press.

Chapter 11

Trans-/Multilingual Language in Different Contexts

Using Scaffolding to Assist Multilingual Learners

Verbra Pfeiffer

Introduction

In many higher education institutions in South Africa, the majority of students who choose English as the preferred medium of instruction are additional language speakers (Haberland et al., 2013; Van der Walt, 2013; Carstens, 2016). Teaching in today's multilingual/multicultural classrooms should focus on communicating with all students and negotiating challenging academic content by building on their different language practices, rather than simply promoting and teaching one or more standard languages (Garcia & Sylvan, 2011). One of the major challenges for designers of academic literacy programmes is to accommodate culturally and linguistically diverse students. Against a multilingual backdrop, this study examines how pre-service teachers at a university in South Africa use translanguaging, including their home languages, to search for an understanding of "good writing" through an in-class task.

Focusing on the challenges that multilingual students face while writing for academic purposes, this chapter aims to aid our future teachers' mindfulness of (what may be defined as) good writing, examining ways multilingualism can be an advantage in the classroom. To clarify, academic writing is defined in this chapter as writing that is clear, concise, focused; it has a formal, but not complex, tone and style. Additionally, this chapter hopes to show pre-service teachers how students can use their home language to support their academic writing, making instructors conscious that what multilingual students bring from their homes and communities are funds of knowledge that are valuable for themselves and others (Gonzalez et al., 2005; Canagarajah, 2011). The goal is to make pre-service teachers cognizant of the importance of writing efficiently and encourage them to progress towards finding methods to help improve learners' writing skills.

Literature Framework

Nationally and internationally, higher education institutions have become increasingly multilingual. Often, international students develop academic literacy in a language different from the main language of learning and teaching of their host institution. Ergo, English, often viewed as a high-status academic language, is introduced at the postgraduate level, resulting in this situation for many domestic students.

DOI: 10.4324/9781003124665-13

When considering language as a resource, Duff (2010) finds that

> Academic discourse is therefore a site of internal and interpersonal struggle for many people, especially for newcomers or novices. . . . Affective issues and tensions . . . may be especially acute in intercultural contexts—in which local and global (or remote) language codes, cultures, and ideologies of literacy may differ.
> (p. 170)

For university students studying in a medium that is not their home language, the academic language can be quite daunting. It may cause them tension because not only do they have to learn and understand academic language, but they are also introduced to different codes and cultures.

Multilingual students thus use a variety of language practices to make meaning (Van der Walt & Dornbrack, 2011). However, there is very little research on the effect of using more than one language of learning and teaching (LoLT) on the output produced by students. Students tend to exploit the linguistic and cultural resources available to them to define their relationship to the world they live in as they shuttle between languages and modalities in their learning (Canagarajah, 2011; Makalela, 2015; Velasco & García, 2014; Motlhaka & Makalela, 2016, p. 253). In Kramsch's (2000) study, students increase their control over written discourse when they become aware of the interpretive contexts for their texts and develop a metalanguage from which to analyse these contexts (Motlhaka & Makalela, 2016, p. 253). In the study presented later, I touch on the way that students shuttle between languages when they are allowed to use their home languages while discussing a task in class, which leads to students' freedom and confidence to understand and grasp a text better.

Various researchers have come up with their understanding of the term *translanguaging*. For example, Palfreyman and Van der Walt (2017) found translanguaging to be linked to strategies and practices in teaching that use the languages that are available to students to help them make sense of academic content (p. 9). Canagarajah (2011) defines translanguaging as "the ability of multilingual speakers to shuttle between languages, treating the diverse languages that form their repertoires as an integrated system" (p. 401). Translanguaging in writing can support creativity in bilingual and multiliteracy pedagogy. Hélot (2014) argues that using translanguaging in literary texts legitimizes language mixing and that, furthermore, translingual texts offer an excellent basis for both discussing what it means to be bi- or multilingual and exploring the notion of identity. Because translingual authors break the traditional ideological barriers that separate languages, new bi/multilingual voices and identities emerge. Canagarajah (2013) perceives translingual writing as a means to resolve challenges of writing pedagogy, arguing that it is a "pragmatic resolution that is sensitive and important for challenging inequalities of languages" (p. 113). Individuals who translanguage are learning the dominant languages for social and educational means at the same time. Velasco and García (2014) argue that students use translanguaging in writing to achieve higher standards of thought, creativity, and language use compared to the writing of a monolingual. In this study, the students made use of translanguaging when they were discussing the task in their groups.

Experiment—Using Semantic Mapping and Scaffolding

Academic writing exhibits multiple features such as clarity, conciseness, focus, and formality. Translanguaging may be our best vehicle for improving learning of these features, since students use their translanguaging in writing to achieve higher standards of thought, creativity, and language use (Velasco & García, 2014).

To demonstrate how translanguaging can benefit students' learning of academic writing, I conducted a study of pre-service teachers' use of the technique of semantic mapping. Semantic maps are graphic displays of word meanings that offer students a visual representation of how words and concepts are related through a network of organized knowledge (Heimlich & Pittelman, 1986). In classrooms, semantic mapping exercises assist multilingual students by providing visual representations of how words and concepts are related in academic writing. Because academic language involves a range of words with highly specific and technical meanings, the strategies of both translanguaging and semantic mapping can thus be especially useful tools for students learning how to navigate lexical choices when reading and writing academic texts.

In my experiment, pre-service teachers from all subjects were instructed to discuss an article (see Support Material) and record themselves in their various groups during the discussion. The students had to comment on words they knew and words they did not know (e.g., *nap*, *uniform*, and *ubiquitous*). Finally, they had to discuss how they could use the article in relation to their subject via the technique of semantic mapping. There were ten groups, as seen in Table 11.1; in the second column we see the home languages of each student in the group, and in the third column we see the language used for the discussion.

Table 11.1 Home languages of the students in the groups and the language of discussion in their groups

Group	Home language	Language of discussion
1.	Afrikaans, Afrikaans, Afrikaans	English
2.	English, English, Afrikaans	English
3.	Afrikaans, English, English, Afrikaans, IsiXhosa	English
4.	Afrikaans, Afrikaans, Afrikaans, Afrikaans	English
5.	Afrikaans, Afrikaans, Afrikaans, Afrikaans	Afrikaans
6.	English, Afrikaans, Afrikaans, English	English
7.	Afrikaans, Afrikaans, Afrikaans, Afrikaans	Afrikaans and English
8.	English, Afrikaans	English
9.	Afrikaans, Afrikaans, Afrikaans	Afrikaans and English
10.	Afrikaans, Afrikaans, Afrikaans, Afrikaans	English

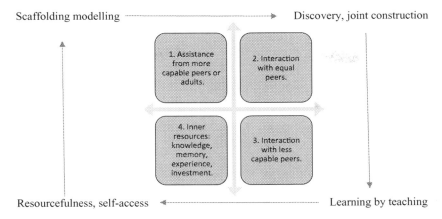

Figure 11.1 Schematic representation of van Lier's scaffolding model

For the exercise used in class, I used van Lier's scaffolding model (2004). Van Lier moves away from the top-down approach and highlights how shifts in agency may occur during the process of scaffolding (Carstens, 2016, p. 4). This model is represented by the four-quadrant structure in Figure 11.1.

The top-left quadrant (1) represents the canonical understanding of scaffolding—namely, support by more experienced peers or teachers using scaffolds such as textual models. The top-right quadrant (2) represents support by equals, which is typically collaborative. The bottom-right quadrant (3) focuses on a less prototypical understanding of scaffolding, namely that more experienced peers may achieve learning gains by explaining difficult concepts to less advanced peers. And the bottom-left quadrant (4) represents the individual's internalisation of scaffolding, which entails the development of cognitive and meta-cognitive structures that facilitate learner autonomy (Van Lier, 2004 cited by Carstens, 2016, p. 5). In my lesson plan (see Support Material), this scaffolding model is discussed further. At the start of the lesson, students identified words they knew and found words they did not know. While doing this, they also defined words that they knew and created meanings of words they did not know. The students were divided into groups which could consist of more experienced peers in the English language. While discussing the article in their groups, the less experienced students were writing down new words with the help of their experienced peers. During the process of writing down new words, the students were learning new words with meanings they were not familiar with. In this instance, this activity may be viewed as collaborative work taking place. In the lesson found at the end of this chapter, readers will notice that more experienced peers in the English language may have achieved learning gains through writing down and explaining difficult concepts to less advanced peers in the English language.

Discussion

The students understood that their knowledge and meaning of the words (e.g., *nap* and *uniform*) were not the same as what was used in the text. In other words, their understanding of the word *nap* meant 'short sleep' and *uniform* was 'a specific dress code.' But in the text (see Support Material) *nap* meant 'the fuzzy covering of the tennis ball' and *uniform* meant 'the outer surface of the ball which can be white or yellow in color.' Students, therefore, had to consult a dictionary since the contextual meanings of these words were different from the students' initial understanding of their meaning. The students found it extremely interesting that these "common words" had different meanings from what they know, for example, words like *nap* and *uniform*. After the class discussion, the students had to write down the new meanings of the words from the dictionary, which had emerged through group work.

As mentioned earlier, academic writing can become quite daunting for multilingual students. As seen in my lesson at the end of this chapter, students had to create their own meanings of the words and then learn the new meanings. Because English words can have more than one meaning, this may be challenging for non-native speakers. Students then used the new words they learned by creating questions which they had written down related to the article since now they understood the words differently. I then asked them about their challenges in academic writing, some of which were identified as follows:

1. Time pressure, meaning they did not have enough time to complete a task in class or during an exam.
2. Doing academic/factual writing.
3. Writing short sentences in English, since many languages like Afrikaans or German privilege the writing of long sentences (e.g., as a sign of intelligence).
4. Difficult sentence structures in English.
5. Writing in the passive voice accurately.

Teachers should keep these challenges in mind when assigning tasks to students: for example, by allowing students enough time to complete a task. Another important aspect that teachers should consider doing in class is more writing exercises in the passive voice as this appears to be a huge problem for L2 students.

In light of the challenges brought forward earlier on, students were able to pull from their own personal experiences to complete the activity, as seen in the lesson plan found at the end of this chapter. Especially if English is not their home language, students would often see a word that they think they know, just to find out that their understanding or knowledge of the word is very different from the way the word is used in a different or academic context. While writing down the meanings of the words, the student could better understand and remember the words. In addition, constructing a sentence using the new words they learned from the text also assisted in them seeing the words in a different academic context.

Even though the students were allowed to speak in their home language (e.g., Afrikaans) during the discussion of the article, they preferred speaking in English. A reason for this could be that very often once a student starts studying at a higher education institution, the language of teaching and learning will be in English, which is the case in many South African universities. However, there were groups that preferred discussing the article in their home language (which was not English) because then they felt they would have a better understanding of the article and the new words that they learned.

Translanguaging When Learning Academic Language

This exercise was to assist teachers with the teaching of new academic/content subject words. Second language (L2) students who were struggling at the word level did not link it to their own experiences. When students have time to discuss an academic article in their home language, they have a better understanding of the words in the text as well as the overall meaning of the text. In relation to discussing the article, they also get to write down the meanings of the new words, which may also assist in the meaning of the word from an academic perspective.

L2 students should keep in mind that in academic language the writer is selecting and ordering words related to the text. Cognitively, they are searching for their understanding of the word in their home language and then relating it to the text. It is important that students know the ordinary meaning but also know the specialist meaning as they will need it in the future. For example, Student 13 in Group 4 and Student 16 in Group 5 understood how to navigate the fact that *nap* had multiple meanings in English only after they spoke about this observation in Afrikaans. Often, students only know the minimum of words required to write exams or tests, and they forget that the new academic words that they learn will be to their advantage for future use.

What students should be aware of is that there is no "switch" from one language to another—rather, multiple languages have an integrated quality. Translanguaging strategies can help "to mediate cognitive, social and affective processes in literacy and learning" (Palmer et al., 2014, p. 759). The problem is that students have become so used to speaking in the language of the medium of instruction that they fail to speak in their home language. Students must realise that when they are using their home language to understand a task given to them, they will have a better understanding and grasp of the work. They then can express themselves better because they understood the text better with the help of their peers and teachers.

Final Thoughts and Implications

If bi/multilingual students have time to develop their ideas, we get better results in their writing. Allowing translanguaging in class gets them to develop confidence in themselves and in writing. As teachers, we need to create groups in which students speak different languages, encouraging students to speak in a language that is understood by all. This strategy could help students get over their fear of speaking in English. The influence of language proficiency on people's ability to express themselves becomes vitally important in educational contexts (Van der Walt, 2013, p. 635). I will have to agree with Carstens (2016) when she states that

> It is useful to think of scaffolds (the tools used in the scaffolding process) as a set of semiotically flexible sociocultural strategies with lasting cognitive gains, while the process of scaffolding involves introducing, using and removing the scaffolds at appropriate stages to allow students to become legitimate and autonomous members of their discourse communities.
> (p. 9)

Teachers need to consider using more scaffolding tools when teaching non-native speakers' new words.

Lesson Plan: Semantic Feature Analysis—Comparing and Contrasting Features of Words

Recommended Level(s)

The level of this lesson is B2 as identified by Common European Framework of References for Languages (CEFR, 2001, p. 24). The grade level for which this lesson is intended is for tertiary and secondary levels.

Context

This lesson may be used to increase students' academic vocabulary for any subject. This practice may be used whenever a teacher wants to introduce a new topic to learners and scaffold students towards understanding and remembering new vocabulary by writing sentences using the new vocabulary learned in the lesson.

Objectives

Students will be able to:

- recognize and explain words they are familiar with;
- interpret words that are new to them;
- support the use of new words in written sentences.

Procedures

Step 1: Before Reading (5–7 Minutes)

- Hand the passage from "Uniform Variety"[1] to the students.
- Divide students into groups of three or four.
- Students who speak the same mother tongue may sit together in a group.
- The teacher will ask the students: *How would you define the word "vocabulary"?*
- Then the teacher will ask the students: *What is the difference between knowing words and understanding words in an academic text?*
- Next, the teacher will ask the students how they decode new or foreign words.
- The teacher will first read through "Uniform Variety" aloud; then in their groups the students will read through the passage a second time.

Step 2: During Reading: Identifying Words Known and Unknown (20 Minutes)

- Students will first identify words that they know in the passage and give the meanings of those words.
- Then, the students will identify words that they do not know.

---

1 See Support Material for excerpts and a full citation of the text of this reading as well as additional context and guidance for this lesson.

- After, the students will come up with possible meanings of the unknown words in their groups without looking up the meaning of the words in a dictionary or on their phones.
- Students might be confused with the use of the words *uniform* and *nap* in the passage as they might be familiar with only one meaning of the word.
- At this stage, students will learn to compare and contrast. They will learn that words they are familiar with can be used differently in various contexts.
- Once the students have identified both words they are familiar with and new words they are not familiar with, their groups will discuss the article and their understanding of what the article is about.
- They are free to discuss the article in their home language if it is not English.
- The students will be handed a table like the following, which they will complete:

Keywords	Features	Comment and Definition

Step 3: After Reading: Creating Sentences (20 Minutes)

- Next, students will write five interrogative sentences in English using the new words that they learned in the lesson. These interrogative sentences need to be in the form of questions.
- While the target is English, students can draw from multiple languages in their actual writing of the sentences.
- After writing their questions, they will exchange their questions with another group who then has to answer the questions, writing down their answers.
- It should be noted that translanguaging is encouraged during the oral components of this lesson to facilitate writing in English.

Step 4: Reflection (5 Minutes)

Students will tell the teacher the new words they have learned and the meaning of those words.

References

Canagarajah, S. (2011). Codemeshing in academic writing: Identifying teachable strategies of translanguaging. *The Modern Language Journal*, 95(3), 401–417. https://doi.org/10.1111/j.1540-4781.2011.01207.x

Canagarajah, S. (2013). *Translingual practices: Global Englishes and cosmopolitan relations*. Routledge.

Carstens, A. (2016). Designing linguistically flexible scaffolding for subject specific academic literacy interventions. *Per Linguam*, 32(3), 1–12. https://doi.org/10.5785/32-3-690

Common European Framework of References of Languages: Learning, teaching, assessment. (2001). *Companion volume*. Council of Europe.

Duff, P. (2010). Language socialization into academic discourse communities. *Annual Review of Applied Linguistics*, 30, 169–192. https://doi:10.1017/S0267190510000048

Garcia, O., & Sylvan, C. (2011). Pedagogies and practices in multilingual classrooms: Singularities in pluralities. *The Modern Language Journal*, 95(3), 385–400. https://doi.org/10.1111/j.1540-4781.2011.01208.x

Gonzalez, N., Moll, L., & Amanti, C. (2005). *Funds of knowledge*. Lawrence Erlbaum.

Haberland, H., Lønsmann, D., & Preisler, B. (2013). *Language alternation, language choice and language encounter in international tertiary education*. Springer Science & Business Media.

Heimlich, J. E., & Pittelman, S. D. (1986). *Semantic mapping: Classroom application*. International Reading Association.

Hélot, C. (2014). Rethinking bilingual pedagogy in Alsace: Translingual writers and translanguaging. In A. Blackledge & A. Creese (Eds.), *Heteroglossia as practice and pedagogy* (pp. 217–238). Springer.

Kramsch, C. (2000). Second language acquisition, applied linguistics, and the teaching of foreign language. *Modern Language Journal*, 84(3), 311–326.

Makalela, L. (2015). Moving out of linguistic boxes: The effects of translanguaging strategies for multilingual classrooms. *Language and Education*, 29(3), 200–217. https://doi.org/10.1080/09500782.2014.994524

Motlhaka, H. A., & Makalela, L. (2016). Translanguaging in an academic writing class: Implications for a dialogic pedagogy. *Southern African Linguistics and Applied Language Studies*, 34(3), 251–260. https://doi.org/10.2989/16073614.2016.1250356

Palfreyman, D. M., & van der Walt, C. (2017). Introduction: Biliteracies in higher education. In D. M. Palfreyman & C. van der Walt (Eds.), *Academic biliteracies: Multilingual repertoires in higher education* (pp. 1–18). Multilingual Matters.

Palmer, D. K., Martinez, R. A., Mateus, S. G., & Henderson, K. (2014). Refaming the debate on language separation: Toward a vision for translanguaging pedagogies in the dual language classroom. *The Modern Language Journal*, 98(3), 757–772. https://doi.org/10.1111/modl.12121

Van der Walt, C. (2013). *Multilingual higher education: Beyond English medium orientations*. Multilingual Matters.

Van der Walt, C., & Dornbrack, J. (2011). Academic biliteracy in South African higher education: Strategies and practices of successful students. *Language, Cultural and Curriculum*, 24(1), 89–104. https://doi.org/10.1080/07908318.2011.554985

Van Lier, L. (2004). *The ecology and semiotics of language learning*. Kluwer Academic.

Velasco, P., & García, O. (2014). Translanguaging and the writing of bilingual learners, bilingual research journal. *The Journal of the National Association for Bilingual Education*, 37(1), 6–23. https://doi.org/10.1080/15235882.2014.893270

Part 3
Perceptions and Ideologies

Chapter 12

Speak Locally, Listen Globally
Training Listeners to Understand the Diverse Accents of Englishes Around the World

Vance Schaefer and Isabelle Darcy

Introduction

It is a myth that a "standard" accent exists. Everyone has an accent. We recognize accents, and they are part of our identity. Some accents are related to stereotypes. Ultimately, the way we perceive accents is shaped by our linguistic and life experience. In an interconnected world, we have greater exposure to a wide range of accents associated with not only regional dialects but also sociolects (i.e., the phonological patterns of specific groups that share social characteristics such as socioeconomic status, gender, sexuality, age, and/or ethnicity), including many marginalized accents. However, all of us understand some accents more easily than others. Why this is the case is not well understood. What is known is that familiarity with diverse accents can improve understanding and reduce linguistic prejudice and intolerance. Monolingual and multilingual speakers of English need greater training in perceiving and comprehending unfamiliar accents to better function in international contexts. Explicit instruction and guided exposure are advocated to improve perception of the accents of World Englishes, focusing on *both* first and second language listeners.

This chapter covers the following. Section 1 describes the central concepts characterizing the pronunciation of accents. Section 2 overviews the mechanisms behind accent perception, and why understanding unfamiliar varieties is not always easy. Section 3 briefly reviews perception training. Finally, Section 4 offers lesson plans to incorporate global listening into the classroom.

Central Concepts for Describing Pronunciation

An accent (i.e., pronunciation of a language variety) can vary by many elements:

1. Segments (i.e., speech sounds, which are consonants and vowels);
2. Suprasegmentals (which include stress and intonation);
3. Phonotactics (which guides how sounds are organized into words, what makes possible syllables, and delineates the possible sequences of segments and suprasegmentals);
4. Phonological processes (which refer to phenomena such as flapping /t/ to sound something like a /d/ (i.e., the flap [ɾ]) as in *water* in American English).

DOI: 10.4324/9781003124665-15

Every variety of English differs in one or several of these elements, illustrating the difficulty of pinpointing exactly how accents differ from each other. Beyond speech sounds (see Support Material for a thorough discussion), suprasegmentals are heavily involved in how listeners detect a different accent—through the "music" of the language, which refers to the rhythm, intonation or prosody, and stress patterns.

Stress in English is described by four physical characteristics. A stressed syllable is longer, higher in pitch, louder, and the vowel (quality) remains unchanged. An unstressed syllable is shorter, lower in pitch, quieter, and the vowel may become centralized (or "reduced") to a comfortable resting position in the center of the mouth as a schwa (/ə/ 'a' in *about*) or /ɪ/ in *bit* or /ɛ/ in *bet* in many global dialects of English. Minimal stress pairs such as *a RE.cord* versus *to re.CORD* (capitalization indicates stressed syllable) highlight that stress matters in English. Varieties differ according to which syllable is stressed. American English speakers typically say *RE.search* with initial stress whereas UK English speakers often use final stress: *re.SEARCH*.

Stress varies by word type. Functional or grammatical words (e.g., determiners, pronouns, prepositions, conjunctions, helping verbs, the *be*-verb) are less stressed than content words (i.e., words containing greater lexical meaning and less strictly grammatical meaning). Sentence structure determines an added layer of stress, on top of word-stress patterns. When words combine into phrases (i.e., thought groups or syntactic units), the last content word is the most stressed in some varieties. However, stress (or sentence accent) is also used to introduce new or contrasting information: **HE** ate the cake (not someone else).

While lexical stress is a property of words in English, it is not the case in other languages. French does not use lexical stress to distinguish words. Consequently, speakers using French as their first language (referred to as their L1) who learn English as a second language (referred to as their L2) do not store stress as part of their phonological representation of L2 English words and often do not realize stress in the same manner that other speakers of English do. Different realizations of stress may influence intelligibility and comprehensibility in recognizing words and meaningful prosody. Similarly, some Englishes may not use stress in the same way. In some varieties of English, each syllable has approximately the same length, i.e., syllable-timed Englishes. Stress is also exploited in wordplay and rhythm in humor, advertisement, poetry, rap, emotional appeal, and mnemonic devices. Thus, improving perception of stress differences can not only enhance comprehension but also promote cultural appreciation.

Every variety of English uses specific intonation: pitch rising in yes-no questions, falling in statements and wh-questions (e.g., who, what), remaining up when listing items (e.g., "apples↗, oranges↗, and bananas↘"), and so on. Some varieties feature uptalk (i.e., statements having rising intonation), which might be viewed negatively (e.g., lack of confidence) or positively (e.g., pragmatic usages: wishing to continue the conversation, politely softening statements). Pitch range can differ by variety and/or situation. Importantly, pitch level, patterns, and magnitude may convey various attitudes differing by variety: uncertainty, boredom, reserve, enthusiasm.

Phonotactics dictates allowable sequences in syllables but may vary by English variety. A CCCVCCC syllable structure (C = consonant, V = vowel) as in *strengths* is possible in some varieties, but ease of articulation or differing phonotactics can reduce such sequences. In Japanese, initial C clusters (consonant clusters) are prohibited, and in Spanish, initial [sC] clusters are disallowed. Consequently, Japanese and Spanish learners of English often insert a vowel to break them up: *school* [sku:l] as [sɯ.kɯ:.rɯ] and [ɛs.ku:l], respectively.

Processes cover many phenomena. In addition to /t/, some varieties may flap /d/ to [ɾ] (i.e., sounding like a softer and shorter [d] in both *writer* and *rider*). Sounds may assimilate as in *gimme* (*give me* [v] to [m]). An intrusive r, as in the phrase *China(r) and Japan*, may occur in non-rhotic varieties (i.e., many Englishes in Britain, parts of the United States where /r/ is not pronounced before consonants: *part* [pa:t]). In these varieties, [r] may be inserted between words ending in a vowel (e.g., *China*) and words beginning with a vowel (e.g., *and*). However, some varieties, including L2 varieties, may not apply these processes.

Mechanisms Behind Accent Perception

Accents are complex but not random. They are expressions of someone's background and identity: "(A)ccent is a fluid, contextualized expression of our personal and social identity as well as our communicative stance" (Moyer, 2013, p. 10). Accents are shaped by many factors. Speakers' accents differ depending on when they started learning English [first (L1) vs second language (L2) speaker], or whether they are monolingual or multilingual (i.e., presence of other languages). The L1 of a bilingual speaker affects the specific features of their L2 accent—so clearly in fact that one speaks of a "French accent" or "Swedish accent." The amount and type of interaction, i.e., L1 and L2 usage, also impacts accent as reflected in the three circles of World Englishes (inner, outer, expanding) (Kachru, 1985). A speaker's sociolinguistic background likewise shapes accent: age, gender, sexuality, regional upbringing, ethnic affiliation, socioeconomic status, education, and cultural norms regarding politeness. Speakers have a linguistic repertoire of more than one accent and, cued by the (in)formality of the situation, may shift between accents systemically or in the pronunciation of specific words. A person's accent may change over their lifetime, e.g., Queen Elizabeth's vowels (Harrington et al., 2000). In short, a speaker's accent is not static but in constant flux throughout one's life, daily interactions, and within one conversation.

We now turn to why unfamiliar accents are difficult to understand. Unfamiliar varieties can impede word recognition and understanding. However, **with more exposure, understanding improves**. For example, speakers of General American (GA) who had just moved within the United States to NYC for college did not activate *-er* words in perception such as *baker* as much when they heard it pronounced in a NYC accent without the final /r/ (i.e., bak[ə] not GA bak[ɚ]) (Sumner & Samuel, 2009). This shows that bak[ə] in its NYC form did not act like a word to them (unlike for people born and raised in NYC): GA speakers had difficulty recognizing words spoken with a NYC accent. L2 varieties also pose difficulties for word recognition. If familiarity with variant accents improves comprehension, it suggests that to some extent, variation can be acquired through training.

Understanding how we perceive speech explains why it is hard to decode unfamiliar accents. Our speech perception system is tailored to the L1, influencing perception of segments, suprasegmentals, phonotactics, and phonological processes. When we hear speech containing unfamiliar sounds or structures, we interpret them according to our L1 system. Thus, L2 English listeners may map sounds onto their nearest L1 category: English /θ/ (one of the interdental "th" sounds in words such as *thanks*) may be consistently perceived as [t], [s], or [f]—correspondences that also exist among inner-circle varieties. Beyond segments, speakers may transfer L1 or D1 (native dialect) stress patterns to L2 English or its varieties. Speakers are constrained by L1 phonotactics, e.g., "school" [sku:l] as [sɯ.kɯ:.rɯ] (again L1 Japanese/L2 English). Speakers may not implement L1 English processes or implement different ones, e.g., assimilating L2 English sounds differently from L1 English speakers. Universal tendencies also influence perception. Some sounds occurring more often in the world's languages are more easily perceived and/or pronounced, whereas less common sounds are more difficult to perceive and/or pronounce (e.g., /θ/, the "th" sound in *think*).

These L1-specific and universal factors that shape L2/expanding-circle perception also impact accent formation in outer- and inner-circle English varieties. Thus, accents undergo similar phonological processes, generating great variation within all three circles. L2 speakers appear not to store L2 words with the same robust phonological representations as L1 speakers, impeding recognition of L2 words (Pallier et al., 2001) for the same reason listeners may not recognize words spoken in non-native L1 accents (Sumner & Samuel, 2009). Furthermore, social biases potentially skew perception, motivating speakers to evaluate some varieties as more correct, pleasant, and intelligible (Preston, 1996), with some varieties [e.g., Received Pronunciation (RP), the accent traditionally regarded as the British standard] being more robustly encoded in L1 listeners' mental representation (Clopper, 2017), facilitating understanding. Additionally, a speaker's perceived ethnicity (as seen in photos) may trigger listeners to detect a phantom foreign accent or experience cognitive mismatch, reducing comprehension (Rubin, 1992). To counteract such biases, it is important to cultivate global listening skills by exposing students to different varieties, accompanied by explicit instruction.

Mechanisms and Challenges for Accent Training

Perceptual Training

Which aspects of training for the global listening classroom are important? We argue that raising awareness through explicit instruction on differences/similarities and providing exposure to variability are key. Our lesson plan at the end of this chapter incorporates both. Raising awareness can improve perception, increase familiarity, and ultimately mitigate social biases. Because it draws attention onto the form of speech—and not only onto meaning—explicit instruction leads to more phonological learning. Global pronunciation instruction increases comprehensibility over segment-only training (Derwing et al., 1998). Similarly, training with stimuli that use multiple speakers and varying phonetic environments ("High-variability") enhances L2 perception (Bradlow et al., 1999), and for L1 English, augments perceptual learning of unfamiliar varieties (Clopper & Pisoni, 2004). Contextual exposure is important, as hearing entire words helps L2 English listeners differentiate between difficult-to-hear sounds while hearing words within phrases boosts understanding over words spoken in isolation (consider puns: *Be kind to your dentist because she has fillings too*). Exposure to diverse accents is critical for developing listening comprehension (Scales et al., 2006; Walker, 2010), particularly as local accents are promoted for speaking. However, exposure to phonological features that minimally impede listening comprehension (i.e., low functional load) may be deemphasized: e.g., /θ/ pronounced as [t] or [s] appears to have minimal impact on intelligibility/comprehensibility (Jenkins, 2000). Drawing from these research findings, using multiple speakers and "learning to decode" auditory materials step by step are the cornerstones of our lesson plan.

We summarize our suggestions:

1. Explicit instruction (features, rules, systematicity) and guided exposure for L2 learners and L1 speakers.
2. Variability in voices (e.g., number, gender, ethnicity, age) and contexts [feature; segment; word (including minimal pairs); phrase; rhetoric; monologue; dialogue; (in)formality; practiced versus spontaneous speech; reading; genre (business, academic, and so on)].
3. Comprehensive ("global") exposure across (a) regional/social varieties, including inner-, outer-, expanding-circle, marginalized varieties, and registers; (b) four pronunciation areas (segments, suprasegmentals, phonotactics, processes); and (c) accentedness versus intelligibility versus comprehensibility versus impression (e.g., pleasantness).
4. Strategic training to mitigate social biases toward non-native or marginalized accents.
5. Specific learner needs and background (considering L1, dialects spoken, English-language experience).

We conceptualize a template of activities structured around (1) enhancing metalinguistic awareness; (2) listening to a variety of speakers/contexts; (3) analyzing varieties (referencing RP, GA, or the learner's variety) by phonological areas; (4) evaluating samples for characteristics (see Table 12.1) and discussing biases affecting perception; and (5) creating activities to meet individual/group needs. Activities include intensive/extensive listening, interaction, optional production, and comprehension strategies {e.g., applying knowledge about stress, context, common patterns—e.g., substituting [s] or [t] for /θ/—to "decipher" words and "fill in the blanks" where a listener cannot catch what is being said}.

Table 12.1 Characterizing accents, based on Munro and Derwing (1995)

Term	Definition
Accentedness	Degree of difference from one's own or reference accents such as GA or RP
Intelligibility	Ability to understand the meaning of an utterance
Comprehensibility	Ease/difficulty of understanding an accent
Pleasantness	Subjective judgment by listeners of an accent

Challenges of Implementing Training

Implementing training can be challenging. First, understanding accents in terms of linguistics, specifically phonology, is not an easy matter. As such, instructors should adhere to simple, clear explanations guided by student learning outcomes and objectives for each lesson. For example, instructors should break stress down into tangible characteristics of vowel length, quality, loudness, and pitch; phrase-level stress patterns should be clearly connected to function/content words. Listeners should apply what is learned step by step with clear visuals. To illustrate, instructors can project a transcript onto a whiteboard and ask guiding questions, marking the transcript for each phonological element one by one (see lesson plan discussed later, Step 1): What are the function words? Content words? Where do we pause to create phrases? Where do we link words?

Starting simple and recycling activities in progression, while applying what is learned, are crucial. Learners listen to and analyze "easier" accents: their own, speakers of their dialect, familiar accents. Afterward, they move onto unfamiliar accents (see lesson plan, Step 2), building on what was practiced with easier accents. Listeners analyze samples alone, in pairs, or small groups, and then, as a full class. Listeners identify the accent and describe features that cue that accent. They then search for phonological differences that impede understanding and systematic patterns/correlations to better understand the accent. Additionally, listeners expand exposure: a variety of voices, situations, content, length. They listen to the same passage spoken in different accents and advance to samples from other sources. Listeners do dictations to test their listening (i.e., intelligibility) and move onto longer passages to increase ease of understanding (i.e., comprehensibility).

Social aspects of accents cannot be ignored (cf., communicative competence, biases, etc.), but they also represent a potential minefield of stereotypes and attitudes, requiring careful thinking and classroom control. Instructors should take an objective stance emphasizing that all accents are equal linguistically, with distinct complex phonological systems of features and rules, and that so-called nonstandard, marginalized accents and L2 accents are merely different rather than deficient. It is challenging to clarify the difference between L2 varieties (where differing pronunciations may be L1-influenced) versus L1 varieties (where differing pronunciations are considered variants). In short, instructors should describe but not prescribe accents. Accents may be negatively stereotyped, but they are a natural part of language development such that many people are bi- or multidialectal, just as people are bi- or multilingual. The most productive way to address this issue is to frame it with the question, "How can we learn to understand each other better?"—whether one is an L2 speaker/listener, L1 speaker/listener, or D1/D2 (dialect 1 versus dialect 2) speaker. To explore potential correlations between understanding and biases, instructors might ask students to compare and rank accents or pronunciation features in terms of accentedness, intelligibility, and comprehensibility using rating scores, or to evaluate accents according to subjective characteristics such as pleasantness and correctness (Preston, 1996). This approach jump-starts discussion of social aspects (e.g., stereotypes, attitudes toward accents) as real-life unavoidable concerns which impact comprehension. Again, we recommend careful discussion.

Lastly, we address materials. Student learning outcomes and a template of activities (see lesson plan) guide instructors in creating materials. Although time-consuming, the internet, entertainment media, and software ease the work. Samples can be played back for listening practice and analysis as excerpts or in their entirety from their source or recorded with software (e.g., Audacity). Instructors create transcripts for visual analysis or activate subtitles which incidentally can provide insight when incorrectly transcribed (e.g., *sauce* as *source*).

Videos offer accent samples for extensive listening or discussion of (socio) linguistic aspects of accents (e.g., features, identity) (see Support Material for materials). Entertainment media (e.g., stand-up comedy, TV shows, movies) provide insight into how differences and stereotypes of particular accents, including those deemed "accentless" (e.g., a common perception of a white, middle-class American accent), are exploited to create humor or add instant backstories to characters. This reality can be eye-opening and unsettling, requiring instructors to be hypervigilant and objectively focus discussion to avoid triggering negative reactions. Lastly, we recommend inviting guest speakers to provide natural accent samples, insider viewpoints on social issues, and interactive situations where listeners must respond to what is said in the target accent.

Lesson Plan: Accent Detective—Breaking Accents Down Into Their Components

Recommended Grade Level(s)

High school, university (under)graduate students.

Context

Speakers of inner-, outer-, expanding-circle, and marginalized Englishes. Courses for EFL/ESL/EAL pronunciation, World Englishes, second language phonology, TESOL teaching, international communication. The goal of this lesson plan is for students to increase their understanding of their accent and enhance perception/comprehension of unfamiliar accents across four phonological dimensions to better interact in international contexts. Listeners should speak locally, listen globally.

Objectives

Students will be able to:

- explain how segments are produced (e.g., features) and describe differences between segments in the same words in different varieties;
- list the characteristics and functions of stress;
- identify content words, function words, and the focus word in a phrase;
- describe basic intonation patterns for sentence types;
- explain pronunciation processes with simple rules;
- systematize pronunciation differences between varieties.

Procedures

Step 1: Analyzing Familiar Varieties (30 Minutes)

Sample: Learners record themselves reading the Speech Accent Archive passage (Weinberger, 2015: http://accent.gmu.edu/) and/or use recordings of the passage by speakers of the listeners' accent(s) or reference accents: General American, Received Pronunciation.

  * See Support Material for an example, markings of the passage, extra suggestions, and activities.

Analysis:

1. Learners record themselves reading the passage.
2. Learners analyze their sample(s) from their accent, using handouts of the passage with space between lines and below for notes.
   a. Mark the passage for pauses using slashes.
   b. Circle content words.
   c. Put a mark above/below stressed syllables, including primary and secondary.
   d. Put a dot above focus words.

Speak Locally, Listen Globally 121

  e. Use arrows to show rising, falling, continuing high intonation pitch.
  f. Use half-circle lines to connect words read together.
  g. Use horizontal lines with varying heights above phrases to mark different pitch levels.
  h. Put a triangle under unstressed, reduced vowels.
  i. Put an X over potentially deleted sounds.
  j. Put a capital P over processes, e.g., flap (i.e., /t/ in *water*).

* Learners might focus on one pronunciation feature per passage, building up to the full range of features.

Step 2: Analyzing Unfamiliar Varieties (60 Minutes)

Sample: Speech Accent Archive recording of target dialect(s)

1. Learners evaluate samples on a scale from 1 to 5 for accentedness, intelligibility, comprehensibility, pleasantness, etc.
2. Learners analyze samples:
  a. Learners repeat steps A-J from Step 1. Additionally, they transcribe differing pronunciations using the International Phonetic Alphabet (IPA) below words, e.g., [fɪŋ] '*thing*', and note correlations, e.g., <th> [θ] to [f].
  b. Learners describe correlations between sample(s) and their accent/reference accent(s).
  c. Learners note unfamiliar or difficult-to-understand features.
  d. Learners devise strategies to enhance understanding of target accents.
  e. Learners identify varieties or describe their impression of speakers, e.g., regional/social background. Instructors hide the ID on screen or record sample(s) for playback.
  f. Learners determine direct or inverse relationships between factors: accentedness, intelligibility, comprehensibility, pleasantness, etc.
3. Learners discuss stereotypes, biases toward target accents (e.g., Do you find this accent pleasant, friendly, etc.? Does your impression of the accent influence intelligibility or comprehensibility? What stereotypes about accents are you familiar with?).

References

Bradlow, A. R., Akahane-Yamada, R., Pisoni, D. B., & Tohkura, Y. (1999). Training Japanese listeners to identify English /r/ and /l/: Long-term retention of learning in perception and production. *Perception & Psychophysics*, *61*, 977–985. https://doi.org/10.3758/BF03206911

Clopper, C. G. (2017). Dialect interference in lexical processing: Effects of familiarity and social stereotypes. *Phonetica*, *74*, 25–50. https://doi.org/10.1159/000446809

Clopper, C. G., & Pisoni, D. B. (2004). Effects of talker variability on perceptual learning of dialects. *Language and Speech*, *47*(3), 207–238. https://doi.org/10.1177/00238309040470030101

Derwing, T. M., Munro, M. J., & Wiebe, G. (1998). Evidence in favor of a broad framework for pronunciation instruction. *Language Learning*, *48*(3), 393–410. https://doi.org/10.1111/0023-8333.00047

Harrington, J., Palethorpe, S., & Watson, C. I. (2000). Does the queen speak the queen's English? *Nature*, *408*(6815), 927–928. https://doi.org/10.1038/35050160

Jenkins, J. (2000). *The phonology of English as an international language*. Oxford University Press.

Kachru, B. B. (1985). Standards, codification and sociolinguistic realism: The English language in the outer circle. In R. Quirk & H. G. Widdowson (Eds.), *English in the world: Teaching and learning the language and literatures* (pp. 11–30). Cambridge University Press.

Moyer, A. (2013). *Foreign accent: The phenomenon of non-native speech*. Cambridge University Press.

Munro, M. J., & Derwing, T. M. (1995). Foreign accent, comprehensibility, and intelligibility in the speech of second language learners. *Language Learning*, *45*(1), 73–97. https://doi.org/10.1111/j.1467-1770.1995.tb00963.x

Pallier, C., Colomé, A., & Sebastián-Gallés, N. (2001). The influence of native-language phonology on lexical access: Exemplar-based vs. abstract lexical entries. *Psychological Science*, *12*(6), 445–449. https://doi.org/10.1111/1467-9280.00383

Preston, D. R. (1996). Where the worst English is spoken. In E. W. Schneider (Ed.), *Focus on the USA* (pp. 297–360). John Benjamins Publishing.

Rubin, D. L. (1992). Nonlanguage factors affecting undergraduates' judgments of nonnative English-speaking teaching assistants. *Research in Higher Education*, *33*(4), 511–531. https://doi.org/10.1007/BF00973770

Scales, J., Wennerstrom, A., Richard, D., & Wu, S. H. (2006). Language learners' perceptions of accent. *TESOL Quarterly*, *40*(4), 715–738. https://doi.org/10.2307/40264305

Sumner, M., & Samuel, A. G. (2009). The effect of experience on the perception and representation of dialect variants. *Journal of Memory and Language*, *60*, 487–501. https://doi.org/10.1016/j.jml.2009.01.001

Walker, R. (2010). *Teaching the pronunciation of English as a lingua franca*. Oxford University Press.

Weinberger, S. (2015). *Speech accent archive*. George Mason University. http://accent.gmu.edu

Chapter 13

Implementing Global Englishes Real-World Activities in a Thai Tertiary Setting

Yusop Boonsuk and Eric A. Ambele

Introduction

English is used as a global lingua franca among speakers of varied linguacultural backgrounds. This pluricentric phenomenon has brought about educational dilemmas into English language teaching (ELT): which English variety should be incorporated into pedagogies, and which learning activities would yield effective learning results amidst English diversity? These controversies are trending and, hence, worth addressing.

This chapter presents Global Englishes Language Teaching (GELT) learning-based activities (Rose & Galloway, 2019) as useful prompts to raise students' awareness of Global Englishes (GE) issues, ELT ideologies in Thailand, and beliefs and attitudes towards Standard Englishes (British and American). The chapter also discusses the relationship between the GELT framework and ELT and presents the suitability of GELT in the Thai context. The scope of this chapter is within a tertiary classroom in a public university in Southern Thailand, adjacent to the Malaysian border. This university accommodates a diverse range of Thai and international students, serving as a unique linguacultural setting. Many international students enroll into this university every year, especially those from Asia (e.g., Malaysia, Indonesia, China, Cambodia, Myanmar, and Vietnam). With such superdiversity, this university has become the optimal choice as different English varieties are heard/used on campus. The implemented activities targeted undergraduate students who were enrolled in a Global Englishes course. The course ran for 15 weeks throughout a semester. The course primarily focused on introducing students to global English varieties and variations.

The authors believe that this topic can offer alternative ELT methods of learning English through a more practical framework addressing real-world usage of English, its pluricentricity, and its diversity—where English is no longer tied to the native speaker group and where real-life English dialogues might not always involve native English speakers. Through pedagogical alterations, students can receive essential preparation to apply the in-class learning experiences to solve their out-of-class communicative problems. Furthermore, the activities can convince students, instructors, policymakers, and curriculum designers that monocentric or single-variety-biased English pedagogies cannot respond to the current trends and requirements of English diversification, as English speakers from different backgrounds speak English differently.

DOI: 10.4324/9781003124665-16

ELT Ideology in Thailand

Language and ideology are interrelated, especially in terms of attitude, identity, and language planning and policy (Lippi-Green, 2012). They reflect people's actual language use in a particular society with regard to the trends in which they speak, what they think of the language, the language options they choose to use, and their sociopolitical positions with regard to different languages. Thailand is an Expanding Circle country with English as a foreign language. The Thai government has clearly stated that the development of English skills is one of the most important factors for developing the ability of Thai people to cope with globalization (Ambele & Boonsuk, 2020; Kaur et al., 2016). This kind of government policy will certainly have an impact on the English language ideologies of Thai learners.

Teaching, learning, and curriculum policies are entirely initiated by those who have power. Consequently, Thai English teachers take a passive role in taking charge of their own teaching. These teachers have been expected to follow a particular set of theoretical principles and pedagogical techniques, which are conceptualized and materialized by Western theorists and considered by those theorists to be suitable teaching and learning methods. Thus, English language education in Thailand is still based on the traditional pedagogy of English as a Foreign Language (EFL), which generally encourages students to behave in accordance with native speakers' norms (Boonsuk et al., 2021; Jindapitak & Teo, 2012). To put this phenomenon in perspective using English pronunciation as an example, speakers who have a more native-like accent often look down on Thai people who speak English with a "Thai accent." This notion is supported by a study conducted by Jindapitak and Teo (2012) on the reactions of Thai English learners towards varieties of English. They found that Thai learners perceived people who could speak in a native accent to be of higher status than those with non-native accents.

English pronunciation has thus become one of the most valuable criteria used by Thais to distinguish whether a person is of a higher or lower class. Because of this, most Thais attempt to pronounce English like native speakers in order not to be discriminated against. If this notion is embedded and accepted by the majority, then the Thai English accent may have no place in society. Those who speak English with a Thai accent will be marginalized as second-class people.

Global Englishes and ELT

Global Englishes (GE) is a paradigm in sociolinguistics designed to diminish sociolinguistic boundaries while embracing the dynamics of English diversity. The paradigm does not project English users as failed speakers but rather successful communicators. The GE approach values the emergence of English language diversity and existing English varieties in different contexts. Different English-usage patterns are not accounted as problematic in GE communication, just as native English speakers (NES) are not the only ideal models for non-native users to learn the English language from. GE prioritizes communicative skills such as linguistic accommodations and meaning negotiations as they allow English language learners to be more flexible in multilingual situations and adequately open-minded to get messages across in culturally diverse settings. Finally, the GE framework does not project that English should be owned by specific ethnicities or sovereign territories: any English user in the global community can claim ownership, too.

The availability of studies on the implementation of GE-oriented pedagogies remains limited (Boonsuk et al., 2021; Fang & Ren, 2018; Galloway & Rose, 2018). Among them, Galloway's (2011) Global Englishes Language Teaching (GELT) was identified as the most cited framework. This research-originated framework offers vital insights on GE-based curriculum development. GELT competes with conventional English language learning pedagogies through the support for English-diversity awareness. It shows that English conversations could take place in any situation with English users simultaneously acting as interlocutors and owners of an English variety. This condition means that flexible English can be used in conjunction with specific cultural codes establishing diversely local English norms. Using GELT pedagogies, ELT is set free from native standards as it addresses real-world possibilities in English communication across the Inner, Outer, and Expanding Circles. When compared with conventional ELT, GELT is almost on the opposite pole, as the traditional approach emphasizes NES-inspired benchmarks and standards to determine English proficiency.

GELT admirably provides a more practical solution to counter stereotypes that are deeply rooted in ELT practices, widely incorporated in instructional materials, and excessively influential to learning ideologies. However, with English as a global language, the teaching status quo needs to be re-conceptualized with the help of GELT to embrace the evolutionary dynamics of how English is now employed. Through GELT, learners are no longer involuntarily forced into English nativeness but instead, given a flexible opportunity to explore the lingua franca as it is, establish new perceptions of English, adopt more practical linguistic norms, and understand that the language has become pluricentric. At the same time, educational service providers—e.g., instructors, curriculum designers, and policymakers—can incorporate GELT as an alternative framework to expand ELT beyond strict native standards and prepare learners for mainstream and non-mainstream communicative encounters in English that might take place just outside the classroom (Rose & Galloway, 2019).

Scholars have applied the ELT paradigm in studies covering many student groups (Sung, 2014; Galloway, 2017; Rose & Galloway, 2017). Typical of these is Galloway and Rose (2018), which investigated GELT and its ability to enhance the awareness of English diversity among tertiary learners in Japan. This academic investigation directly challenged traditional ELT approaches. The learners were tasked to choose and discuss an English variety of interest, and results indicated that they became more aware of and had more positive attitudes towards English diversity. The approach not only helped students understand and value phonological, grammatical, lexical, and pragmatic differences among English varieties but also enabled them to "reflect on the linguistic history of a nation in order to understand the process that helped shape the English spoken there" (Galloway & Rose, 2018, p. 10).

In Thailand, relevant literature in past years indicates that the ELT status quo does not favor GE. The primary reason is that ELT in the Thai society still adheres to EFL pedagogies where NES are positioned as optimal learning models who provide satisfactory language-learning experiences, whereas instructors have not been open-minded enough to embrace GE instructional approaches. To prevent learners from having prejudiced reactions against non-native English varieties, Jindapitak and Teo (2012) organized a three-stage activity. The task in Step 1 was to have the learners collect and prepare speech samples from different non-native communities. In Step 2, the learners presented their audio-sample selections to the class as well as offered an analysis of the speakers. Finally, Step 3 was the time when the learners jointly accumulated the findings and discussed the outcomes as a class. A post-activity assessment revealed that the learners became more open-minded about and interested in the concept of English diversity. The learners also realized that international contexts of English communication might not always involve mainstream English varieties such as British or American English and that interlocutors could speak English using other accepted English varieties. As Galloway and Rose (2015) illustrated, exposing learners to many existing varieties of English could be a more constructive teaching method than merely encouraging them to adhere to a specific English variety that belongs to a nation.

Student-Foreigners GELT Exposure Activity

Inspired by the Transformative Learning Theory (Jarvis, 2009), this course-based activity was designed for a 15-week semester covering three learning measures (i.e., disjuncture, reflection, and feedback) and a two-phase organization (i.e., in-class videos and out-of-class fieldwork). Transformative learning is grounded on the premise that learners adjust their thinking as they receive new knowledge, evaluate their past ideas and understanding, and constantly shift their views on learning when they receive new information through critical reflection.

In-Class Video-Based Learning Activity

The learners worked in groups of fewer than five to choose a video of English users from various linguacultural Asian countries. The learners subsequently evaluated the videos and identified which English varieties were employed, stated if they felt comfortable listening to such varieties, listed advantages or disadvantages of such varieties, and compared them with Thai English, British English, and American English. Eventually, every group shared their insights with the class, led a discussion, and ran a Q&A session. In this phase, diverse English varieties were introduced to the class. Despite the occurrence of norm-related conflicts and standard disagreements, the learners managed to negotiate for meanings and accommodate communication to preserve communication quality. Consequently, the learners began to notice that real-world conversations might not always involve NES, meaning that learning a native English variety might not always be something compulsory. In contrast, some learners demonstrated their pride in speaking Thai English as the variety represents their collective identity.

Nevertheless, some instructors reported that this implementation was impractical because it was impossible to teach every existing variety of the world. Therefore, to tackle this practical concern, instructors should prioritize which varieties to introduce and when it would be proper for those varieties to be introduced. For instance, for ELT classes in countries within the Association of Southeast Asian

Nations (ASEAN), it would make sense to start with the ASEAN English varieties and subsequently expand to the rest of Asia, and non-Asia. This prioritization is based on the probability of communicative exposures learners might encounter in their futures.

In terms of practices, listening activities with sample conversational videos involving English speakers from multiple origins should be employed. If the scope is ASEAN, then the activities should be designed consistently using ASEAN-relevant contents. The primary purpose is to familiarize learners with the surrounding English reality, which could be regionally based but internationally recognized. Here are examples of related topics and phrases available online, searchable via sites such as YouTube and Google: "Does the Thai English accent confuse foreigners?"; "Varieties of English"; "Thai English Accent"; "American English Accent"; and "British English Accent."

Field-Trip Learning Activity

In small groups of fewer than five students, the learners went out for a field survey at famous destinations in Thailand, which were populated with tourists from many countries around the world. Learners were tasked to jointly conduct interviews with foreigners who came from many places in all three circles: Inner, Outer, and Expanding.

During interviews, the learners had to be creative about their interview questions as no pre-determined questions were assigned. Going through random conversational topics, the learners discussed freely with their interlocutors, and they were also free to talk to as many visitors as they desired under the only condition that these interviewees should be from various geographic origins such as Europe and Asia. This condition was given so that the learners received maximum exposure to English diversity by involving interviewees from multiple ethnicities in their interview quest. The activity outcomes were interesting and profound because, after the interviews, the learners returned to the class with a task to associate parts of the interviewees' demographic data with the course themes and present their insights in front of the class. After some presentations began, the audience in the room became active and raised many thought-provoking questions.

This activity was outstanding in the sense that the learners observably gained awareness of how communicative English could practically be employed and how distinctive classroom English could be when compared with real-world interactions. More importantly, the learners recognized that speakers from different ethnic origins might be using different English varieties in conversations, and it is not wrong to be different. The learners understood that even though the tourists were speaking different versions of English, they could still try to accommodate different communicative styles and gain fruitful results from the interactions. Although these communicative encounters had exposed the learners to English diversity, they reported still feeling significantly positive about it. In fact, they even began to perceive that achieving native English might not have much to do with success in communication in these multicultural contexts where meaning negotiations are more vital for mutual understanding. Based on these positive notions, this course was perceived as a potential awareness activator.

Activity Reflection

After going through both activities (In-Class Video-Based Learning Activity and Field-Trip Learning Activity), the learners completed another attitudinal evaluation activity. Results showed that their attitudes towards English diversity remained positive, and their perceptions of English ownership changed in the sense that nobody nor any nation could now claim to be the sole owner of the language. More specifically, English was reportedly believed to be a language of the world, and any English speakers could proudly say English is their language. Furthermore, the learners indicated that all English varieties, including Thai English, deserve international recognition and that ELT should not seek to pressure speakers into adopting native Englishes if their linguistic outputs produce intelligible messages. Moreover, the learners stated that the activities were valuable as they had opportunities to be critical in their views of English. They recognized that English has different roles and benefits at national, continental, and global levels.

On the basis of these reports, we confirm that these activities were effective at promoting positive learning attitudes and English conceptualization among this group of learners, resulting in a significant ideological shift towards the learning targets. Previously, the learners had continuously cultivated a value that favors native English varieties, and native English speakers from the Inner Circle as the owner of the language. After this course, students had evidently adopted a more open-minded perception and determined to recognize that English has been diversified at a macro level among speakers from different linguistic and cultural roots across the world. Another benefit was that the learners proudly accepted Thai English as their identity and felt less awkward starting a conversation since they were now more comfortable with their accent. The ultimate perceivable benefit was that most learners gained a boost in confidence to engage in an interview with foreigners regardless of their perceived imperfect English capacities. After reviewing these notions, it was quite convincing that the concept of nativeness, which favors British English and American English, is becoming obsolete in pragmatic ELT.

Conclusion

Modern ELT should recognize that English is a pluricentric language, meaning that there are multiple acceptable standards and conventions. Educational stakeholders should incorporate feasible language-learning approaches, ideologies, and contents that focus more on communication efficiency than fancy native-like imitations. English-learning objectives should be re-conceptualized. Educators should move away from achieving nativeness or monocentricity and towards English diversity or pluricentricity. Learning priorities should also be reconsidered as practicing opportunities, and English-variety exposures have not been sufficiently addressed in ELT. Implementing GELT offers a realistic preparation for ELT learners as it helps learners recognize existing communicative possibilities and learn to accommodate such communication. The ultimate goal of language learning should be producing an efficient English communicator and not an almost-native speaker. Finally, ELT scholars should collaboratively explore this academic area and help eradicate the deeply rooted false values of achieving native English and neglecting pragmatics.

Lesson Plan: Student-Foreigners GELT Exposure Activity

Recommended Grade Level(s)

Tertiary Level

Context

This lesson exposes students to Global Englishes issues, with a prompt on examining the sociolinguistic use and role of different Englishes. It is suitable for English major students and those using English as a Medium of Instruction (EMI). The lesson is designed for a multicultural/foreign English language context where there are diverse English users from varied linguacultural backgrounds and is estimated for a 90-minute class. However, teachers in monocultural contexts can adapt this lesson to suit the sociolinguistic reality of their unique contexts.

Objectives

Students will be able to:

- identify variations in Englishes;
- be aware of and appreciate the uniqueness of different English varieties.

Procedures

Step 1: Exposure (15 Minutes)

- Place students in small groups to select English videos with different linguacultural speakers using different varieties of English.
- Ask students to evaluate the videos in terms of the English variety used; origin of speakers; accent used; and their attitudes towards the different accents, English variety, and its speakers. Have students compare the varieties with their own local English variety and Standard varieties (British or American).
- Ask every group to take turns sharing their insights on these issues, leaving room for follow-up questions.

Step 2: Real-World Interaction (1 Hour)

This step is broken down into different stages as follows:

Step 2a: Question Preparation (5–10 Minutes)

- Students work as a group to develop their own interview questions on any topic suitable for them and the interviewees before conducting the interview.

Step 2b: Interviews (30–40 Minutes)

- Students work as groups interviewing as many foreigners as they can find.

Step 2c: Interview Summary Presentations (2–3 Minutes/Group; 10–20 Minutes)

- Students briefly present on their interview experiences with the foreigners, leaving room for follow-up questions from other groups and the teacher.

Step 3: Reflection (10 Minutes)

Ask the students what they noticed about how different people use English—what they observed and why? Engage the students in an attitudinal evaluation activity on Global Englishes (e.g., their attitudes towards English diversity; their perceptions of English ownership, English varieties, and recognition; and accent differences and use). The instructor might relate these aspects to the students' own local English variety and attitude about accents, identity, and ELT focus in a world of different Englishes.

Step 4: Exit (5 Minutes)

Ask students to explain how such Global Englishes knowledge might be useful for learning English.

Extension Activities

1. Instruct students to observe their friends' and foreign peers' use of language and write up a report to be shared at the next class meeting.
2. To lead into a lesson on attitude, identity, and language use in ELT, the students can be instructed to ask any foreigner about their perception of their own local English accents and those of other English users.

References

Ambele, E., & Boonsuk, Y. (2020). Voices of learners for Thai ELT classrooms: A wake up call towards English as a lingua franca. *Asian Englishes*, *23*(2), 201–217. https://doi.org/10.1080/13488678.2020.1759248

Boonsuk, Y., Ambele, E., & McKinley, J. (2021). Developing awareness of global Englishes: Moving away from 'Native Standards' for Thai University ELT. *System*, *99*. https://doi.org/10.1016/j.system.2021.102511

Fang, F., & Ren, W. (2018). Developing students' awareness of Global Englishes. *ELT Journal*, *72*(4), 384–394. https://doi.org/10.1093/elt/ccy012

Galloway, N. (2011). *An investigation of Japanese university students' attitudes towards English* (Doctoral dissertation, University of Southampton).

Galloway, N. (2017). *Global Englishes and change in English language teaching: Attitudes and impact*. Taylor & Francis.

Galloway, N., & Rose, H. (2015). *Introducing global Englishes*. Routledge.

Galloway, N., & Rose, H. (2018). Incorporating global Englishes into the ELT classroom. *ELT Journal*, *72*(1), 3–14. https://doi.org/10.1093/elt/ccx010

Jarvis, P. (2009). *Learning to be a person in society*. Routledge.

Jindapitak, N., & Teo, A. (2012). Thai tertiary English majors' attitudes towards and awareness of World Englishes. *Journal of English Studies*, *7*, 74–116.

Kaur, A., Young, D., & Kirkpatrick, R. (2016). English education policy in Thailand: Why the poor results? In *English language education policy in Asia* (pp. 345–361). Springer. https://doi.org/10.1007/978-3-319-22464-0_16

Lippi-Green, R. (2012). *English with an accent: Language, ideology and discrimination in the United States*. Routledge.

Rose, H., & Galloway, N. (2017). Debating standard language ideology in the classroom: Using the "speak good English movement" to raise awareness of global Englishes. *RELC Journal*, *48*(3), 294–301. https://doi.org/10.1177/0033688216684281

Rose, H., & Galloway, N. (2019). *Global Englishes for language teaching*. Cambridge University Press.

Sung, C. C. M. (2014). English as a lingua franca and global identities: Perspectives from four second language learners of English in Hong Kong. *Linguistics and Education*, *26*, 31–39. https://doi.org/10.1016/j.linged.2014.01.010

Chapter 14

Code-Switching in Hong Kong
Key to Implementing a Hong Kong English Curriculum?

Ka Long Roy Chan

Introduction

Influenced by World Englishes (WE), scholars have been studying different varieties of English in the traditional Kachurian Outer Circle Englishes, such as Hong Kong English (HKE) and Singaporean English, for decades. Recently, the studies of these post-colonial Englishes started to shift from phonetics, phonology, and syntax to applied linguistic studies of English Language Teaching (ELT). The suitability of these varieties in traditional English as a Second Language (ESL) classrooms has been questioned, and scholars have started to make theoretical assumptions regarding how to implement these Englishes into curriculums for pedagogical purposes. There are abundant studies on HKE features, particularly in the past decade, including phonetics and phonology (e.g., Hansen Edwards, 2019; Chan, 2020a); syntax (e.g., Chan, 2003; Setter et al., 2010); and semantics (e.g., Chan, 2003; Deterding et al., 2008)—all of which provide a rich foundation for implementing HKE into ELT in local contexts.

Preliminary studies in the early 2010s suggested that HKE may be applicable for pedagogical use in classrooms (Sewell, 2012) and that teachers in Hong Kong were generally positive toward HKE (Chan, 2016/2017). Meanwhile, more studies have posed evidence that bilingual code-switching (CS) has played a major role in Hong Kong and serves as an identity marker (Chan, 2018), in addition to strengthening the identity of being a Hongkonger (Chan, 2019). CS could be considered an important tool of the English curriculum due to its high relevance to language and identity. Therefore, this chapter aims to provide a theoretical discussion on the possibility of implementing HKE into the local ESL curriculum, with the potential benefits to both teachers and learners within Hong Kong. The discussion further extends to whether the implementation could apply to other contexts globally. Along with other chapters in this book, the discussion will be conveyed in a more practical tone, which fits the need of both language practitioners and linguists. At the end of the chapter, an activity that includes a task-based guided role-play on CS will be introduced for teachers.

Code-Switching in Hong Kong and HKE Teaching

Code-switching (CS) requires some context before the main discussion, since it has been defined differently over the years (Wang & Kirkpatrick, 2019). For example,

DOI: 10.4324/9781003124665-17

there is a distinction between inter- and intra-sentential CS: speakers who shift *inter*-sententially move between different codes (different languages, dialects, or other varieties) at a clause (or sentence) level, while speakers who shift *intra*-sententially alternate on a word level (Chan, 2003). However, CS is generally agreed to be a common language behavior in any multilingual society with multiple languages in the community.[1]

CS has been well-researched in Hong Kong, as Hongkongers are known as bilinguals in Cantonese (L1) and English (L2), attributed to its colonial background. Since the 1970s, the CS behavior among Hongkongers has been documented in either written or spoken form. The spoken form of CS was widely used as a communication tool among a spectrum of Hongkongers for intra-ethnic solidarity and as an in-group identity marker (Chan, 2018). Three ethnolinguistic studies of CS were done within two decades by Li and Tse (2002), Sung (2010), and Chan (2018), with the latter two identifying themselves as "replication studies" of the prior. The trio provided longitudinal-like evidence of CS in Hong Kong. Even though the three did not exactly duplicate each other, with the abundant informants ranging from students to lecturers, the results showed coherently that CS seems essential to Hongkongers, as the languages in Hong Kong have been heavily mixed, and both Cantonese and English complement each other in a sentence for completing a meaningful utterance (Chan, 2018). In Chan (2019), a follow-up study of Chan (2018), it is found that trilingual CS (Cantonese, English, and Mandarin) may have taken place because of the growing trilingualism in Hong Kong. However, despite the high popularity of CS in Hong Kong, it has never been a part of the curriculum in Hong Kong's ELT classrooms, partly because of the stigma that is attached to CS as an informal form of language use (Chen, 2015).

The ELT environment in Hong Kong is highly (and traditionally) monolingual—English is the preferred medium of instruction (MOI) in classrooms. This can be evidenced in two ways. First, schools in Hong Kong were divided as either EMI (English as the MOI) or CMI (Cantonese/Chinese as the MOI), and EMI once accounted for almost 90%; meanwhile, English has been the MOI of almost all Hong Kong universities (Evans, 2016). Second, the strong English orientation from teachers and parents shows how monolingual teaching is favored in Hong Kong. Even after the handover to China, parents and business sectors urged the government to change the mother tongue policy, which shows how parents preferred EMI. English teachers in Hong Kong also expressed their preference for using English as the only MOI (Harwood & Lai, 2017).

The EMI teaching in Hong Kong is strongly monolingual and perhaps exonormative, which largely ignores the growing concerns of WE—the inclusion of English varieties in both a local and global sense. In the WE paradigm, the understanding of different varieties of English resulting from different L1s should be encouraged by teachers because the opportunity for communication between ESL learners is estimated to be much higher, given that the number of ESL learners have already exceeded the number of native English speakers (Crystal, 2003). In other

---

1 For a more detailed description, refer to Chan (2003) and Li (2000).

words, the teaching focus of ESL should, therefore, emphasize an acknowledgement of the inclusiveness of English varieties and an acceptance of their varieties. In this regard, the current ELT environment in Hong Kong discourages students from understanding different English varieties and, also, the use of local elements in any circumstance. Chan (2016/2017) interviewed teachers of English in Hong Kong, ranging from primary school teachers to university lecturers, to investigate their attitudes towards English, especially their preferences towards English during teaching. The results demonstrated that teachers in Hong Kong prefer to use exonormative forms of English, for instance, British or American English, as the "standard form." The same preference was also discovered among students of different levels in Hong Kong (cf. Chan, 2019). However, interestingly, despite preferring an exonormative form of English, the teachers and students surveyed in Chan (2016/2017) and Chan (2019) also acknowledged the fact that a local English variant (HKE) is commonly used by Hongkongers. Therefore, there is a discrepancy between the ESL situation in Hong Kong and the actual WE paradigm: the English varieties that are taught in ESL classrooms do not comprehensively reflect the local linguistic environment in Hong Kong nor an inclusive range of global Englishes.

HKE and CS are widespread linguistic features adapted by Hongkongers and not only demonstrate functional communication usage among the community but also show the cultural identity of the language users, as well, despite having never been part of the curriculum. More importantly, while one may argue that different varieties of English may perform differently in communication and students should learn one that is more well understood by others, numerous studies have also demonstrated that there is not a necessary correlation between "nativeness" and intelligibility. This means the so-called non-native English used by the ESL learners could be as intelligible as, or even more intelligible than, the exonormative form of English, depending on the context and the listeners. Hansen Edwards et al. (2018) examined the intelligibility of four English varieties for different listeners, and the result showed that HKE has high intelligibility, even compared to the so-called native English like American English. This result is consistent with Chan's (2020b) research on the intelligibility of HKE for people worldwide, in which HKE shows a high intelligibility to most of the participants. Along with other research, such as Matsuura (2007) and Sewell (2012), they show that HKE, even with unique linguistic features, is useful for international communication.

Thus, the preceding discussion suggests that HKE and CS are parts of Hong Kong culture while at the same time largely ignored by the ESL curriculum. So what would it be like if they were implemented into ESL teaching? Or would it even be feasible? Sewell's (2012) research on the intelligibility of HKE concluded that HKE could be acceptably used for "pedagogical purposes (in ESL teaching)" (p. 14). Sung (2010) also comes to a similar conclusion—that CS could be a "feasible and effective means" for teaching ESL in Hong Kong (p. 418). Yet, so far, discussions to take these assumptions further into practice have been rare. Therefore, this book chapter serves as a theoretical attempt to address this very issue of integrating HKE and CS into the curriculum.

However, what is the basis for implementing such an attempt in the curriculum? Also, what are the benefits of doing so for both teachers and learners? The following sections aim to provide answers to these questions.

Implementing HKE Into ESL Curriculum

To understand the implementation of a local ESL curriculum, it would be better to start with Hino's (2018) and Chan's (2020a) models. In his monograph, Hino (2018) presented a vision to *liberate* Japanese English from the traditional "Anglo-centric" English norm via a seven-phase model. His major attempt was to create a Japanese English that is easy to learn for Japanese students and is also useful for communication worldwide. Chan (2020a, 2020b) modified Hino's (2018) model into the Hong Kong context and suggested a four-phase model for HKE to be fully liberated from the exonormative norm of English:

- Phase I: Inclusion of a WE Belief in Teachers' Training
- Phase II: Design of a Standardized HKE Curriculum
- Phase III: Implementation of Curriculum and Further Research
- Phase IV: Birth of Users of HKE and Continuous Evaluation (Chan, 2020b, p. 228)

Among the four phases, a draft of how to modify the ESL curriculum is outlined in *Phase II* and *Phase III*.

In *Phase II*, standardization of HKE is suggested, as a "standard" is essential before the curriculum is finalized for teachers to follow. Codification of HKE in a form of reference books covering both lexical and phonological levels would set a guideline for teachers to follow. While standardization is more the job of linguists and researchers, teachers are also important in implementing the curriculum by (1) understanding the concepts of WE and (2) participating in small-scale trials of HKE teaching and providing feedback to researchers. Linguists and researchers alone could not complete their studies without teachers' help to see how the curriculum works in real life, as well as how the students react and respond. Also, teachers are encouraged to design their lesson plans and activities based on the new curriculum to enrich the content. The feedback from teachers would help linguists in modifying and adjusting the curriculum; under several rounds of trials and errors, the curriculum would be used in *Phase III*, with continuous evaluations from teachers and researchers to measure the outcomes from students and teachers.

This curriculum will be an example of a local curriculum that fulfills a local and global need simultaneously. The benefit of having a local curriculum is that ESL students would likely spend less effort in the learning process. Also, ESL teachers could teach with ease and more flexibility. Moreover, a local curriculum also helps strengthen the solidarity among students towards their cultures, which has been proven to be long neglected under rapid globalization. However, a local curriculum applying the WE concept could also provide learners with sufficient input concerning the world, especially an awareness of the multi-centric nature of the world, which involves people of different cultures and languages that need to be appreciated. Sadly, as mentioned earlier, there have been few attempts in Hong Kong to bend local linguistic features into a teaching curriculum. Even though teachers may have tried, they are left with no reference to follow. Therefore, in the following, exactly how CS and HKE could benefit students and teachers and how these elements could be incorporated into teaching will be briefly outlined as an initial trial for teachers worldwide.

The benefits of using HKE and CS as tools in ESL teaching are multifaceted for both ESL learners and teachers. For learners, the first advantage would be increasing their learning efficiency. Sakaria and Priyana (2018) pointed out that the use of students' L1, probably similar to daily-like talks, helps in learning an L2; this is especially true for understanding difficult grammatical items. Cook (1997), also supported the use of L1 in L2 learning since L1 is still easier to learn complex information than L2, even for very proficient L2 users. Apart from the ease in understanding concepts, the use of a more familiar tone may help develop solidarity among learners towards their own culture and their identity. As Evans (2014) stated, language is always interlinked with identity, and therefore, the use of local language to teach certain concepts strengthens students' affection towards their own culture, which facilitates an identity construction. Chan (2018, 2019) showed that, in Hong Kong, CS and HKE are crucial in daily communication, as well as being an identity marker of being a Hongkonger. An in-group solidarity will be developed within the language community that shares the same language behavior, thus benefiting the learning process and encouraging a more positive learning attitude and greater motivation (Skiba, 1997).

For teachers, it is believed that their teaching practice would be enhanced, partly because they would feel more at ease communicating in their own L1s. Previous studies showed that L2 teachers tend to doubt their teacher-identity and even L2 learners themselves (Chan, 2016/2017); this causes a problem in their teaching as it further passes on the traditional concepts of exonormative Englishes. Bilgin (2016) suggested that CS is associated with the teacher's identity and their teaching practices and ended with a note that teachers should be educated about the use of CS in classes. This use of CS in classes is sensible, as it helps build up the rapport between students and teachers, thus creating a better learning atmosphere in classrooms (Liu, 2010).

The discussion has shown how the use of CS could benefit the teaching and learning process; at the end of this chapter, several concrete ideas on how to implement the teaching of CS and HKE in practice are suggested. As Sung (2010) stated, there are "pedagogical benefits that mixed code [CS] may bring to the students' learning experience of the English language" (p. 418). Hence, CS should always be taken into consideration if modification is made to the existing curriculum. Similarly, Creese and Blackledge (2010) suggest pedagogies in promoting bilingual teaching, and three of them are thought to be relevant to the discussion here:

(1) Use of bilingual label quests, repetition, and translation across languages;
(2) Recognition that languages do not fit into clear bounded entities and that all languages are "needed" for meanings to be conveyed and negotiated;
(3) Recognition that teachers and students skillfully use their languages for different functional goals such as narration and explanation (Creese & Blackledge, 2010, p. 113)

These items emphasize the importance of (a) the use of multiple languages during teaching, (b) the benefits of immersing classrooms with WE concepts for both teachers and students, and (c) the understanding of the different uses of CS in teaching and other social contexts. To develop a local curriculum, teachers need to collect real examples of CS and HKE and to understand how these are culturally connected. In Hong Kong, these could be done by using different cultural texts, such as movies and magazines, which reflect local culture and local language use.

The making of a new curriculum is surely tough. As Sung (2010) and Chan (2020b) both agreed, policy makers should cooperate with researchers and teachers to understand the needs of teaching and learning. If the new curriculum is beneficial to both educators and learners, as well as fitting in a global context, it is surely important to investigate the possibility.

The following lesson plan illustrates one way in which CS and HKE could be implemented as a part of the ESL curriculum in Hong Kong, given its benefits for teachers and learners.

Lesson Plan: Role-Play of Code-Switching in Hong Kong

Recommended Grade Level(s)

Bilingual senior high school to university students

Context

This 45-minute task-based guided role-play on code-switching (CS) helps students learn more about language learning and the culture of Hong Kong. This task works best as an introductory activity for lessons like language varieties or language contact in areas with bilingualism for a class size of 15 to 20.

Objectives

Students will be able to:

- identify instances of CS in Hong Kong contexts;
- identify and describe why CS is used in Hong Kong;
- appreciate language varieties and language contacts.

Procedures

Pre-Task: Group Ethnographic Research

Readings of the definitions and common examples of CS in Hong Kong are delivered to students one week before the lesson, as well as a summary of a research from Chan (2018). Students are asked to form groups to conduct data research.

Students should conduct one-day data research on a group basis, in which they should note down or record (if possible) their conversation in different environments as a simplified version of Chan (2018). They should notate every incidence of CS made by them and/or others they encounter during the day. Then, they have to formulate a table with the details of the examples and the context (a restaurant, a class, a conversation, etc.)

Step 1: Group Sharing and Preparation (15 Minutes)

Students should sit in groups and present the data they collected. Groups with examples from a similar context (e.g., restaurant) should sit together and share with other groups their examples. They should prepare for a short role-play using the examples that they have under the same context (e.g., waiter and customers in a restaurant).

Step 2: Role-Play (20 Minutes)

Students should perform a short role-play of one to two minutes. Other students are given a peer evaluation form for notetaking. At the end, representatives from each group should vote the most memorable CS example from other groups and share with the whole class.

Step 3: Debrief (10 Minutes)

The teacher should explain the reasons of CS as a tool of communication in Hong Kong, including language contact and the history of the language(s). And they should explain how CS may benefit language learning at the end of the class with an emphasis on the contextualized use of CS.

Post-Task: Reflective Journals

Students should write a report using the data gathered from the ethnographic study.

References

Bilgin, S. S. (2016). Code-switching in English language teaching (ELT) teaching practice in Turkey: Student teacher practices, beliefs and identity. *Educational Research and Reviews, 11*(8), 686–702. https://doi.org/10.5897/ERR2016.2802

Chan, B. H. S. (2003). *Aspects of the syntax, the pragmatics, and the production of code-switching: Cantonese and English*. Peter Lang.

Chan, K. L. R. (2016/2017). Attitudes towards Hong Kong English: Native English teachers and local English teachers. *Asian Journal of English Language Teaching, 26*, 85–110.

Chan, K. L. R. (2018). Being a "purist" in trilingual Hong Kong: Code-switching among Cantonese, English and Putonghua. *Linguistic Research, 35*(1), 75–95. http://dx.doi.org/10.17250/khisli.35.1.201803.003

Chan, K. L. R. (2019). Trilingual code-switching in Hong Kong. *Applied Linguistics Research Journal, 3*(4), 1–14. https://doi.org/10.14744/alrj.2019.22932

Chan, K. L. R. (2020a). The future of Hong Kong English: Codification and standardisation?. In W. Tang (Ed.), *Hong Kong: Past, present and future* (pp. 69–88). Nova.

Chan, K. L. R. (2020b). *The intelligibility of the segmental and suprasegmental features of Hong Kong English to listeners in the inner, outer, and expanding circles* (Ph.D. thesis, The Chinese University of Hong Kong).

Chen, K. H. Y. (2015). Styling bilinguals: Analyzing structurally distinctive code-switching styles in Hong Kong. In G. Stell & K. Yakpo (Eds.), *Code-switching between structural and sociolinguistic perspectives* (pp. 163–184). De Gruyter. http://doi.org/10.1515/9783110346879.163

Cook, V. (1997). Monolingual bias in second language acquisition research. *Revista Canaria de Estudios Ingleses, 34*(1), 35–49.

Creese, A., & Blackledge, A. (2010). Translanguaging in the bilingual classroom: A pedagogy for learning and teaching? *The Modern Language Journal, 94*(1), 103–115. https://doi.org/10.1111/j.1540-4781.2009.00986.x

Crystal, D. (2003). *English as a global language*. Cambridge University Press. https://doi.org/10.1017/CBO9780511486999

Deterding, D., Wong, J., & Kirkpatrick, A. (2008). The pronunciation of Hong Kong English. *English World-Wide, 29*(2), 148–175. https://doi.org/10.1075/eww.29.2.03det

Evans, D. (2014). *Language and identity: Discourse in the world*. Bloomsbury. https://doi.org/10.5040/9781474242035

Evans, S. (2016). *The English language in Hong Kong: Diachronic and synchronic perspectives*. Palgrave Macmillan. https://doi.org/ 10.1057/978-1-137-50624-5

Hansen Edwards, J. G. (2019). *The politics of English in Hong Kong: Attitudes, identity and use*. Routledge. https://doi.org/10.4324/9781315178547

Hansen Edwards, J. G., Zampini, M. L., & Cunningham, C. (2018). The accentedness, comprehensibility, and intelligibility of Asian Englishes. *World Englishes, 37*(4), 538–557. https://doi.org/10.1111/weng.12344

Harwood, C., & Lai, C. (2017). Linguistic capital: Language medium of instruction policy in Hong Kong. *Language Problems & Language Planning, 41*(2), 159–167. http://doi.org/10.1075/lplp.41.2.05har

Hino, N. (2018). *EIL education for the expanding circle: A Japanese model*. Routledge. https://doi.org/10.4324/9781315209449

Li, D. C. S. (2000). Cantonese-English code-switching research in Hong Kong: A Y2K review. *World Englishes, 19*, 305–322. https://doi.org/10.1111/1467-971X.00181

Li, D. C. S., & Tse, E. C. Y. (2002). One day in a life of a "purist". *The International Journal of Bilingualism*, *6*(2), 147–203. https://doi.org/10.1177%2F13670069020060020301

Liu, J. (2010). Teachers' code-switching to the L1 in EFL classroom. *The Open Applied Linguistics Journal*, *3*, 10–23. https://doi.org/10.2174/1874913501003010010

Matsuura, H. (2007). Intelligibility and individual learner differences in the EIL context. *System*, *35*, 293–304. https://doi.org/10.1016/j.system.2007.03.003

Sakaria, S., & Priyana, J. (2018). Code-switching: A pedagogical strategy in bilingual classrooms. *American Journal of Educational Research*, *6*(3), 175–180. https://doi.org/10.12691/education-6-3-3

Setter, J., Wong, C., & Chan, B. (2010). *Hong Kong English*. Edinburgh University Press.

Sewell, A. (2012). The Hong Kong English accent: Variation and acceptability. *Hong Kong Journal of Applied Linguistics*, *13*(2), 1–21.

Skiba, R. (1997). Code switching as a countenance of language interference. *The Internet TESL Journal*, *10*(3), 1–6.

Sung, C. C. M. (2010). Being a "purist" in Hong Kong: To use or not to use mixed code. *Changing English*, *17*(4), 411–419. https://doi.org/10.1080/1358684X.2010.528875

Wang, L., & Kirkpatrick, A. (2019). *Trilingual education in Hong Kong primary schools*. Springer. https://doi.org/10.1007/978-3-030-11081-9

Chapter 15

Translanguaging in University Direct-Entry Pathway English Courses
An Australian Case

Michelle Ocriciano

Introduction

As higher education around the world experiences a boom in internationalisation (Teichler, 2017), countries where English is the primary language have experienced a dramatic increase in the numbers of international students. English has often become the official medium of instruction at universities throughout the world. With that, university direct-entry pathway courses have gained greater importance and status. The vast number of countries focused on international education justifies a broader interest in university direct-entry pathway English courses, and the frameworks used in their design.

Despite the growing focus on internationalisation in higher education and the language diversity it brings, pathway English language programs remain deeply rooted in purist language ideologies (Lin, 2013). Pervasive monolingual ideologies are present in educational settings since there is still an ingrained belief that monolingualism in a society, and subsequently universities, is the only valid possibility (Gogolin, 1997). Furthermore, monolingual ideologies are detrimental not only to international students but also to those speaking heritage and Indigenous languages at home (Tupas, 2015).

As a linguist, migrant, and someone whose English is a second language, I became increasingly uncomfortable each time I had to teach a heavily prescribed and monoglossic curriculum. Whereas I was, unfortunately, unable to make changes in the curriculum itself, I had freedom to transform my delivery. In this chapter, I describe how I have approached and reinterpreted such curriculum in a direct-entry university pathway so that it would both allow my students' voices to be heard and encourage the use of their full repertoires

The contemporary debate surrounding social justice focuses on disadvantages and discrimination based on gender, race, religion, sexual orientation, and ethnicity; it is rare that language is considered a factor by which individuals, communities, or nations can be excluded (Piller, 2016). However, it cannot be denied that "linguistic racism is present on Australian university campuses because while some students experience linguistic invisibility others experience linguistic privilege" (Dobinson & Mercieca, 2020, p. 789). Therefore, it is urgent to recognize institutional disadvantages and discrimination based on language. Such discrimination was defined over 30 years ago as "ideologies and structures which are used to legitimate, effectuate, and reproduce unequal divisions of power and resources (both material

DOI: 10.4324/9781003124665-18

and non-material) between groups which are defined on the basis of language" (Skutnabb-Kangas, 1989, p. 41). And yet, such discrimination is easily recognized in pathway English language courses such as when teachers require students to use only English, or when students receive a "red card" for speaking their first language in school premises. These actions and acts of discrimination are disguised in the discourse of intelligibility and readability. They validate, reproduce, authorize, and reinforce imperialist and monolingual views of language, which only emphasize the relationship of domination and exploitation (Young, 2011).

Translanguaging offers a theoretical and pedagogical lens to address these sociolinguistic issues as it legitimizes the voices of students who would otherwise be silenced during the teaching/learning process. Translanguaging can be defined as "multiple discursive practices in which bilinguals engage in order to make sense of their bilingual worlds" (García, 2009, p. 45). Therefore, it promotes and enforces the use of students' full multimodal repertoire as they draw on all their semiotic resources to communicate and make meaning, thus shifting students as recipients of knowledge to active co-authors of the teaching and learning process.

Translanguaging supports language learning and teaching without a deficit lens. As a result, students can smoothly slip in and out of either L1 (first language) or L2 (second language) as best suits their needs. A translingual approach also understands that bilinguals are not, and do not function as, two monolinguals in one (Grosjean, 1982). In addition, translanguaging moves beyond the shift of language to the discursive practices developed over time for and by an individual, such as moving from topic to topic while interacting.

Although monolingual bias continues to dominate TESOL by privileging linguistic purism and the idealization of the native speaker (Ortega, 2014), translanguaging boldly challenges these assumptions (Vogel & García, 2017), as well as colonial and structuralist ideologies of language standardization (Makoni & Pennycook, 2006). Therefore, in university pathway English language courses, academic English should be understood as an ideologic and socio-political construct which maintains the hegemony, power, and interest of privileged groups.

Envisioning TESOL through a translanguaging lens (Tian, 2020) also challenges the usual focus on the four skills (speaking, listening, reading, and writing) and leads to the discovery of language as a social semiotic system (Halliday, 2014). The diversity of modes of communication—linguistic codes, visuals, sounds, and gestures—are socially and historically constructed. Therefore, teaching must go beyond instruction in technical skills; it also needs to consider the metaknowledge necessary to understand different media and their functions.

Multimodality questions if it is impossible to interpret texts paying attention only to the written language, since a multimodal text must be read in conjunction with all other semiotic modes of that text (Kress & van Leeuwen, 2001). Towards this reconceptualization, from traditional skills to a multimodal framework, we can begin by looking at "classrooms as semiotic spaces in which human beings who are the agents of their own meaning making produce multimodal texts" (Stein, 2000, p. 333). In this sense, systematizing the multimodal work can be a way to critically approach different linguistic modalities used in the online environment.

As students in direct-entry pathway English programs are constantly faced with pervasive monolingual ideologies and are steadily under pressure to achieve the required results, it is important to be empathic and invest in student-teacher relationships. Empathy is a concept with an increasing number of constructs and definitions, but my praxis is informed by Segal (2011), who defines it "as the ability to more deeply understand people by perceiving or experiencing their life situations and as a result gain insight into structural inequalities and disparities" (p. 266).

As neoliberalism becomes increasingly present in education (Ball, 2016; Giroux, 2003), and education becomes consistently focused on "evidence" or the "what works" movement (Biesta, 2009), it is appropriate to revisit Freire's educational framework (1998): teaching is a political activity, and teachers can affect policies and create change. Neoliberal practices and ideologies reinforce the *status quo* and discourage critical inquiries into the tensions of education. I have been led to question this status quo, due to ongoing reflection on my praxis, particularly regarding the monoglossic views of the direct-entry program curriculum. Inspired by Freire's suggestion that teachers have "consciously taken the option to intervene in the world" (p. 122), I have transformed my classes into a vehicle of social change as I believe that translanguaging has the power to "transform relationships between students, teachers and the curriculum" (Vogel & García, 2017, p. 9).

Educational Setting/Context

University direct-entry pathway English courses provide pre-entry academic and language preparation, and language assessment for university admissions purposes to non-English speaking background international students (NESB). As part of the admission process, all NESB students must provide the results of an English language proficiency exam such as the Test of English as a Foreign Language (TOEFL), and the International English Language Testing System (IELTS). If the results are below the requirements, students will receive a conditional offer to their desired course, meaning they must enrol in the pathway English language program and meet minimum assessment results. Depending on a student's English language proficiency exam score, they will join modular pathway courses, which usually run for up to 30 weeks in blocks of 5 to 10 weeks.

The students described in this chapter were part of a five-week, direct-entry pathway course in an Australian university. Each class had 18 students, and the vast majority were from mainland China, a few from Saudi Arabia, Japan, and Thailand. They were between 17 and 26 years old, and B2 according to the *Common European Framework of Reference for Languages*. Since the most popular exam is the IELTS, the direct-entry pathway English language course is designed in such a way that by the course's conclusion, students have similar language skills as those described in the IELTS band descriptors. The interventions I used with these students had the following objectives:

- to bring social justice by using translanguaging as both a theoretical and pedagogical construct (Tian, 2020);
- to offer students scaffolded preparation for the type of multimodal learning they will face in the Australian higher education system;
- to inform my praxis with social empathy as a way to more deeply understand students in an attempt to gain insight into inequalities and disparities.

The First Lesson: Let's Get to Know Each Other and Uncover the Hidden Repertoire

It is common during the first class of any course to use *getting to know each other* activities. The focus on designing this activity was to connect with students, so it was important to use a topic that most students would feel like discussing, which is why I chose food.

On the first day of class, as students talked about their favourite dishes, I opened Google Translate, and asked them to go to the computer and dictate the dishes in their L1 so we could see the translation to English. We then discussed the accuracy of English translations, and students suggested better translations. We continued the activity by also looking for an image that was close to the authentic dishes they described. By talking about food in the first class, students normalized the use of their home languages, the use of technologies for translation, and the use of multimodality.

As students continued to share stories about their favourite food, we also learned about each other's backgrounds. Most students were from China, so they shared the names of their provinces and all the languages they speak. I printed and laminated the flags of each country, state, or province so we could build a classroom board that says, "*In this classroom, we proudly speak [name of language]*."

Many pathway courses require a discussion of the course structure and the academic skills expected from students in the first class. Part of the expected behaviour in many programs is that students do not speak their home languages during English classes and, at times, not even in the university corridors. However, it is common to see them whispering and hiding their faces when trying to use their home language. During the first day, as we reviewed the course structure and expectations, I showed them statements about learning in general, and we discussed typical students' beliefs, such as "writing word lists is an efficient technique" and "rewriting essays is unnecessary." The last part of this discussion started with "in the English class we should only use English," which led them to analyse their beliefs about English-only policies. I concluded the activity by assuring them that the use of their first language was not only permitted but also encouraged.

Towards the end of the lesson, we listed famous people who speak English as an additional language and started building a bank of successful examples of NESB speakers. The ongoing homework task was to collect published interviews of these people and add them to the NESB bank.

Throughout the lesson, I tried to set the tone for an inclusive culture, focusing on deconstructing the myths of the superiority of the English language and of those who speak it as a first language.

Multimodal Weekly Online Platform

To address the gap between an exam-centred curriculum and the academic skills required in Australian universities, I also developed a weekly online platform framed around translanguaging and multimodality. As a response to students' requests for writing prompts, I used backwards design (Richards, 2013) and placed the weekly essay question at the centre of the lesson. From there, I looked for keywords related to the topic in the coursebook and added others that students might need. The list was then converted to be used in an online flashcard tool such as Quizlet. This type of resource can be efficient to assist students with spaced repetition and memorization.

The next step was to curate resources that supported students' knowledge of the essay topic. I often choose 2–3 reading passages (The Conversation[1] is particularly good as it is short and approachable) and 2–3 audio/video examples such as TED-Talks. Providing resources with a range of viewpoints and representing a variety of Englishes assisted students through navigating the waters of critical reading.

The resources were then shared using Padlet—a virtual wall where users can add links, videos, files, and images, organizing them in a variety of ways. A useful feature of this tool is that students can rate the resources with stars—which has helped me reflect on my praxis and adapt resources to better assist students.

In order to expose students to different varieties of English so they would feel more comfortable with and aware of connected speech, I used TubeQuizard,[2] an online application that uses YouTube videos with subtitles to automatically create quizzes. There are many choices; however, I usually chose the quizzes under the *pronunciation for listening* category as it deals with linking and disappearing sounds, which often hinder understanding.

With all resources ready, I used Padlet to create ten columns with headings and placed the corresponding pre-selected resources under each heading: Essay question, Vocabulary, Reading 1, Reading 2, Reading 3, Listening 1, Listening 2, Listening 3, and Suggestions from Students. The last column allowed students to contribute their own suggestions of resources in any language they please.

Putting It All Together

Once Padlet is ready, the activity is rather simple, with most of the interaction between students happening online. In the first step, students need to read and watch all the resources and choose one where they leave a comment in their *home language*. The comment can be a reply explaining how they feel about the topic, a comparison using their home country, their general understanding of the resource, a summary, or anything else relevant for the group.

The second comment is written in English and is a reply to another student's original comment written in a language other than English. In case students do not share the same language, they can use electronic translators such as Google Translate to understand the content. The final step is the classroom procedures found as a lesson plan at the end of this chapter.

Embracing the use of students' first language in the English class can be daunting. Particularly in multilingual contexts, it is unrealistic to imagine that teachers will have some knowledge of all the languages being used. To assist in this challenge, teachers need to build a trusting environment from the first class, explaining the reasons for the unusual use of L1 in the classroom. In addition, embracing a multilingual classroom can put the teacher in a vulnerable position. Instructors

---

1 The Conversation Media Group Ltd. (2021). https://theconversation.com/
2 TubeQuizard. (2021). http://tubequizard.com/

can use this vulnerability to show students their curiosity about their students' language. Teachers can also focus on tone, intonation, and body language as students speak languages other than English, as these features carry much information. Technology, in the form of electronic translators, can also play a key role in class preparation and teaching in general. Even if the translation is inaccurate, the instructor can take advantage and use the inaccuracy as a teaching tool by asking for clarification and reasons. This can be a great opportunity to learn about and teach language awareness, metalanguage, and register.

Lesson Plan: Multimodal Flipped Writing Class

Recommended Level(s)
Young adults and adults B2 and above

Context
The lesson is aimed at tertiary students in direct-entry pathway English language courses but can be used in a variety of contexts and levels with minor adaptations. This lesson is particularly suitable for those who use theme-based lessons. This lesson is the last step of the procedure indicated in the multimodal weekly online platform. It revolves around a writing task that will take place at the end of a week/theme. In this blended/flipped lesson, students will have previously worked with multimodal resources to learn about the essay topic. The lesson consists of an error-correction activity, followed by essay planning and writing, and concludes with students reading, analysing, and discussing each other's essays.

Objectives
Before class, students will be able to:

- recognize and engage with authentic resources presenting a variety of Englishes;
- experience and practice interactions in online forums;
- interact with other students outside classroom hours;
- analyse and differentiate forms of connected speech;
- collect and compare information from a variety of sources.

During class, students will be able to:

- explore and practice their voices as writers;
- examine and propose corrections to mistaken sentences;
- read, analyse, and discuss each other's essays.

Procedures

Preparation

After students have engaged with the resources in Padlet throughout the week and before the last class of the week, the teacher reads all comments from Padlet and selects language items that require corrections.

- Copy the language items to a document and divide the number of sentences by the number of groups you would like to have.
- Print each different document as big as possible.
- Copy all sentences from the original document to slides as it is often easier for students to see.

Step 1: Sentence Correction (30 Minutes)

Teacher hands out one set of sentences to each group. Students work together to find and correct mistakes. Encourage the use of any language while discussing the sentences. Students go to the board/computer and share their corrections. Teacher monitors and confirms corrections and/or proposes new ones.

Step 2: Essay Planning (30 Minutes)

After the correction activity, students use their notes related to resources in Padlet and work in small groups to plan the essay. Each group shares their suggestions, and students can add to their original notes. Remind students that note-taking can be done in the language that they feel most comfortable and that mixing languages is also allowed.

Step 3: Essay Writing (65 Minutes)

Before students write the essay, remind them to write the words they do not know in their home language and come back to them only after they have finished writing the whole essay. If time allows, they can look up the words and add the word in English, or this can be done during teacher-student feedback later. Students then write their essays individually.

Step 4: Essay Sharing and Feedback (Can be Used as Extension Activities)

Students exchange their essays and read, analyse, and discuss each other's essays. Students receive their essays back and make any changes they wish. Finally, the teacher collects the essays and concludes by requesting comments about the writing process.

References

Ball, S. J. (2016). Neoliberal education? Confronting the slouching beast. *Policy Futures in Education*, *14*(8), 1046–1059. https://doi.org/10.1177/1478210316664259

Biesta, G. (2009). Good education in an age of measurement: On the need to reconnect with the question of purpose in education. *Educational Assessment, Evaluation and Accountability (Formerly: Journal of Personnel Evaluation in Education)*, *21*(1), 33–46. https://doi.org/10.1007/s11092-008-9064-9

The Conversation Media Group Ltd. (2021). *The Conversation*. https://theconversation.com/au

Dobinson, T., & Mercieca, P. (2020). Seeing things as they are, not just as we are: Investigating linguistic racism on an Australian university campus. *International Journal of Bilingual Education and Bilingualism*, *23*(7), 789–803. https://doi.org/10.1080/13670050.2020.1724074

Freire, P. (1998). Pedagogy of freedom: Ethics, democracy and civic courage. Rowman & Littlefield Publishers.

García, O. (2009). *Bilingual education in the 21st century: A global perspective*. Wiley, Blackwell.

Giroux, H. (2003). Utopian thinking under the sign of neoliberalism: Towards a critical pedagogy of educated hope. *Democracy & Nature*, *9*(1), 91–105. https://doi.org/10.1080/1085566032000074968

Gogolin, I. (1997). 'The "monolingual habitus" as the common feature in teaching in the language of the majority in different countries. *Per Linguam: A Journal of Language Learning*, *13*(2). https://doi.org/10.5785/13-2-187

Grosjean, F. (1982). *Life with two languages: An introduction to bilingualism*. Harvard University Press. https://doi.org/10.2307/2545800

Halliday, M. A. K. (2014). Language as social semiotic. In *The discourse studies reader* (pp. 263–272). John Benjamins. https://doi.org/10.1075/z.184.52hal

Kress, G., & Van Leeuwen, T. (2001). Multimodal discourse. In *The modes and media of contemporary communication*. Arnold Publishers. https://doi.org/10.1017/S0047404504221054

Lin, A. (2013). Toward paradigmatic change in TESOL methodologies: Building plurilingual pedagogies from the ground up. *TESOL Quarterly*, *47*(3), 521–545. https://doi.org/10.1002/tesq.113

Makoni, S., & Pennycook, A. (2006). *Disinventing and reconstituting languages* (Chapter 1, pp. 1–41). Multilingual Matters. https://doi.org/10.21832/9781853599255-003

Ortega, L. (2014). *Understanding second language acquisition*. Routledge. https://doi.org/10.4324/9780203777282

Piller, I. (2016). *Linguistic diversity and social justice: An introduction to applied sociolinguistics*. Oxford University Press. https://doi.org/10.1093/acprof:oso/9780199937240.001.0001

Richards, J. C. (2013). Curriculum approaches in language teaching: Forward, central, and backward design. *RELC Journal*, *44*(1), 5–33. https://doi.org/10.1177/0033688212473293

Segal, E. A. (2011). Social empathy: A model built on empathy, contextual understanding, and social responsibility that promotes social justice. *Journal of Social Service Research*, *37*(3), 266–277. https://doi.org/10.1080/01488376.2011.564040

Skutnabb-Kangas, T. (1989). Multilingualism and the education of minority children. *Estudios Fronterizos*, 18–19, 36–67. https://doi.org/10.21670/ref.1989.18-19.a02

Stein, P. (2000). Rethinking resources in the ESL classroom: Rethinking resources: Multimodal pedagogies in the ESL classroom. *TESOL Quarterly*, *34*(2), 333–336. https://doi.org/10.2307/3587958

Teichler, U. (2017). Internationalisation trends in higher education and the changing role of international student mobility. *Journal of international Mobility*, 5(1), 177–216. https://doi.org/10.3917/jim.005.0179

Tian, Z. (2020). *Envisioning TESOL through a translanguaging lens: Global perspectives*. Springer Nature. https://doi.org/10.1007/978-3-030-47031-9

TubeQuizard. (2021). *TubeQuizard*. http://tubequizard.com/

Tupas, R. (2015). Inequalities of multilingualism: Challenges to mother tongue-based multilingual education. *Language and Education*, 29(2), 112–124. https://doi.org/10.1080/09500782.2014.977295

Vogel, S., & García, O. (2017). *Translanguaging*. Oxford Research Encyclopedia of Education. https://doi.org/10.1093/acrefore/9780190264093.013.181

Young, I. M. (2011). *Justice and the politics of difference*. Princeton University Press. https://doi.org/10.2307/j.ctvcm4g4q

Chapter 16

Global Englishes and Oral Communication

Perceptions of Multilingual Speakers

Nasiba Norova

My English as a second language (ESL) teaching practice started as an international student at a Midwestern university, where I was completing a master's degree in TESL. At the time, I was aware of British English and American Englishes only. However, this university exposed me to different Englishes, which made me reflect on my teaching philosophy. I would wonder why students coming from African and Asian countries, where English is spoken as an official or second language, were placed in remedial EAP (English for Academic Purposes) 125: Introduction to Oral Communication class, a class I taught. Those students were fluent in English, spoke varieties of Englishes, and there was almost nothing to teach them in terms of English vocabulary and fluency. The students also questioned why they needed to take the class when they were already fluent. However, they also admitted that their international and domestic friends would ask them to speak clearly, slowly, and in "American English," stating that their Englishes "are not intelligible enough." I also witnessed this in my class when speakers of Global Englishes (GE) were asked to slow down and make their speech more intelligible.

The inquiry regarding perceptions towards different Englishes started from my personal interest, which later turned into my capstone project. While teaching Introduction to Oral Communication for the second semester, I incorporated a GE Unit in my syllabus in response to three values and needs found during my first-year practice: (1) a need to value learners' English (Farrell & Martin, 2009), (2) a need to prepare global citizens (Matsuda, 2003), and (3) a need for comity (to foster solidarity and understanding among GE speakers) (McKay, 2002). This action research study attempted to create space for acknowledging my students' language abilities, to assist in building their confidence in their Englishes, and to prepare them as global citizens who are aware of English varieties, thus fostering solidarity and understanding among them.

Global Englishes

Today, the English language is one of the most used global languages for communication. In many developed countries, English is a native or official second language, while in developing countries it is a foreign language used in many international organizations as a "work" language (Galloway, 2017). The globalization of English is related to the current economic power and global role of English-speaking countries as well as their historically shaped foreign policies. According to Galloway and

Rose (2015), there are four channels through which English spread widely across the globe.

Channel one is through the policy of colonization, in which emigrants from the UK spread English to colonized communities such as the current United States, New Zealand, Canada, and Australia. Channel two is through slavery and the imposition of English into Indigenous populations of African countries. Channel three was opened through the exploitation of colonies, imposing English for communication purposes in countries such as Nigeria, Singapore, India, and Hong Kong. Channel four occurred through globalization, which boosted the global prestige of the English language due to the economic and political power of English-speaking economies such as the United States, the United Kingdom, and Canada. *Global Englishes* is an umbrella term that unites research interests and scopes of the fields such as World Englishes, English as lingua franca, and English as an international language (Canagarajah, 2013; Galloway, 2017; Rose & Galloway, 2019).

The sociolinguistic reality of English shows that it can no longer uphold its monolithic legacy. In fact, the term *Global Englishes* itself depicts the language's reality and describes the complex nature of English in multiple varieties, which can be explained through "sociolinguistically and socioculturally diverse" (Canagarajah, 2013; Pennycook, 2007) and "fluid" attributes (Rose & Galloway, 2019).

English Language Perceptions

Although GEs play a major role in the globalization of English, perceptions towards them vary and manifest through emotions, behavior, facial expressions, or verbal statements (Galloway, 2017). Perceptions can also reveal a person's beliefs and dogma. Attitudes that emerge from these perceptions often reveal language preferences and motivations for learning and teaching language, and these attitudes impact how people view speakers of those languages and varieties. Studies show Englishes spoken in "English speaking countries" (i.e., as a native variety) are perceived as positive and favorable, with preference mostly given to American English and Received Pronunciation (Butler, 2007; Galloway, 2017). Matsuda (2003) also found that Japanese students have a positive attitude toward *native varieties* of Englishes and express a desire to sound like them, demonstrating *native speakerism* ideology. Other studies also yielded similar "preferism"' towards American or British Englishes (Ladegard & Sachdev, 2006), familiarity (Zhang & Hu, 2008), and high prestige degree (Rindal, 2010). However, research shows that other global varieties of Englishes are perceived as socially unattractive (Rezaei et al., 2019) or having less status and solidarity (Chan, 2016). They are also described as *broken* or *deficient* and even *uneducated* (Canagarajah, 2013) and can be perceived negatively (Jenkins, 2015).

The major reason for the biased and/or negative stereotypical perceptions towards Global Englishes and their speakers is lack of awareness and exposure to them in academic settings (Kachru, 2011). Moreover, the dominance of *native speakerism* and *standard English* (SE) ideologies also prevents GEs from being "preferred" varieties. Therefore, in order to eliminate such ills and contest these views, there is a need for both including GEs concepts in the framework of English language teaching and also exposing students to Global Englishes (Evans, 2010; Galloway, 2013, 2017; Godley & Reaser, 2018; Kirkpatrick et al., 2016; Kubota, 2001; Nelson, 2011; Matsuda, 2003; Rose & Galloway, 2019; Timmis, 2002; Wang & Jenkins, 2016).

As Yamuna Kachru (2011) asserts,

> Learning and teaching of world Englishes *do not mean learning and teaching of each regional variety* [emphasis added] to everyone in the Inner Circle classrooms or everyone learning English in Brazil, China, Japan, Saudi Arabia, or Southern Africa. It means *making learners aware of the rich variation that exists* [emphasis added] in English around the world at an appropriate point in their language education in all three Circles and of giving them the tools to educate themselves further about using their English for effective communication across varieties.
>
> (p. 167)

Therefore, by including podcasts from a variety of Global Englishes perspectives into my EAP 125 course curriculum, I embraced a call for contributing to my students' awareness of existing Englishes. I also attempted to identify my students' perceptions towards different Global Englishes. With this purpose in mind, I explored the following research questions: "How do multilingual speakers perceive the use of GE discourse in an EAP oracy course? How might these perceptions inform L2 oracy pedagogy?" The following sections describe the action research I conducted to answer these questions.

Participants

Research on my EAP 125 course was conducted during the spring semester of 2017—my second time teaching the course. Enrolled were 13 international students from India, Ivory Coast, Kenya, Kuwait, Nepal, Nigeria, Pakistan, Panama, and Vietnam. Apart from English, they spoke eight different languages and represented nine different majors. Their ages ranged from 18 to 20 and all of them were taking the class in their first year of college.

Data and Data Collection

During the GE Unit, which lasted six classes, the students viewed six GE podcasts, representing African American Vernacular English, British English, Korean English, Jamaican English, Nepali English, and Nigerian English. Before the podcasts, students responded to a prompt: "*Do you use different variations of a language (i.e., English or any of your other languages)? If so, how do the different variations relate to your identity? If not, why do you think this is the case?*" After viewing the podcasts, students wrote another essay: "*After viewing and listening to six Global Englishes videos/podcasts, what is your understanding of language variation? What role does language variation play in speaking? In what ways has your study of language variation impacted your speaking and listening skills?*" After each podcast, the students also responded orally to three questions:

(1) Is the video/podcast representative of good English? Why or why not?
(2) Is the video/podcast representative of a strong speech?
(3) How does the language variety used add to/detract from the speaker's presentation?

The recorded responses were transcribed, and all data were coded with the help of MAXQDA 2018 qualitative data analysis software. Recursive content analysis was carried out to identify the perceptions of students towards the six Global Englishes used in the podcasts.

Continuum of Development

After listening to the podcasts, students generated responses to the questionnaire, revealing insights into resistance, awareness, experience, and empowerment.

Resistance

Multilingual students resisted listening to Global Englishes podcasts, finding them unintelligible: they seemed different from their way of speaking as well as different from a standardized variety of English. According to their responses, this was caused by pronunciation and grammar. Student 7 stated,

> In this video is not a representative of a good English because of incorrect pronunciation unorganized grammar structure completely terrible accent seriously difficult to catch up and understand.

Student 5 also found the accent distracting because it was different from their own:

> She is distracting because my accent is totally different from her accent or the way of talking is my mine totally from her so, thus is she is totally distracting me.

Student 2 resisted the English spoken in Nigeria because it differs from the one spoken in Britain:

> For me good English is Britain English and Nigerian accent, or English is really different from the British one.

Awareness

Even though some of the Englishes were challenging to students, some students expressed variation recognition. It became evident that Student 6 was aware of the Jamaican English that was assigned. The student wrote,

> The English she spoke is from Jamaican-Patois. It is a mix of French, Creole, and English. It detracts from the speaker's presentation because I am not able to understand most of her speech.

Evidently, the student possesses some information about this particular variation as they include some factual information about it. Some students also showed their awareness of traits that belong to their own linguistic repertoire. Student 10 wrote that they recognized the variety spoken in the podcasts because this is the language they speak:

> I heard everything she said clearly including the broken English because broken English is spoken in my country and I also speak broken English when I am around people that understand.

Experience

It became evident that some students already had experience listening to and speaking with speakers of different English varieties, which should be obvious since they themselves are speakers of English varieties. For instance, Student 1 expressed their familiarity with African American Vernacular English (AAVE) because of their social milieu:

> I am familiar with the way she speak because I used to talk most of the time to black American, to some friend; this is why I am comfortable with the way she speak.

Student 4 also wrote that s/he is a speaker of certain variety:

> . . . this is kind of English that I used to listen to and yeah am used to it because that the English that learn is British English we used to speak that kind of English like /ˈlet.ə/ /ˈmʌð.ə/.

Empowerment

While judging if the English spoken in the podcasts is good or bad, the students also voiced how empowered they grew because they understood the core function of language—a means of communication and a means to express one's identity (Cummins, 2001). Specifically, Student 3 wrote that Nigerian English, which s/he refers to as "broken English," is the language that reflects her/his identity. The student stated,

> For the broken English, I feel vert relax when I speak it because of course it is broken, and it does not required enough. Also, it reflects my personality because I like "Naija music" which is made of broken English.

Another student wrote that

> This [Global Englishes podcast] helps me to know that the most important is not to speak like American people do, but to speak so that you can be understandable and convincing. The most important is to succeed in sending the message that you have to give.

Last but not least, listening to different English varieties during the class increased the students' knowledge of English varieties.

Student 6 related the following:

> Honestly, [listening to Global Englishes] had a tremendous impact on my language skills. As I am an international student, I have a lot of international friends as well. I wondered myself why was so complicated to understand students from Ivory Coast, and Nigeria. I understood that after colonization and the oppression of British, they acquired that broken language; their language was stolen, and that is why their variation is different than mine.

Significance

It is important to consider resistance, awareness, experience, and empowerment—the attitudes of students towards Global Englishes—because reflecting on their attitudes can help create and adopt better educational and pedagogic policies in classrooms. Moreover, this study is significant because it exposed me to my students' perceptions of GEs in the classroom, but it also exposed them to the value of language. As one of the students mentioned, it is not important if one speaks in American English or any other variety—what is important is being able to send the message, to keep the communication, to make it convincing. The GE unit was intended to foster solidarity among different multilinguals who were speakers of Englishes. With this study, I endeavored to show that all varieties are valuable, including the Englishes spoken in students' home countries. I hope that valuing my students' Englishes gives them confidence and empowers them.

Conclusion

Although this action research involved overt exposure to GEs and lasted only six class meetings, the students enrolled in the EAP 125 course were able to easily discuss their attitudes towards English language varieties. They perceived GEs as challenging and unintelligible; hence, they resisted. Despite this, all the students' responses showed that they were in a continuum of development, where they expressed awareness, experience, and empowerment. Incorporating GEs does not involve total transformation of syllabi and curriculum, but it prevents perceiving English as a monolithic entity and shows a different perspective on the English language. My lesson plan later demonstrates how GE content can support EAP course goals. It encourages students to study and consider pluralistic, inclusive, and ever-evolving angles of Englishes (Matsuda, 2003), avoiding inaccurate understanding of status quo English communication. It may also help prevent negative attitudes towards other varieties of Englishes (Matsuda, 2018). In today's global economy, the ability to speak English proficiently is a form of linguistic, cultural, and economic capital (Bourdieu, 1986; Pennycook, 2017); however, students need to be empowered by all Global Englishes and use them as their advantageous capital in the global world.

Lesson Plan: Language Varieties and Linguicism—Empowering Ourselves

Recommended Grade Level(s)

The lesson plan is recommended for high school students and students in undergraduate first-year English skills courses.

Context

The lesson plan can be placed along with such units as Culture and Language, Language and Identity, Language and Power. No scaffolding is necessary before this lesson.

Objectives

Students will be able to:

- distinguish Standard American English (SAE) and African American Vernacular English (AAVE);
- explain *linguicism* (discriminatory treatment based on the use of less prestigious language; linguistic racism) and reasons behind it;
- develop strategies to empower speakers of different Englishes.

Procedures

Step 1: Warm-Up Discussion (5–10 Minutes)

Please See Support Material for a PowerPoint with Handouts for Each Step Found in This Lesson

Students answer discussion questions related to language varieties:

(1) What language do you speak at home, at school with your family, friends, teachers?
(2) Do you change your language depending on social circumstances? If so, why?

Students can share their own experiences with standardized and other vernacular varieties of languages they know. The warm-up also serves to activate their schematic knowledge on language use.

Step 2: Pre-Listening Activity (5–10 Minutes)

Step 1 leads them to the concept of *linguistic discrimination*:

(1) What can you tell about people by their speech?
(2) Can you identify people's socioeconomic status, race, ethnicity, and nationality by their speech?

Discuss. After this, the instructor introduces *linguicism* and provides the definition.

Step 3: Clip Listening (2 Minutes)

The instructor presents a table with open-ended demographic information questionnaire (see Support Material). The students will first listen to a clip from the movie *Sorry to Bother You* (no visual) and will complete the questionnaire in order to construct the speakers' linguistic profiles. After that, students share and compare their responses with their groupmates.

Step 4: Clip Viewing (2 Minutes)

After students share their questionnaire responses, the instructor shows the video clip, scenes included, for students to verify the speakers' linguistic profiles.

Step 5: Working with a Transcript (15 Minutes)

Students work with transcripts (see Support Material). The instructor shows the scene image and relevant dialogue.

While working with the transcript, students make sure to differentiate between standard English and AAVE. The dialogue between the two speakers also mentions *white voice*, which in this example indicates SAE. Standard English is stereotypically (and mistakenly) associated with eloquence, education, intelligence, and elite class. So, here, "white voice" indexes not only "race" but also other social identities and meanings.

Step 6: Critical Thinking Questions (30 Minutes)

Students work in pairs. The first strategy is to *Define the problem* (see Support Material). The instructor guides students to identify the primary problem: linguistic racism. Instructors can further explain it as a type of discrimination against people who speak English varieties other than SAE, discussing examples such as linguistic profiling during job applications or linguistic discrimination in the workplace.

Then students move to the second strategy, *Identify available solutions*. Students work in pairs to solve the problem. At this stage, students critically consider why the problem mentioned in the movie scene is problematic, why it needs to be resolved, how they might solve it.

The last critical thinking strategy is *Select your solution*. Students share their solutions with the group and the best solution to combat linguicism will be chosen.

Students then discuss linguicism in light of Title VII of the Civil Rights Act, which prohibits certain forms of discrimination.

Homework: I Care Why?

Students explain the relevancy of the linguistic discrimination to their life and write a journal entry and analyze bell hooks' (2015) quote,

> By transforming the oppressor's language [SE], making a culture of resistance, black people created an intimate speech that could say far more than was permissible within the boundaries of standard English. The power of this speech is not simply that it enables resistance

to **white supremacy,** but that it also forges a space for alternative cultural production and alternative epistemologies—different ways of thinking and knowing that were crucial to creating a counter-hegemonic worldview. **That power resides in the capacity of black vernacular to intervene on the boundaries and limitations of standard English** [bolded mine].

(pp. 224–225)

References

Bourdieu, P. (1986). The forms of capital. In J. G. Richardson (Ed.), *Handbook of theory and research for the sociology of education* (pp. 241–258). Greenwood.

Butler, Y. (2007). How are nonnative-English-speaking teachers perceived by young learners? *TESOL Quarterly, 41*(4), 731–755.

Canagarajah, S. (2013). *Translingual practice: Global Englishes and cosmopolitan relations*. Routledge.

Chan, J. (2016). A multi-perspective investigation of attitudes towards English accents in Hong Kong: Implications for pronunciation teaching. *TESOL Quarterly, 50*(2), 285–313. https://doi.org/10.1002/tesq.218

Cummins, J. (2001). *Negotiating identities: Education for empowerment in a diverse society* (2nd ed.). California Association for Bilingual Education.

Evans, B. (2010). Chinese perceptions of inner circle varieties of English. *World Englishes, 29*(2), 270–280. https://doi.org/10.1111/j.1467-971X.2010.01642.x

Farrell, T. S., & Martin, S. (2009). To teach standard English or world Englishes? A balanced approach to instruction. *English Teaching Forum, 47*(2), 2–7.

Galloway, N. (2013). Global Englishes and English language teaching (ELT) bridging the gap between theory and practice in a Japanese context. *System, 41*(3), 786–803. https://doi.org/10.1016/j.system.2013.07.019

Galloway, N. (2017). *Global Englishes and change in English language teaching: Attitudes and impact*. Routledge.

Galloway, N., & Rose, H. (2015). *Introducing global Englishes*. Routledge.

Godley, A., & Reaser, J. (2018). *Critical language pedagogy: Interrogating language, dialects, and power in teacher education*. Peter Lang.

Hooks, B. (2015). *Yearning. Race, gender, and cultural politics*. Routledge.

Jenkins, J. (2015). *Global Englishes: A resource book for students*. Routledge.

Kachru, Y. (2011). World Englishes, contexts, and relevance for language education. In E. Hinkel (Ed.), *Handbook of research in second language learning and teaching* (pp. 155–171). Routledge.

Kirkpatrick, A., Walkinshaw, I., & Subhan, S. (2016). English as a lingua franca in East and Southeast Asia: Implications for diplomatic and intercultural communication. In P. Friedrich (Ed.), *English for diplomatic purposes* (pp. 75–93). Multilingual Matters.

Kubota, R. (2001). Teaching world Englishes to native speakers of English in the USA. *World Englishes, 20*(1), 47–64. https://doi.org/10.1111/1467-971X.00195

Ladegard, H., & Sachdev, I. (2006). "I like the Americans . . . But I certainly don't aim for an American accent": Language attitudes, vitality, and foreign language learning in Denmark. *Journal of Multilingual and Multicultural Development, 27*(2), 91–108. https://doi.org/10.1080/01434630608668542

Matsuda, A. (2003). The ownership of English in Japanese secondary schools. *World Englishes, 22*(4), 483–496. https://doi.org/10.1111/j.1467-971X.2003.00314.x

Matsuda, A. (2018). Is teaching English as an international language all about being politically correct? *RELC Journal, 49*(1), 24–35. https://doi.org/10.1177/0033688217753489

McKay, S. L. (2002). *Teaching English as an international language*. Oxford University Press.

Nelson, C. (2011). *Intelligibility in world Englishes*. Routledge.

Pennycook, A. (2007). *Global Englishes and transcultural flows*. Routledge.

Pennycook, A. (2017). *The cultural politics of English as an international language*. Routledge Linguistics Classics.

Rezaei, S., Khosravizadeh, P., & Mottaghi, Z. (2019). Attitudes toward world Englishes among Iranian English language learners. *Asian Englishes, 21*(1), 52–69. https://doi.org/10.1080/13488678.2018.1440367

Rindal, U. (2010). Constructing identity with L2: Pronunciation and attitudes among Norwegian learners of English. *Journal of Sociolinguistics*, *14*(2), 240–261. https://doi.org/10.1111/j.1467-9841.2010.00442.x

Rose, H., &. Galloway, N. (2019). *Global Englishes for language teaching*. Cambridge University Press.

Timmis, I. (2002). Native-speaker norms and international English: A classroom view. *ELT Journal*, *56*(3), 240–249. https://doi.org/10.1093/elt/56.3.240

Wang, Y., & Jenkins, J. (2016). "Nativeness" and intelligibility impacts of intercultural experience through Englishes a lingua franca on Chinese speakers' language attitudes. *Chinese Journal of Applied Linguistics*, *39*(1), 38–58. https://doi.org/10.1515/cjal-2016-0003

Zhang, W., & Hu, G. (2008). Second language learners' attitudes towards English varieties. *Language Awareness*, *17*(4), 342–347.

Chapter 17

Using (Critical) Applied Linguistics to Negotiate the Teaching of Dominant Englishes

Ribut Wahyudi

This chapter discusses how I taught (Critical) Applied Linguistics (CAL) to fifth-semester undergraduate students. The original course was Introduction to Applied Linguistics (AL). However, as a lecturer, I have the autonomy to deliver materials that cover both AL and CAL (Pennycook, 2010). Inspired by post-structural works (e.g., Foucauldian Discourse Analysis) and post-colonial resources such as Alatas' (2003) *Academic Dependency* in social science, I am committed to promoting critical understandings in the course. I want students to have a critical positioning toward dominant Englishes (e.g., British and American), which have become the regime of truth in Indonesian contexts (Wahyudi, 2018). To achieve these goals, I give students critical reading materials such as *Post-Method Pedagogy* (Kumaravadivelu, 2001), *Translanguaging* (Li, 2017), the revisit of *Linguistic Imperialism* (Canagarajah & Said, 2011), *Native Speaker Fallacy* (Canagarajah, 1999a), and other related materials. Also, I ask students to explain (in a final test question) how CAL has or has not altered their views as English students and the possible benefits of CAL for their status as multilingual speakers.

Classroom Context

The students I taught had an English Literature and Linguistics background, were from different parts of Indonesia, and were multilingual. They may or may not become an English teachers in the future. However, the materials given were designed to encourage all students to be critical users of English.

Some Relevant Previous Studies and Theories

Due to limited space, only some related studies and theories are discussed subsequently, primarily those which most resonate with this chapter's focus on AL/CAL approaches to English learning.

Sung (2015) conducted a pilot project on implementing a Global Englishes component in a university English course in Hong Kong. He asked the students to discuss whether they agree or not with the notions of a Native Speaker (henceforth, NS) and Standard English, along with its reason(s). The students were also asked to describe the accents on "English in China CCTV News," whether they were Chinese, British, or American English. Sung found that the students had a

DOI: 10.4324/9781003124665-20

positive response to Global English and were confident to speak English with local accents. However, he also found students' "lingering desire" (p. 47) toward an NS model and "standard" English.

Through English as International Language (EIL)-informed pedagogy, Zacharias (2019) investigated teacher-learners' positioning toward Native English Speaker Teachers (NEST) versus Non-Native Speaker Teachers (NNEST). The data collection was conducted at a private university in Indonesia, which hired both NEST and NNEST. The students were asked to write an initial position essay with the following theme: "Who is the best teacher of English? NESTs or NNESTs?" (p. 120). And at the end of the course, students were asked to write an autobiographical paragraph as a component of a final paper. The paper included students' position toward the class theme, the definition of NEST and NNEST, the relevant incidents that support their position, readings that support their position, and a conclusion. The results showed that most students who favored NEST shifted to NNEST at the end of the course.

Dyches and Gale (2019) introduced new strategies to increase student and teacher agency through the detailed collaboration between a linguist and high school English teacher. The linguist and the teacher designed lessons together, which opened the discussion of linguistic ideologies and the established system of power in *The Adventures of Huckleberry Finn*. The researchers used Critical Race Theory (CRT) to analyze the story as it discusses racism, oppression, and Whiteness. The designed goals for the students were, among others, to understand CRT and apply it to examine American canonical literature.

The works of Canagarajah (1999b) and Pennycook (2019) resonate to some extent with the way I taught in the classroom. Canagarajah (1999b) proposes that language learning should be *personal*, *situated*, *cultural*, and *political*. He contends that knowledge is ideological and negotiated. Pennycook (2019) introduced the concept of *translingualism* to disrupt the dominance of English by outlining the need to understand the interconnection of "English in the local and global relations of desire" (p. 180), such as discrimination, disparity, and difference. It also provincializes and decolonizes English from Eurocentric categories, including power, politics, coloniality, and modernity. Thus translingualism, the combination of two ideas—*translingual* and *activism*—contests our current pedagogical discourses.

Overall, my teaching resonates with the critical pedagogy promoted by Canagarajah (1999b), especially when making learning personal, cultural, and political. It also resonates with Pennycook's (2019) idea of translingual activism, the deconstructed native-speakerism concept (Zacharias, 2019), open attitudes to local Englishes (Sung, 2015), and increased students' agency (Dyches & Gale, 2019).

How to Design the Course

The materials of the course are a combination of AL and CAL. The introductory issues include AL but also CAL (broadly defined) and its possible critical positioning toward the dominant Englishes. The course's critical dimension can be traced through the selection of the materials, take-home assignments, the questions for middle and final tests, and the students' critical reflection on the (C)AL course as written in the final test answer.

The Selection of Materials and the Reason(s) for Selections

I chose the introductory chapter of Bunce et al. (2016) to familiarize the students with three constructions of English: *progress, modernity*, and *consumerism*. This chapter was to raise students' awareness that English teaching is not limited to the language per se, but the reproduction of the dominant Western thoughts where English is identified as the symbol of progress and modernity.

Coleman's (2016) "English Language as Naga in Indonesia" was selected to demonstrate that the dominant British and American Englishes have been pervasive in Indonesian daily life, as seen in TV programs and news media. Coleman contends that English devours the Indonesian language and simultaneously the Indonesian language devours local languages.

I selected Canagarajah's (1999a) article "Native Speaker Fallacy" to disrupt the privileging of the Native Speaker (NS) over the Non-Native Speaker (NNS). Canagarajah argues that the prevailing myth on the dominance of NS over NNS could be traced back to Chomsky's idea of the NS's *grammaticality judgment*, which (supposedly) the non-native counterparts do not possess. Canagarajah problematized this idea and argued that the NNS can occupy an equal position.

I also deliberately chose Mahboob's (2009) article on "English as an Islamic Language" in order to make students aware that English teaching can fulfill particular *religious needs*. The use of Mahboob (2009) was also motivated by the similarity of the Muslims in both Pakistan and Indonesia. At the same time, Kachru's (1998) work on "English as an Asian Language" was chosen to stress that the English user's localized function (how the use of standard English is shaped by a local context) is legitimate.

I also used Li Wei's (2017) keynote on translanguaging in the TESOL classroom in order to make students aware that using Indonesian and/or local languages in addition to English is theoretically and pedagogically justifiable. The purpose was, among others, to make the students engage more emotionally with the materials. I also introduced an article on Post-Method Pedagogy (Kumaravadivelu, 2001) to accommodate students' sociocultural contexts.

Finally, I also selected Canagarajah's and Said's (2011) article on the revisit of Linguistic Imperialism to deconstruct dominant Englishes.

How to Teach the Materials

Using Cook's *Applied Linguistics* book (2006), I added critical and deconstructive concepts to counternarrative the monolingual approach occasionally found in this text. For example, while preparing for class, I circled the phrase "native speaker" (p. 22) in Chapter 3 ("Languages in the Contemporary World") and then put an arrow pointing to the right. At the end of the arrow, I wrote the phrase "multilingual speaker," which meant that the class needed to deconstruct the idea of a "native speaker" (NS).

Canagarajah's (1999a) article "Native Speaker Fallacy" (NSF) opened space to discuss NS and NSF. After explaining NSF, we discussed the disadvantage of being a Non-Native Speaker (NNS): because it is always compared to NS status, which is often considered "superior." Therefore, I encouraged students to shift their subject position from NNS to "multilingual speaker." Such a shift can encourage students to deconstruct their supposed disadvantaged position as NNS (Wahyudi, 2021).

Since Cook's (2006) textbook didn't include alternative teaching methods, I added EIL, translanguaging (Li, 2017), and Post-Method Pedagogy (PMP) (Kumaravadivelu, 2001), stressing that these concepts allowed the use of Indonesian and local languages in the classroom, in addition to English, to better understand the course materials. I also emphasized that using locally situated materials is good classroom discussion, for example, promoting local tourism using English. The use of English to promote Islamic values was also an alternative. When explaining the *possibility* principle of the PMP (Kumaravadivelu, 2001), the need to discuss social, political, and economic aspects, we discussed that the Native Speaker position is *politically advantageous* for the dominant Englishes. The NS position asks that we strictly "imitate" the NS's ideals, and any deviation of the concept would be considered illegitimate.

When explaining Coleman (2016)'s discussion of English as Naga (i.e., dragon) in Indonesia, English dominance in Indonesia's school context became a focal point; we considered the possibility that if English was not taught, parents might protest or at least question such a decision. But, if the local languages (e.g., Javanese or Madurese) were not taught, the students' parents may not complain about it. No students disagreed with my hypothetical. I also highlighted the fact that local languages are only offered up to the junior high school level, while English is taught up to university levels. Students were then asked to react to a hypothetical—to imagine how school would be different if a Minister of Education declared that local languages were compulsory up to the university level.

In teaching Canagarajah's and Said's (2011) revisit of Linguistic Imperialism (LI), we focused on the key concepts in the chapter, such as LI itself and its central constructs, including ideologies, linguicism (seeing one language as more prestigious than another) (Phillipson & Skutnabb-Kangas, 2013), native-speakerism, and monolingualism. I asked the students to pay attention to these keywords, explaining them in both English and Indonesian languages to strengthen students' comprehension and understanding. We also contextualized the concept of linguicism to the local context. I said that mastering English and being proficient in English is good, but if doing so made someone look down on local or national languages, this would be an example of linguicism, as it creates a hierarchy among the languages.

Assignment, Middle, and Final Tests

Take-Home Assignment

The take-home assignment aimed to make students understand the content of the given materials and the possible benefit for them as students in an English Department. I asked them to write one paragraph focused on the key content for the given materials and one paragraph about the possible benefit. The goal was for students to contextualize the materials relative to their lives so that learning could be meaningful. This activity resonates with one principle of critical pedagogy, which necessitates that learning is personal (Canagarajah, 1999b). To disrupt English dominance, the questions for middle and final tests sought to raise their critical thinking and agency, negotiating the hegemony of the dominant Englishes.

Middle Test

In the middle test, students were to explain Canagarajah's (1999a) article on Native Speaker Fallacy, and its possible benefit to them as a "multilingual subject." Moreover, they were also required to briefly explain the concept of Communicative Language Teaching (Cook, 2006) versus the concept of Post-Method Pedagogy (Kumaravadivelu, 2001) and their potential suitability in the Indonesian context. Situated in the Islamic university, I felt it necessary to ask students to explain Mahboob's (2009) article "English as an Islamic Language" and students' possible positioning as researchers in Applied Linguistics. Moreover, the students had to briefly explain what translanguaging is (Li, 2017) and its possible benefit in the English classroom.

These middle test questions exposed students to diverse aims: disrupting native-speakerism; contextualizing pedagogy to the Indonesian situation through PMP, institutional context, and need (English in an Islamic context); and engaging and democratizing learning through translanguaging. All these resonate with critical pedagogy, which includes personal, political, and cultural (Canagarajah, 1999b) and translingual activism (Pennycook, 2019).

Final Test

For the final test, students were required to explain how CAL either has or has not altered their views as English Department students. They were to briefly explain whether there are benefit(s) of CAL for them as *multilingual speakers*. Second, I asked them to briefly explain the three dominant constructions of English as *progress*, *modernity*, and *consumerism* (Bunce et al., 2016) and asked their opinions about how the three dominant constructions of English do or do not relate to Linguistic Imperialism (Canagarajah & Said, 2011). Third, I asked the students to write the main content of Coleman's (2016) "English as Naga in Indonesia" and the learned lesson(s) for students as *responsible intellectuals*.

These questions reflect both the personal and the political as discussed by Canagarajah (1999b) and the spirit of activism, since they encourage students to counter dominant thoughts such as native-speakerism and monolingualism (Pennycook, 2019).

Students' Reflections

The following are examples of two students' (SNA and SNR) reflections on the course in their final test answer.

> Critical Applied Linguistics has changed my view against native speaker or the usage of English. The notion about native speaker is more superior than others has disapeared in my mind. Also, if I encountered some of my friends who speak English in a wrong pronunciation or grammar, I preferred to realize that it was usual thing and admitted that we are Indonesian, and should not always speak as right as native speaker.
>
> (SNA)

SNA's answer suggests that she has been successful not only in getting rid of the hegemony of native-speakerism but also in changing her attitude to both being more tolerant to her friends' "wrong" pronunciation or grammar and considering that Indonesians should not speak as perfectly as Native Speakers (NS). Her explanation appeared to resonate with my explanation in the classroom that NS should not be positioned as superior due to their grammaticality judgment, as criticized by Canagarajah (1999a).

Similar positioning in terms of freeing herself from the superiority of English, SNR raised the issue of using English to promote local languages in the global context:

> Critical applied linguistics has altered my view in case of appreciate local languages. As a student of English department, I realize that English is not superior, and we can take benefit of learning English to promote or introduce our local languages internationally.
>
> (SNR)

SNR's written answer indicates that she has shifted from seeing English as superior to seeing that English has a complex position in the world. She has been able to speak "Otherwise" (Pennycook, 2019). Her English learning seemed to be more political—that is, to promote local languages internationally. This positioning appeared to resonate with what I had explained in the classroom: English needs to be a language to promote Islamic values, Indonesian language, culture, and tourism. SNR's answer resonates with the idea of activism linked to the learning of English.

Conclusion

My teaching in the (C)AL course aims to critically negotiate the dominant Englishes (see lesson plan in the next section), promote local languages and cultures, Islamic values, and tourism. It is political and has an advocatory function. Initial answers for the selected students suggest that students deconstructed the hegemony of the monolingual approach of the dominant Englishes. It is very important to think of English teaching alongside the promotion of local languages, cultures, tourism, and products because in this way English teaching serves our own interests and needs rather than serving the West.

Lesson Plan: Critically Negotiating Monolingual Concepts of Dominant Englishes

Recommended Grade Level

Upper-level undergraduate

Context

This lesson is appropriate for university students majoring in Linguistics/Applied Linguistics in the Outer Circles (e.g., India, Malaysia) and Expanding Circles (e.g., Indonesia, Thailand). The activities are a good fit for fifth-semester students (third year) or above, where they have been familiar with the dominant constructions of Englishes (e.g., British or American). It is worth noting that before deconstructing the prevailing assumptions, students need to know the constructions of the dominant narrative (Grbich, 2004).

Objectives

Students will be able to

- deconstruct the dominant monolingual concepts such as Native-Speakerism, ELT methods, and related ideas (e.g., progress, modernity);
- reconstruct their understanding and positioning toward dominant Englishes.

Classroom Activities

The teacher provides the students with the chance to voice their understanding of both mainstream texts (Cook, 2006) and critical readings such as Canagarajah (1999a), Kumaravadivelu (2001), and Mahboob (2009). The teacher asks the students critical questions such as the following:

- How are the dominant concepts of Native Speaker, English Language Teaching Methods, progress, and modernity associated with dominant Englishes, and what are the possible disadvantages for students as multilingual speakers?
- What are some of the political, social, and economic benefits for the United Kingdom and the United States if the dominant concepts are not challenged or contested?
- How do the critical readings in the field help students identify the dominant English constructs and help students reconstruct new understanding and positioning?
- How might the critical readings help transform students to be responsible intellectuals for their own country through their disciplines/knowledge(s)?

Procedures

Step 1: Discussion of Contested Topics (20 Minutes)

The student will come to class having read the Introduction to Cook's *Applied Linguistics* (2006). Students and teacher discuss contested topics in the introduction, such as native-speakerism and dominant ELT Methods. The teacher can ask the following questions:

- Who is being privileged and disadvantaged if the notion of native-speakerism prevails?
- Do the dominant ELT Methods provide a space for EFL teachers' agency in theorizing their own pedagogy?

Step 2: Introduction of Alternative Materials (20 Minutes)

The teacher then introduces alternative materials such as Canagarajah's (1999a) chapter on Native Speaker Fallacy, Canagarajah's and Said's (2011) chapter on Linguistic Imperialism, and Kumaravadivelu's (2001) article on Post Method Pedagogy. When discussing Native Speaker Fallacy, the teacher refers to Canagarajah's problematization of the concept of *native speaker*, which is associated with their grammaticality judgement, Chomsky's idea. This grammaticality judgement places *native speaker* as superior to *non-native speaker*. When discussing the chapter on Linguistic Imperialism, the teacher can highlight the fact that English dominates other languages and is positioned higher than others. The teacher can then discuss that this imperialistic nature of the dominant English needs to be critically negotiated. When discussing Post Method Pedagogy, the teacher can explain the transformative potential of this pedagogy to empower the EFL teacher.

Step 3: Asking Students' Opinions (15 Minutes)

The teacher asks students to provide their own opinions about the contested concepts mentioned in Step 1. Possible questions include the following:

- Who will get benefits from the binary concept of *native speaker* versus *non-native speaker*?
- What is the possible benefit if the idea of *non-native speaker* is replaced with *multilingual speaker*?
- How do students have to position themselves strategically against the dominant Englishes?
- Which is more empowering for EFL teachers: dominant ELT Methods or Post Method Pedagogy? Why?

Step 4: Explanation and Contextualization (10 Minutes)

The teacher explains and contextualizes the alternative materials mentioned in Step 2 to students' sociocultural contexts. For example, the teacher explains that Canagarajah's (1999a) article can be used to justify that all users of English(es), regardless of their ethnicities or countries, have equal space in teaching English(es). Therefore, students do not have to feel inferior when competing with "native speakers" in the future.

Step 5: Disruption of the Dominant Concepts (20 Minutes)

The teacher makes use of the alternative materials in Step 2 to disrupt the dominant concepts in Step 1. For example, the teacher can explain that Post Method Pedagogy emerged from the dissatisfaction of existing ELT Methods, since these methods fail to empower teacher's agency in creating their own methods and also fail to accommodate local and sociocultural contexts. The teacher then asks the students to provide an example for each of the principles of Post Method: particularity, practicality, and possibility.

Step 6: Explanation of Alternative Materials and Raising Awareness of Local Contexts and Needs (15 Minutes)

The teacher explains that the alternative materials in Step 2 can be used to theoretically support the need to teach English in order to promote sociocultural contexts and fulfil local needs. For example, using a *particularity* principle of the Post Method, Islamic cultures and local tourism can be discussed in the English classroom.

References

Alatas, S. F. (2003). Academic dependency and the global division of labor in social science. *Current Sociology*, *51*(6), 599–613. https://doi.org/10.1177/00113921030516003

Bunce, P., Phillipson, R., Rapatahana, V., & Tupas, R. (2016). Introduction. In P. Bunce, R. Phillipson, V. Rapatahana, & R. Tuppas (Eds.), *Why English: Confronting the hydra* (pp. 1–20). Multilingual Matters. https://doi.org/10.21832/9781783095858-003

Canagarajah, S. (1999a). Interrogating the "native speaker fallacy": Non-linguistics roots, non-pedagogical results. In G. Braine (Ed.), *Non-native educators in English language teaching* (pp. 77–92). Lawrence Erlbaum Associates Inc. https://doi.org/10.4324/9781315045368-15

Canagarajah, S. (1999b). *Resisting linguistic imperialism in English teaching*. Oxford University Press.

Canagarajah, S., & Said, S. B. (2011). Linguistic imperialism. In J. Simpson (Ed.), *The Routledge handbook of applied linguistics* (pp. 388–400). Routledge. https://doi.org/10.4324/9780203835654.ch27

Coleman, H. (2016). The English language as Naga in Indonesia. In P. Bunce, R. Phillipson, V. Rapatahana, & R. Tupas (Eds.), *Why English: Confronting the hydra* (pp. 59–71). Multilingual Matters. https://doi.org/10.21832/9781783095858-007

Cook, G. (2006). *Applied linguistics*. Oxford University Press.

Dyches, J., & Gale, C. (2019). "Standard" English, "classic" literature: Examining canonical and linguistic ideologies in Huck Finn. In M. D. Devereaux & C. C. Palmer (Eds.), *Teaching language variation in the classroom strategies and models from teachers and linguists* (pp. 157–164). Routledge. https://doi.org/10.4324/9780429486678-25

Grbich, C. (2004). *New approaches in social research*. Sage. https://doi.org/10.4135/9781849209519

Kachru, B. (1998). English as an Asian language. *Link & Letters*, *5*, 89–108.

Kumaravadivelu, B. (2001). Toward a post method pedagogy. *TESOL Quarterly*, *35*(4), 537–560. https://doi.org/10.2307/3588427

Li, W. (2017). *Translanguaging and the goal of TESOL*. Summit on the Future of the TESOL Profession, TESOL.org. Retrieved May 20, 2021, from www.tesol.org/docs/default-source/ppt/li-wei.pdf

Mahboob, A. (2009). English as an Islamic language. *World Englishes*, *28*(2), 175–189. https://doi.org/10.1111/j.1467-971x.2009.01583.x

Pennycook, A. (2010). Critical and alternative directions in applied linguistics. *Australian Review of Applied Linguistics*, *33*(2), 1–16. https://doi.org/10.1075/aral.33.2.03pen

Pennycook, A. (2019). From translanguaging to translingual activism. In D. Macedo (Ed.), *Decolonizing foreign language education: The misteaching of English and other colonial languages* (pp. 169–185). Routledge. https://doi.org/10.4324/9780429453113-7

Phillipson, R., & Skutnabb-Kangas, T. (2013). Linguistic imperialism and endangered languages. In T. K. Bathia, & W. C. Ritchie (Eds.), *The handbook of multilingualism and bilingualism* (pp. 495–516). Wiley-Blackwell.

Sung, C. C. M. (2015). Implementing a global Englishes component in a university English course in Hongkong. *English Today*, *31*(4), 42–29. https://doi.org/10.1017/s0266078415000383

Wahyudi, R. (2018). *Situating English language teaching in Indonesia within a critical, global dialogue of theories: A case study of teaching argumentative writing and cross-cultural understanding courses* (Unpublished dissertation, Victoria University of Wellington).

Wahyudi, R. (2021). A transnational TEGCOM practitioner's multiple subjectivities and critical classroom negotiations in the Indonesian university context. In R. Jain, B. Yazan, & S. Canagarajah (Eds.), *Transnational identities, pedagogies, and practices in English language teaching: Critical inquiries from diverse practitioners* (pp. 240–258). Multilingual Matters.

Zacharias, N. T. (2019). EIL pedagogy in an initial teacher education program in Indonesia: The case of an academic writing class. In S. Zein (Ed.), *Teacher education for English as a lingua franca: Perspectives from Indonesia* (pp. 115–130). Routledge. https://doi.org/10.4324/9780203730522-7

Index

academic discourse xixn7, 103; *see also* discourse
academic writing xxviii, 92, 102, 104, 106; *see also* translanguaging; writing
accent: accentedness 117–118, 121; American English 127; British English 127; characterization **117**; definition of 113–114; exercises 29; foreign 116; L1/L2 115–116; native 53; NYC 115; perception 113, 115–116; resistance 155; standard 113; Thai 124, 127–128; training 118–121; variations 77; vocabulary 84; *see also* context; identity; L1; L2; linguistics; pronunciation; World Englishes
anglosphere 3, 4
ASEAN (Association of Southeast Asian Nations) 126–127
assessment 15, 16, **24**; major/final 86, 87, 89, 90; language 144; post-activity 126
attitudes: authors' 9; beliefs 123; investigation of 134; learners' language/non-adversarial 4; open 164; perceptions 153; positive 125, 128–130; questions of xxii; reflection and discussion of 157; stereotypes 118; various xxix, 114; *see also* language
audiovisual texts 36–39; *see also* multimodality
authority xiii, 5n1
awareness: cross-cultural 92–94, 96, 98, 125, 127, 135, 147; demonstrate 29; lack of 153; languaging 14, 69; metalinguistic 71, 117; raising 26–27, 34–35, 39, 63, 116, 123; students' 4, 6, 26, 35, 123, 154, 155, 157, 165; *see also* Global Englishes

bilingual: activity 34; communication 48; code-switching 132; dictionary 37; emergent 43–44, 48–50, 53; Hongkongers 133; learner 38; speaker 35, 115; students 20, 43; teaching 136; translanguaging 63–64, 68–71, 77, 103, 143; users 26
bilingualism 6, 43, 63, 76, 138; *see also* bilingual
borrowing 7, 64, 78; *see also* loanwords

CAL (Critical Applied Linguistics) 163–165, 167–169, 171; *see also* linguistics; translanguaging
circles (Kachru) 27, 35–37, 39, 115–116, 125, 127, 154, 169
CMC (Computer-Mediated Communication) **94**, 96, 98
CMI (Chinese as a Medium of Instruction) 133
code-meshing xviii–xix, xixn7; *see also* code-switching; dialects; languaging; translanguaging
code-switching i, xviii–xx, 64, 76, 78, 79, 132–139; *see also* dialects; languaging; translanguaging
coloniality 3, 164
colonization xiv–xv, xvn5, 83–84, 153, 157
Common Core 84, 84n2
communication: bilingual 48; effective xiv, xixn7, 27, 92–94, 96–98, 128; English xi, 125–126, 134; everyday 63; 76; functional 134; Global Englishes 38, 124, 152–159; intercultural 4, 93, 97–98; international 120, 134; learning 34; meaningful 53; mode 143; opportunity 133; practices **97**; quality 126; skills 30; strategies 39; successful 26, 127; tool 133; translanguaging 52, 63, 74, 76, 135, 136
communicative approach 27, 29
comprehensibility 114, 116, 117, **117**, 118, 121
context: academic 106; accent 115; classroom xi, xx, xxv, 163; course 93;

disciplinary xii; diverse 93; educational 4, 7, 15, 107, 144; EFL 43; exposure 116; global/cultural xi, xxii, xxv, xxviii, xxix, 9, 15, 28, 137, 168; high 97–98; historical xvii; Hong Kong 135; Indonesian 163, 167; institutional xxii, 4, 15, 167; intercultural 103; international 113, 126; interpretive 103; Italian academic 5; languaging 64; lesson plan 9, 16, 29, 39, 49, 59, 70, 79, 89, 99, 108, 108n1, 120, 129, 138, 148, 158, 169; linguistic 16, 26; local 132, 165–166; low 97; meaning xii, xiin3, xiiin4; multicultural 127; multilingual 146; non-native 26; professional xix, xixn7; real-world x; rhetorical 94–95; specific 4, 96; social 136; sociocultural 165; sociolinguistic 7; teaching 27; TESOL 3; Thai 123; translation 34, 37; variety of/different xvii, xxi, 6, 14, 93, 97, 102, 106, 117, 124; WE-inspired 5; *see also* culture
cooperative learning 13, 15, 16
critical thinking xviii, xxi, 13, 34, 49–50, 85, 159, 166; *see also* CAL (Critical Applied Linguistics); pedagogy
culture: xi–xvi, xxi, 35, 76, 98, 103, 135, 136, 158; academic 14; American 85; contrastive 93; different xv, 103, 135; diverse 99; -driven behaviors 98; erasure 85; high-context 97; Hong Kong 134, 138; inclusive 145; Indonesian 168; Islamic 171; local 137, 168; low context 97; representation of 96; resistance 159; various 96; *see also* context
curriculum: bottom-up 26; designers 123, 125; EAP 125 course 154, 157; ELA 82; ESL 132, 134, 135, 137; direct-entry program 144; existing xxii, 136; exam-centered 145; global xiv; global classroom xii; Global Englishes/GE x, 83, 85–86, 90, 125; Hong Kong English 132–135; local 135–136; Middle East 75; monoglossic 142, 144; nationalistic xiv; new 137; objectives 83; pandialectal xi; policies 124; standard 88; structure 83; teachers' xv–xvi, xxvii; teaching 135; writing program 93

descriptive/descriptivism xv
dialects: code-switching xviii, 26; conventions xv; D1 116; different 28, 76, 84, 133; distinctions 84; English xx, 114; global xxv, 114; home xix; intralinguistic diversity xxi; lexicon 84; morphology 84; multiple xx, 118; native 116; regional 113; single xi; stereotypes and perceptions xviii, xxii, 28; student xx, 37, 76, 97, 118; unfamiliar 86; use of xviii; variations/various 82, 84; writing xviii; *see also* Languages and Dialects
dialogue xvii, 28, 53, 117, 123, 159
digital literacy 93; *see also* digital media
digital media 92–95, 97–99, 101
direct-entry courses 142–144, 147–149; *see also* curriculum
discourse xixn7, 26, 64, 67–69, 78, 92–93, 95, 103, 107, 143, 154, 163–164
discrimination 66, 142–143, 158–159, 164
diversity: appreciation/importance/value 28, 30, 37; Beirut 74; classroom 76; cultural 25, 35, 37, 75, 96; English 26, 124–128, 130; global 35; intralinguistic and interlinguistic xxi; jargon 78; language 92–94, 96, 98–99, 142; modes of communication 143; *see also* dialects

EAP (English for Academic Purposes) 152, 154, 157
EFL (English as a Foreign Language) classroom/environment 13, 35, 39, 43, 47, 54, 120; competence 5; definition xxvi, 43, 52; emergent bilinguals 43, 44, 48–50; learners/students 4, 8, 10, 43; pedagogy 124–125; programs 48; teachers 170; translanguaging pedagogy 48; translation 37
EIL (English as International Language) 25, 164, 166
ELA (English Language Arts) 82–84, 84n2, 86–87, 89
ELF (English as a Lingua Franca) xxvii, 25, 34, 83–84
ELT (English Language Teaching): classes/classrooms 126, 128, 133; coursebooks 4; definition xxvi, 123, 132; environment 133–134; field of 34; global Englishes 124; ideology 124; methods and practices 123, 125, 128, 169–170; students/learners 70, 128
EMI (English as a Medium of Instruction) 4, 5, 63, 64, 129, 133
empathy: critical xiv, xvi–xvii, xvi6, 82; social 144; students 84; as translation xvii
empowerment xvii, 155–157
engagement xvii, 14, 75–76, 83, 86, 88, 93
ESL (English as a Second Language): classes/courses 59, 120, 132, 134, 137; definition xxvi, 52, 132, 152;

environment 35; interactions 53; learners/students 52, 133–136; tasks and activities 37, 39, 55; teachers 54, 135–136
ethnicity 3, 65, *66*, 85n5, 113, 115–117, 125, 127, 133, 142, 158, 170
ethnolinguistic study 133
experience: diverse 40; language 48, 58, 85–86, 117, 125; learners/students' 13, 75, 84, 86, 96, *105*, 106, 107, 123, 136, 142, 155–158; linguistic 92, 113; negative xvii; personal xvii, 4, 26, 75, 79, 85, 96, *105*, 106; research 75; speakers' xiv
explicit instruction 35, 113, 116–117

feminism 78, 80
French Mandate 74

gender 18, 20, 36, 78, 113, 115, 117, 142; *see also* feminism; sexuality
global classroom xii–xviii, xiiin4, xxi, xxv
Global Englishes: awareness 35–36; classroom/environment xiv, xxv, 123, 134; communication 38; definition xxvi, 82, 124, 153; different xviii; embracing xiv; field of xxi; learners/students 38, 96, 157; lessons/material xii, xxii, 20, 39, 83, 88–89, 125, 129–130, 163; naming xiii, xxv; pedagogy 38; perceptions/ stereotypes 153, 157; podcasts/videos 154–157; teaching/instruction xi, xxii, 34–35, 123; users/speakers 37, 152; varieties 39, 93, 99, 154; *see also* pronunciation; World Englishes
globalization 92–93, 124, 135, 152–153
global language xii, xvi, xxii, 125, 152
Grammar Translation Methods (GTM) 44
grammaticality judgement 170

heteroglossic ideology xiii
higher education 5, 9, 14, 63, 102, 106, 142, 144
history xi, xiii, xv, xxi, 9, 19, 35, 53, 82, 84–85, 94, 98, 125, 139
home language: conventions xix; emergent bilinguals 43, 48; interactional patterns/ cues 73; learners'/students' 10, 37, 49–50, 102–104, **104**, 106–107, 109, 145–146, 149
hybrid language 7, 9, 10, 77, 80

identity: accent/dialect 113, 115, 119; cultural 134, 136; gender 18; global differences xv; language xi, xvi, 124, 132; learners'/students' 44, 126, 128, 130, 154, 156, 158; marker 132–133, 136; multilingual 103; racial 66; speakers'/users' xv, xvi, 74, 77; teachers' 136
ideology 26, 66, 124, 153; *see also* heteroglossic ideology; monoglossic ideology
IELTS (International English Language Testing System) 144
intelligibility 26, 36, 39, 114, 117–118, **117**, 121, 134, 143
interaction: activities 117; class 40, 75; intercultural 98; learner/student 13, 54, 75, 127, 129, 146, 148; lecturer-student 5, 69, 73; negotiated 14; peer 15, 45, 49, 52–55, 57–59; reflective 35; social 64; sociocultural 50; speaker 115; spoken 45, 47
intercultural communication 4, 13, 15, 19, 92–93, 96–98, 103
internationalization 63, 92, 142
interpersonal skills 13, 79, 103

jargon 67, 77–78, 95

L1: accent and dialect 115–118; backgrounds 34, 53; definition xxvi, 34, 52, 114, 143; emergent bilinguals' 44; groups 54–55; learners/students' 34, 35, 37, 52–56, 64, 68–71, 80, 117, 136, 143, 145; peer 53–55; policies 53; production 53; lecturer/teachers 53, 68, 136; use 54–55, 64, 68, 136, 145; varieties/different 118, 133
L2: accent 114–118; classrooms/ environment 52, 53, 69; definition xxvi, 44, 52, 114; learners/students 34, 37, 52, 64, 68–71, 106–107, 117, 133, 136, 143; pedagogy 26; perception/ stereotype 116, 154; research 55n; speakers 57, 116–118; teacher/ lecturer 68, 136; varieties 115, 118
language: attitudes 4; conventions xv, xxvi, 16, 82; ideologies 83, 124, 142; instruction xi–xii, xxi; shift 15, 18; variants 96
language variation *see* code-meshing; code-switching; dialects; Languages and Dialects; translanguaging
languaging 44, 64, 69; *see also* translanguaging
learning stations 13, 15, 17, 18, 24; *see also* station teaching

lexicon xxvi, 5, 15, 17, 83; *see also* vocabulary
lingua franca xvii, xxi, xxvi, 6, 26, 34, 83–85, 87, 123, 125, 153
linguicism 158–159, 166
linguistics: accents 118; applied xixn7, xxi, 163, 165, 167–169, 171; basic 9; educational xxi; English 3–4, 163; knowledge 10; traditional xx; translanguaging 64, 69; understanding of 22
listening: activities 127; in the classroom xviii; comprehension 117; courses 29; global 113, 116; intensive/extensive 117, 119; learners/students' 126; others' opinions 13; skills 34–35, 118, 143, 154; tasks 26–27, 146, 155–159
literacy xixn7, 67, 84n2, 93, 102–103, 107
literature: class/course 63, 65, 67, 69, 74–79, 82–85, 87–89, 163–164; dialects in xviii; English young adult 44; field xxi; research 3, 102–104, 125; teaching xxii; variety of xxvii
loanwords 7; *see also* borrowing

metacognition 86
methods and methodology xxi–xxii, 13–14, 44, 69, 75, 102, 123–124, 166, 169–170
MOI (Medium of Instruction) 133
monoglossic ideology xiii, 3, 43, 48, 142, 144
monolingual xixn7, xx, 34–35, 37, 45, 63, 69, 104, 113, 115, 133, 142–144, 165–169
morphology 4–6, 8–9, 84
morphosyntactic features 15, 17
mother tongue 64, 67, 70, 84, 108, 133
multicompetence 34
multilingualism 102; *see also* bilingualism
multilingual speakers xiii, xxvi, 64, 103, 113, 152, 154, 163, 167, 169
multiliteracy 103
multimodality 43, 143, 145; *see also* digital media

narrative xi, xiv, xvii, 75, 79–80, 85, 165, 169
native: language 26, 29, 34–37, 39, 68; speaker communities 6; speakerism 153, 164, 166–170; speaker fallacy 163, 165, 167, 170; speaker model 4, 7; speakers xiv, 3, 26, 106–107, 124, 168, 170; *see also* accent; dialects; non-native speakers; varieties

neoliberal practices 144
NESB (non-English speaking background) 144–145
non-native speakers 3, 106, 107; *see also* native, speakers
norms xixn7, 4–5, 26, 93, 98, 115, 124–125

paradigm 4, 25–26, 28, 124–125, 133–134
pathway programs 142–145, 148–149
pedagogy: critical 164, 166–167; EFL 124; EIL 164; ELF 34; English linguistics 4; global classroom xii; Global Englishes 38; L2 oracy 154; multiliteracy 103; postmethod 3, 163, 165–167, 170; teaching 25–26; translanguaging 44, 48, 64; writing 103
perception: accents/dialect xxii, 113–117, 119–120; English 125, 153; English speakers xxii; expanding-circle 116; learners'/students' 36, 75–78, 128, 130, 154–155, 157; multilingual speakers 152; positive 38; speech 115; training 113; varieties 36, 39; *see also* attitudes; Global Englishes
phonology/phonetics 29, 84, 87, 118, 120, 132; *see also* pronunciation; syllable
pluralism 25
poetry 69–70, 85–86, 114
PMP (Post-Method Pedagogy) 3–4, 166–167
PPP model (Presentation, Practice, and Production) 28–29
preferism 153
prescriptive/prescriptivism xv, xxix
pre-service (teachers) i, xviii, xx, 13, 16, 102, 104
pronunciation: accent 113–118, 120–121; differences 27–30; English 27–30, 124; global instruction 116; incorrect 155, 167–168; for listening 146; received xix, 116, 120–121, 153; varieties 30

race xix, 3, 36, 65–67, 84–85, 119, 142, 156, 158–160, 164
register 14–19, 25, 52, 82, 117, 147
religion: background 78; Christianity 74; discrimination 142; Islam 165–168, 171; practices 97–98; references 76; sects 74; teachings 77; topics 67, 69; values 68
repertoire: classroom xx; cultural 43–44; emerging English/bilingual 47, 53; hidden 145; individual/own xviii, xx, 53; Korean 44, 48; linguistic 44,

48, 53, 58, 63, 68, 71, 115, 155; peers' 47; semiotic 43–44, 48; speakers' xix; students' 97, 142–143, 155; translanguaging 52, 103; verbal 47
resistance xixn7, 155, 157, 159
rhetoric xix, 92–95, 97–99, 117

scaffolding 53, 65, 102, 104, *105*, 158
segments 5, 36, 54, 113, 116–117, 120
semantics 4, 104, 108, 132
sexuality xix, 68, 78, 113, 115, 117; *see also* gender
Skopos theory 36
social justice 83–84, 142, 144
sociocultural contexts 4, 34, 48, 50, 75, 77–78, 82, 92, 107, 165, 170–171
socioeconomic status 18, 78, 113, 115, 119, 124, 158–159
sociolect xix–xx, 113
sociolinguistics xxi, 29, 84, 124; *see also* linguistics
solidarity 133, 135–136, 152–153, 157
standardization i, 82, 135, 143; *see also* Standard English (in Languages and Dialects)
station teaching 13; *see also* learning stations
stereotypes xviii, 28, 84, 98, 113, 118–119, 121, 125
stigma/stigmatization xvii, 133
strategy xix–xx, 34, 63, 67, 74–76, 78, 93–94, 97, 107, 159
stress: differences 114; focus words 120; function words 118, 120; lexical 114; patterns 114, 116–118, 120–121; syllable 114, 120; *see also* phonology/phonetics; suprasegmental
suprasegmental 113–114, 116–117
syllable 113–114, 120

taboo 67–69, 77–80
task: consensus 52, 55; conversation 56; interview 57; spot-the-difference 57; Task-Based Language Teaching (TBLT) 52
technology 27, 83, 92, 147
tertiary education xxv, 39, 70, 108, 123, 125, 127, 129, 148
TESOL (Teaching English to Speakers of Other Languages) xxvi, 3, 120, 143, 165
TLT (Transformative Learning Theory) 126
translanguaging: academic writing 104, 107; applied linguistics 163; classroom 64–65, 69, 107; code-switching/meshing xviii–xx, xixn7, 64; definition 52–53, 63–64, 103, 143–144; learners'/students' 52, 55, 57, 67; multimodality 43–44, 48–50; pedagogy/practices xiv, 44, 47–50, 56, 58, 64, 68–69, 102, 109, 145, 166–167; space 48; TESOL 165
translation: activities 34–36, 39–40; asset/tool 34–35, 38, 45; cultural 76; empathy xvii; English 75, 145; fair xvii; Grammar Translation Methods (GTM) 44, 44n1; inaccurate 147; jobs 4; language 97, 136; learning stations 17; literal 78; mechanical 37; pedagogical 34, 69; practice 67; process 37; retention 5; technologies 145; transcript **46**, 65n1; various 70; word-to-word 48; *see also* context
translingualism 74, 76, 78–80, 164

undergraduate classroom 77

variation: accent/dialectal 77, 82, 84, 115; activity 23; Arabic 74–77, 80; circles 116; cross-cultural 99; cultural 93, 96, 99; English xiii, xv, xxi, 129; formal 25; global xviii, xxi–xxii, 14; Global English 92, 123; honoring xv; intercultural 13, 96; intradialectal xviii; language xi–xiii, xx–xxii, 16, 82–83, 88, 93, 154; linguistic 93–96, 99; recognition 155; rich 27, 154; translingualism 76; writing 95
varieties: global 6, 25–27, 29, 31, 153; local xv, 26–27, 29; native 26, 95, 153; nonstandard xv, 3, 7; postcolonial 9; standard xiv–xv, xxi, 3, 129
vocabulary 7, 9, 34, 37, 52–58, 84, 87, 89–90, 95–96, **95**, 108, 146, 152

word formation 5–10
World Englishes: accents/dialects 84, 113, 115, 120; approach 9; circle model 35, 115, 132; differences xvii; examples/models 5–6, 35; features of 4; field xxi, 153; foundation 83; innovations 6; integrate 28; learning 27, 154; norms 98; perspective 8; philosophy 26; sub-discipline 3; teaching 27, 154; word-formation 7; *see also* Global Englishes; Languages and Dialects
writing: academic 92, 102, 104, 106; classroom 92–95, 97, 99, 148; creative xviii, 70; literature xxi–xxii, 82, 88; pedagogy 103

Languages and Dialects

AAVE (African American Vernacular English) 156, 158–159
Afrikaans **104**, 106–107
American English xv, xvii, 3–4, 6, 15–17, 19, 27, 29–31, 84, 95, **95**, 113–114, 126–128, 134, 152–153, 157–158, 163, 165
Arabic 54, 74–80
Australian English 7, 27, 29, 84

Black English xix; *see also* AAVE (African American Vernacular English)
British English xix, 3, 14–15, 19, 27, 30–31, 36, 95, **95**, 126–128, 152, 154, 156

Cameroon English xix, 29
Canadian English 95
Cantonese 133
Chinese languages and Englishes 54–55, 84, 133, 163
Colloquial Arabic 76

Dharuk 7

French 25, 74, 78–79, 114–115, 155

Gujarati 54

Hindi 7
Hokkien 7
Hong Kong English 132–139

Indian English 7, 9–10, 27, 29, 36
Indonesian languages 163–168
Irish English 84

Jamaican English 154–155
Japanese xviii, 98, 115–116, 135, 153
Japanese English 135

Kiswahili 7
Konglish 44
Korean 43–48, 54, 84, 154
Korean English 154

Lebanese 74–77
Lebanese English 75
Liberian English 7

Malay 7
Malaysian English 84, 123
Mandarin 54–55, 133

Nepali English 154
New Zealand English 95
Nigerian English 7, 29, 85, 154–156

Russian 25, 52–57

Scottish English xviii
Singaporean English 132
South African English 27–31, 106
Spanish and Spanish Englishes 36, 52–54, 115
Standard British English xix, xxvi; *see also* British English
Standard English xv, xvii, xx, 7, 10, 22, 36, 40, 77, 79–80, 97, 123, 153, 159–160, 163–165

Thai English 124, 126–128
Tunisian English 27
Turkish 35–36, 63, 65–69

World Standard Spoken English 26; *see also* Standard English

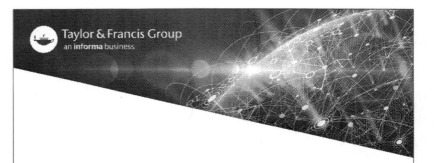